ARCHITECTURE ORIENTED OTHERWISE

Architecture Oriented Otherwise

David Leatherbarrow

PRINCETON ARCHITECTURAL PRESS, NEW YORK

For Lauren

Published by
Princeton Architectural Press
37 East Seventh Street
New York, New York 10003

For a free catalog of books, call 1.800.722.6657.
Visit our website at www.papress.com.

Editor: Jennifer Thompson
Designer: Deb Wood

Special thanks to: Nettie Aljian, Sara Bader, Dorothy Ball,
Nicola Bednarek, Janet Behning, Becca Casbon, Carina
Cha, Penny (Yuen Pik) Chu, Russell Fernandez, Pete
Fitzpatrick, Wendy Fuller, Jan Haux, Clare Jacobson, Aileen
Kwun, Nancy Eklund Later, Linda Lee, Aaron Lim, Laurie
Manfra, Katharine Myers, Ceara O'Leary, Lauren Nelson
Packard, Arnoud Verhaeghe, Paul Wagner and Joseph
Weston of Princeton Architectural Press
—Kevin C. Lippert, publisher

Library of Congress Cataloging-in-Publication Data
Leatherbarrow, David.
 Architecture oriented otherwise / David Leatherbarrow.
    p. cm.
 ISBN 978-1-56898-811-5 (alk. paper)
 1. Architecture—Philosophy. I. Title.
 NA2500.L434 2009
 720.1—dc22

                    2008019134

INTRODUCTION

Architecture Otherwise

Here it is a question of recognizing and actualizing something which I consider to be a presupposition of our being human, namely that the other may not only have a right but may actually be right…
—Hans Gadamer, *The Enigma of Health*

An orientation which goes freely from the same to the other is a work.
—Emmanuel Levinas, "Meaning and Sense"

Forces beyond the architect's control affect architecture's concrete reality, regardless of what was intended in design. What is more, unforeseen influences also bring about the end of the building's freestanding individuality. No tears should dampen this realization, for the defeat of a work's apparent singularity often leads to a victory for the patterns of life it accommodates and represents.

My aim in this book is to explain the ways that buildings sometimes allow themselves to be seen independently, as images, and other times recede from prominence in order to accommodate everyday life. This might be called the advance and retreat of the architectural figure, a two-step performance, alternately in front of and among others, like that of an actor onstage. Considering all the arts, the double task of showing and serving seems to be architecture's unique assignment, a cultural role that is reduced when the building is viewed either as an aesthetic object or a functional solution, or some compromise between the two. I will introduce the lines of thought developed in this book by reconsidering an underappreciated dimension of architectural order, *orientation*. My hope is that this preamble will provide some clarification of the ways that a building can both adhere to and distinguish itself from its "context" and "program," performing in ways that acknowledge existing conditions while enriching them.

Orientation is a familiar term in architecture. Facing eastward is generally assumed. A more basic sense of the word implies movement across the work's borders toward something it holds in common with others.[1] The word "facing" sometimes substitutes for "orientation": with its front facing the street, the Odéon Theater in Paris has an urban orientation. For some historical architectural types, this posture was particularly important. Temples, Vitruvius insisted, should be positioned on their sites "so that those who approach with offerings and sacrifices will look toward the image within the temple beneath the eastern part of the heavens,"[2] unless, of course, some preexisting part of the terrain or town makes this impossible. Etymologically, the word "temple" indicates the separation required for orientation's *reach*, designating a place that is set apart from or cut off—as if with a template, for purposes of contemplation. "Facing," then, means looking at or having a regard for some point or place that stands opposite the building. The *pan-de-verre* and *brise-soleil* of Le Corbusier's Maison Curutchet in La Plata, Argentina, face both northward and the park on the other side of the boulevard. The strong sense of this stance is captured by the word "confronting." That the matter does not end there is clear when one recalls the other meaning of the word "facing," a meaning that is equally common in architecture. When taken to signify looking in a certain direction, the word is used as a verb. But it can also be used as a noun: a facing is a veneer or cladding applied to a building, a lining or surface that provides a protective or figurative covering. The walls of the salon in Adolf Loos's Müller Villa in Prague are faced with cipolin marble; those in the boudoir, with lemonwood. Facing in the first case occurs within the building's site, in the second, on its surfaces. Prearchitectural considerations—environment and use—are implied in each. This means that the movement implied in orientation occurs in two directions, at two distances, and within two kinds of depth: of the location in the first case, of the enclosures in the second case. Neither is optional. Because buildings occupy sites, they must "find their bearings" with respect to their environment. Because they accommodate uses, they must cover their volumes with suitable surfaces.[3]

Assuming that the development of urban, public, or communicative space is impossible as long as architectural methods and techniques remain dedicated to the production of works that proclaim themselves to be internally defined and self-sufficient, I believe that the most pressing task in our time is the description of the ways that better buildings have been oriented or inclined beyond themselves—which is to say, *otherwise*.[4] This movement could be called *counterpositioning*; its result, *counteracting*. I realize that my use of these last two terms is unfamiliar but want to risk it, because I think it may be helpful in offering a productive response to some negative tendencies that are dominant these days. The term "counterpositioning" is best known in art historical scholarship, especially in studies of late-Renaissance and baroque sculpture (*contrapposto*).[5] Medical texts of the same periods and of classical antiquity[6] elaborated an even more basic concept, that of equilibrium (*krasis*) among the parts of a body and, more importantly, between the body and its surrounding milieu, inasmuch as the vicinity combined both attractive and displeasing aspects. The same sort of engagement between an individual and its vicinity can exist in architecture. What is more, the *orientation* that is apparent in the best buildings of the past several decades shows how topography can become genuinely communicative. Contemporary ecological theory may provide a parallel here. If the technical, practical, and representational conditions architecture is to sustain take into account not only natural phenomena but also cultural norms, as embodied in urban situations, my sense of "orientation" can be seen to parallel the mandate to think widely and act locally.

Accepting the actuality of orientation amounts to a sacrifice of the individual building's freestanding self-governance. Colin Rowe and Fred Koetter's chapter in *Collage City* on "the crisis of the object" is perhaps the best known of the many arguments for an architecture of relationships.[7] Leaving aside the peculiarities of a "collage city" theory of the urban field, stating the common view, the relationships the building is to have with its surrounds are generally thought to exist between *designs*, between one's own project and those of other designers. Envisaged here is a reciprocity of professional intentions. This understanding of the urban field is wrong, or at least deficient, in two ways: it makes the wider milieu the outcome of design, which is only part of the story; and it takes for granted precisely what must be explained, the development and the limitations of the building's uniqueness. In this book I attempt to show that the building's exposure or subjection to the many and varied dimensions of its ambient conditions amounts to a disavowal of sovereignty—not just the building's but the designer's, too. While difficult for professional reasons, it seems to me to be

a necessary sacrifice, for only if we finally let go of the idea of
the self-sufficient object will we catch a glimpse of a new—and
newly significant—collective, communicative, or urban order.
The chapter with which this book ends, "The Law of Meander,"
develops this argument through brief studies of the key figures
of twentieth-century architecture: Adolf Loos, Mies van der
Rohe, Frank Lloyd Wright, and Le Corbusier.

     Both communication among people and dialogue
between buildings rest upon the acknowledgment of the limitations of the individuals that enter into conversation.[8] Here I
do not mean to restate the old truism about the reciprocity of
public and private space; rather, my point is that the recognition of privation (in the sense of limitations) increases awareness
of the inevitability of sharing.[9] I use the somewhat paradoxical
term "freestanding participation" in the chapter "Landings and
Crossings" to describe the ways this manner of engagement was
realized in a museum building located next to a river that sep-
arates University College Cork from the city. Communicative
space comes into being when limited conditions give in to what
they lack, to what they want, desire, or are pulled toward: morning light in one case, a theaterlike performance in another, or a
distant prospect. Always a matter of degree, the individuality of
a building, like that of a person, is measured by its participation
in shared conditions.[10] With this observation in mind, one can
also say that the disintegration of urban order is the precon-
dition for the building's objectlike independence. More positively, the dependence assumed in both sharing and privation
suggests that the building is codetermined by conditions that
are not of its own making. This means that the definition of a
location involves a corresponding act of dislocation, a centering
of the building outside itself. Orientation is nothing other than
the acknowledgment of this *ecstasis* or *allocentricity*.[11] Site, the
"dislocated" space between individuals, cannot be the result of

their fusion or cooperation, because they themselves (as selves) presuppose its disintegration. Uniqueness, then, is a second-order concept—not necessarily secondary in importance, but derivative. Dislocated from all forms of internal definition and unfashioned, shared topography is the antecedent condition. I examine this issue several times in this book. In the very first chapter, "Breathing Walls," I describe it with a term borrowed from the painter Georges Braque: anteceding the emergence of the discrete building is a space of *indivision*.

There have been many accounts of the city's demise, also of public life reaching its end. Many of these accounts, however, fall victim to amnesia with respect to the present, or to nostalgia for earlier times when the city seemed to have been more integral and coherent. My understanding and interests are different. I desire neither an urban arrangement that has been lost nor a city possessed of splendid architectural coherence. My concern is with the cities we actually have, particularly their urban potential.[12] Only by accepting the fact that contemporary buildings lack full reciprocity with "the coherent city" can we put ourselves in position to envisage a new urban order, a new sense of what buildings share, and a new understanding of the ways they can, indeed must, communicate with one another and the unbuilt environment. Perhaps the greatest challenge for designers is to work through the nonexpressivity required for this sort of dialogue; the communication I have in mind arises instead out of a tacit form of presence. Articulation in architecture presupposes reticent receptivity, the *silence* that architects such as Loos, Le Corbusier, Kahn, Peter Zumthor, and Ando have recommended in their writings and cultivated in their projects. In the chapter "Materials Matter," I show how both Zumthor and Jean Nouvel developed this point in opposite but complementary ways, Nouvel arguing for architecture's "non-image." When design discovers the building's desire for what it can neither generate nor possess, it also discovers the mutuality of the work's dependencies; it realizes that other buildings are similarly disposed, that they, too, depend on preexisting and undesigned conditions. Shared passions give rise to community, just as they transform sovereign objectivity into true singularity—which is not self-sufficiency.[13]

Several recent texts in and outside of architecture have helped me chart the course of my arguments. Outside of architecture, I have been guided by a number of contemporary studies that approach the problem of urban order from the vantage point of political and ethical philosophy—especially the writings of Giorgio Agamben, Jean-Luc Nancy, Martha Nussbaum, Paul Ricoeur, and Charles Taylor. Although their conclusions often differ, each of them has taken up the related problems of community and communication and has asked about the conditions under which both are possible in our time, a time when there is so much self-interest, self-consciousness, and self-assertion. Ricoeur's title *Oneself as Another* is directly instructive in this context, as are his arguments; likewise, Taylor's *Sources of the Self.* Similarly challenging are the arguments for an "inoperative community" that Nancy has set forth in his book of that title. That his points have bearing on urban and architectural order is plainly evident in a few of his other publications (*La Ville inquiète,* for example); they are even more so in texts by writers in his circle who more commonly address the subject of architecture. I have in mind Benoît Goetz, to whose *La Dislocation* Nancy supplied a wonderful preface outlining in a few pages the demands of thinking "localization" in our time. Goetz, for his part, confronts the "instability of inhabitation" in our "epoch of dislocation," with no illusions about the possibility of a return to or restoration of past urban forms. I will argue in this book that orientation exists, despite urban and cultural fragmentation. The prospect for "communicative space" has been clearly set out by Dalibor Vesely in *Architecture in the Age of Divided Representation*.[14] Particularly helpful to me has been his placement of human praxis, its situations and typicalities, at the center of architectural configuration and representation. For my part, I, too, want to indicate the real possibilities for practical and political *being-in-common*. With this topic in mind, I admit that this present book answers some questions that were left unaddressed in my *Uncommon Ground*—particularly questions about representation. The subject matter for this study, like my earlier one, is a collection of buildings from the past several decades that exemplify my arguments and themes. But like Agamben, I believe communicative space is (and perhaps is always) yet to come.

Each of the three sections in this book contains an implicit critique of current tendencies in architectural theory and design. The first section, which includes studies of the ways buildings perform, develops alternatives to the tendency to view architecture pictorially, to see it as a matter of appearance or "form," especially of technical operations (executed by the designer or the builder). In these chapters I have been prompted by the current fascination with "self-generating form," which is to say, the prospect and imagery of automatism in architecture. This fascination is not new, just newly dominant, and must be thought through again and taken to its limit. Performance is, indeed, a matter of technical understanding, but not only that. In the chapter "Unscripted Performances," I argue that the performances or events we take to be significant are often those that have not been planned.

Performances *take place*. Events require locations. The connections between performance, place, and purpose are described in the studies that make up the second section of this book. The studies of "situations" demonstrate that a physicalistic understanding of architecture—as presented in so many contemporary accounts of architecture's "material" or "tectonic" nature—is inadequate to a building's requirements with respect to human praxis. I show that our concern for a work's concreteness focuses on one of the dimensions of architectural order, only one, and one that is misconceived if taken to be wholly adequate to the architectural task.

The third section of this book, on topography, contains studies that take a stand against the various ways of conceiving the building as a self-sustaining and internally defined product of design. While my several arguments for a "topographical" interpretation of architecture would seem to favor urbanism, or landscape urbanism, as an approach, my intention is just the reverse, as long as the large-size terrain is taken to be another "object of design." Architecture has neither the power nor the responsibility to give rise to communicative space. All the best intentions in the world are useless toward this end, for the city (the concrete embodiment of common culture) is not something that single designs can form, shape, construct, or achieve—only condition and approximate. This is not to say that architecture has no role in this approximation, but that its techniques cannot "bring it about." Its limited, but necessary, role is what I have set out to explain in the pages that follow.

Endnotes

Epigraph 1 Hans-Georg Gadmer, *The Enigma of Health* (Stanford: Stanford University Press, 1996), 82.
Epigraph 2 Emmanuel Levinas, "Meaning and Sense," in *Collected Philosophical Papers* (Dordrecht: Martinus Nijhoff Publishers, 1987), 91.

1   I briefly addressed this topic years ago in *Roots of Architectural Invention* (Cambridge: Cambridge University Press, 1993), esp. 35–38.

2   Vitruvius, *Ten Books on Architecture* 4.5.1., trans. Ingrid D. Rowland (Cambridge: Cambridge University Press, 1999), 59.

3   Considerations of directionality, distance, and depth are central to two chapters in this book, "Skylines" and "Space in and out of Architecture." The fact that depth is the first, not the third, dimension was explained by Maurice Merleau-Ponty in *Phenomenology of Perception* (New York: Humanities Press, 1962), 254ff. Two recent studies elaborate his

arguments in productive ways: Edward Casey, "The Element of Voluminousness: Depth and Place Reexamined," in *Merleau-Ponty Vivant*, ed. M. C. Dillon (Albany: State University of New York, Albany, 1991); and Renaud Barbaras, *The Being of Phenomena* (Bloomington: Indiana University Press, 2004), chap. 12 esp., but elsewhere throughout.

4   Studies of "the other" are so numerous they can be arranged in several categories: investigations of race, sexual difference, "orientalism," and so on. Philosophical studies of "otherness" and of "intersubjectivity" have had a bearing on my arguments about the building's orientation beyond itself. Perhaps the best-known and most influential study on this aspect of philosophical anthropology is Martin Buber's classic *I and Thou* (*Ich und Du*, 1923), (Edinburgh: R. & R. Clark, 1937). Another book of his, published after the second world war but drafted in the years leading to it, *Between Man and Man* (New York: Macmillian, 1948), is equally relevant, especially his "Question to the Single One." Francis Strauven, in *Aldo van Eyck: The Shape of Relativity* (Amsterdam: Architectura & Natura, 1998), demonstrates the parallels between Buber's sense of "*das Gestalt gewordene Zwischen*" and van Eyck's sense of the "in-between," the space of the doorstep, for example. My chapter called "Landings and Crossings" in this book takes up the same theme. Many texts by van Eyck address this topic; "The Medicine of Reciprocity," *Architects Year Book*, no. 10 (London, 1962) is particularly useful. But, granting Buber's importance, the philosopher whose writings serve as the foundation for many contemporary studies of "otherness" is Emmanuel Levinas. See in particular *Totality and Infinity* (Pittsburgh: Duquesne University Press, 1969). Levinas himself described the range of similar investigations in *Outside the Subject* (Stanford: Stanford University Press, 1994). Michael Theunissen's *The Other* (Cambridge, Mass.: MIT Press, 1986) is similarly comparative but carried out in greater depth. The contemporary thinker who has pursued this line of study still further is Edith Wyschogrod.

5   The best short study on this type of configuration is David Summers, "Contrapposto: Style and Meaning in Renaissance Art," *Art Bulletin*, 59, no. 3 (September 1977): 336–61.

6   Gregory Leftwich, in "The Canon of Polykleitos: Tradition and Content," ed. Taisto Mäkelä in *Canon. Thematic Studies in Architecture*, vol. 3 (New York: Princeton Architectural Press, 1998), 37–80, discusses the art theoretical, medical, and philosophical literature relating to this theme, specifically under the heading of the "symmetry of opposites."

7   Colin Rowe and Fred Koetter, *Collage City* (Cambridge, Mass.: MIT Press, 1978).

8   Here, too, a number of recent or contemporary thinkers have guided the development of my arguments; chief among them is Hans-Georg Gadamer.

9   This use of the word "sharing" is meant to allude to a symbolism that is central to architecture—proportion. Just as eating a meal involves the fair distribution, or sharing, of portions, the configuration of an ensemble requires a sensible proportioning of parts. If there is one share, there must be others; one part implies a counterpart. I've chosen the nontechnical term "sharing" over "proportioning," because it preserves a link with the practical dimension of a configuration's primary order.

10   So far as I know, there is only one book on architecture with the term "individuality" as its title: C. F. A. Voysey, *Individuality* (London: Chapman and Hall, 1915). It is an impassioned and eloquent defense. Voysey's opening quotation, "to thine own self be true," plots the book's trajectory. He is at great pains to oppose all forms of "conformism" and "collectivism." The end of the book struggles with attributes that are often attached to individuality: distinction, notoriety, and popularity. Today, these attributes come into focus in debates on "star architects" and "branding." The intellectual and cultural challenge Voysey faced is painfully clear in his concluding chapter on the war that was raging in Europe while he was writing, for he could not avoid the observation that the German emperor also had a strong sense of "individuality." In my Chapter 6, "Sitting in the City," I take up some of Voysey's themes in my discussion of Loos's critique of artistic expression in the domestic realm. The links between individuality, privacy, and privation are set out by Hannah Arendt in *The Human Condition* (Chicago: University of Chicago Press, 1958). See, for example, her chapter on "The Rise of the Social," where she writes: "We no longer think primarily of deprivation when we use the word 'privacy,' and this is partly due to

the enormous enrichment of the private sphere through modern individualism" (page 38). My aim is to show architecture's contribution to this "enrichment," as well as alternative possibilities. I take up another part of this issue in my discussion of praxis and urban order in Chapter 7, "Practically Primitive," arguing that "acting in solidarity" (Gadamer's phrase) is fundamental in both social life and urban architecture.

11　These terms have been discussed in a number of important contributions to philosophical anthropology. For "ecstasis," the key text is Helmuth Plessner, *Die Stufen des Organischen und der Mensch* (Berlin, 1965), particularly chap. 7. On "allocentricity," see Erwin Strauss, "Norm and Pathology in I-World Relations," in *Phenomenological Psychology* (New York: Basic Books, 1966).

12　There is, I think, a similar concern expressed in the concluding section of Marshall Berman's *All That Is Solid Melts into Air* (New York: Simon & Schuster, 1982). He calls that chapter "Bringing It All Back Home."

13　I believe this is the thrust of a short book to which Jean Baudrillard and Jean Nouvel contributed, *The Singular Object of Architecture* (Minneapolis: University of Minnesota Press, 2002). What I've described as an unfashioned space of dislocation—the primary topic of sharing—parallels their sense of the "unsaid surplus" and "seeing and forgetting architecture" (pages 8–13).

14　Dalibor Vesely, *Architecture in the Age of Divided Representation* (Cambridge, Mass.: MIT Press, 2004).

Part 1

Performances

CHAPTER 1

Breathing Walls

The American painter Robert Rauschenberg once explained that throughout his career he had worked on a single problem: bridging the separation between art and life. "Painting," he said, "relates to both art and life. Neither can be made. I try to act in that gap between the two."[1] He was not the first—nor, I suspect, will he be the last—to undertake this task. Friedrich Nietzsche's thought was once described as an effort to overcome the "raging discord" between art and truth.[2] The problem is especially acute in architecture, where the distinction between art and building is taken for granted in most discussions of a project's functionality. In extreme form, the assumption runs as follows: architectural design leads to artistic *works*; building construction results in shelters that actually *work*. Just as Rauschenberg sought to act in the gap between art and life, I would like to describe the connections between one of life's bare necessities (shelter) and its expression (art). To do this I will discuss a single wall in a single building.

Atmosphere

When the Dominican fathers of San Juan, Puerto Rico, first offered Henry Klumb the commission for the Church of San Martín de Porres (1950), he turned them down.[3] In explanation

Henry Klumb, San Martín de Porres, Cataño, Puerto Rico, 1949–66; interior view

of his refusal, he gave two reasons: as a Protestant he felt he could not design a conventional Roman Catholic Church, and as a modern architect he could not build in the Spanish colonial style that everyone on the island had become used to. Eventually he overcame both obstacles and designed a fascinating little sanctuary. My concern, however, is not with the building as a whole, but just one of its parts, an element I will call the *breathing wall*. Obviously, the term is metaphorical. So far as I know, this particular formulation was not used by Klumb, who employed a number of other terms to describe the elements that allow buildings to admit fresh and exhaust stale air. Le Corbusier developed equivalent vocabulary in his proposals for *respiration exacte* in modern buildings.[4] In what follows, I will study this single element in order to use it as a foundation for more basic arguments about architecture and life. The breathing wall is a useful topic because it operates in three ways simultaneously: *technically*, as a device for modifying the climate; *practically*, as a way of structuring the events that define a (religious) institution; and *symbolically*, as the representation of these events. With respect to this last aspect, a single quotation from the architect should be sufficient to indicate the amplitude of meanings implied by the term "breathing wall": "[O]ne of the human necessities of prayer is the ability to breathe, therefore the circulation of air is something that has to be considered by the architect [in the design of a church]."[5] That more is involved than getting oxygen into the blood is clear; both religious and everyday breathing supply the lungs with what they need, but something else is involved in the former. One does not need to be a Catholic to know that the Genesis account of human beginnings hinges on this "something else," for nothing less than mankind resulted from the *inspiration* of soil: "The Lord God formed man of the dust of the ground, and breathed into his nostrils the breath of life; and man became a living soul."[6] Nor is a confession of faith required to see evidences of the extrarespiratory consequences of breathing in the parallel account of origins in the Pentecost myth: communication and community resulted from an inrush of air. The report in Acts 2 is as follows: "Suddenly there came a sound from heaven as of a rushing mighty wind, and it filled all the house where they were sitting... and every man heard [all the others] speaking in his own language."[7] In both stories, breath was simultaneously an instrument and a sign of new life. The Greek word for breath or vapor, *atmos*, clarifies why the mood or quality of an architectural setting, such as the nave of San Martín de Porres, is termed its *atmosphere*.

When entering this little church, a crucifix designed by the client, a Dominican father named Marcolino Maas, attracts one's attention, not the building itself. Maas confirmed the tacit presence of the building by describing an unaffected sort of architecture. The building, he observed, "breathes [an] air of freshness and originality.... There is nothing that could have been copied from somewhere else; yet there is true, honest, and simple building pleasure in and around it without snob-bism or any aim for sensationalism." Father Maas also affirmed the building's suitability for religious practice; its simplicity, he thought, did not prevent it from expressing "a deep religious and quite Catholic and liturgical atmosphere." Nor did the absence of graphic ornament prevent it from revealing the atmosphere of its bayside location. The Dominican father observed that the floor-to-ceiling piers, or fins, on either side of the nave isolate the interior from external distractions when one enters the space or faces the altar. Seclusion, he suggested, "concentrate[d] the attention." Others saw that these piers provided for an intimacy that allowed withdrawn introspection (*recogimiento*). They help focus the parishioner's attention during a service, because they confine his or her perspective; rotated on plan 45° from the axis of the nave, the piers block lateral views. Despite this, the space is far from being closed in, because the fragrance from

Henry Klumb, Museum of Anthropology, History, and Art, UPR, Río Piedras, Puerto Rico, 1953; courtyard

what Maas called "the lavish tropical landscape," together with
the sea air passing from the bay to the town, enters the building through the same fins that give the interior its seclusion.
In addition, when one leaves the building "these pillars visually
open up," Maas observed, allowing the shrine and baptistery,
together with the landscape beyond, to come into view.[8]

All that I want to argue in this study concerns the oper-
ational and the metaphorical substance of these fins, for they
are the means by which the building "*breathes* [an] air of freshness and originality," and also provide its Catholic and liturgical
"atmosphere." With them, or this atmosphere, as my example, I
would like to show that a building's performances are the means
by which it simultaneously accomplishes practical purposes and
gives them legible articulation. Put differently, the appearance
and meaning of an architectural work are essentially tied to the
operations performed by its several elements. Representational
content is not something *added to* the shaping of settings in
response to life's "bare necessities," as suggested by arguments
within the functionalist tradition, but is something intrinsic to
the response to those necessities. My claim is that metaphors
such as "breathing" name an essential dimension of a building's
operations.

The *quiebra sol*: operation and representation

There are well-known precedents for Klumb's use of elements
that regulate the flow of air and light into a building. Perhaps the
best known are those developed by Le Corbusier, particularly
his devices for blocking or breaking the heat of the sun—the
famous *brise-soleil*. Klumb also made use of the sun breaker, or
quiebra sol, throughout his career. It appears prominently in his
early work, across the face of his New York Department Store
in Santurce, San Juan, for example. A number of his buildings
on the campus of the University of Puerto Rico in Río Piedras

(the Lazaro Library and the Law School, for example) are also fitted out with this device. Another elegant example is the central auditorium and library building at the Colegio San Ignacio in Río Piedras. There is great variation in the articulation of these sunshades, however; only the earliest, on the New York Department Store, could adequately be described by Reyner Banham's uncharitable phrase "external egg-crate of vertical and horizontal shades."[9]

Banham suggested that the *brise-soleil* emerged historically as a form of compensation. The development of the load-bearing frame created the possibility of replacing the entire wall with a window. Le Corbusier took this possibility as something of a requirement (see, for example, the Salvation Army Building in Paris or the Clarté Apartments in Geneva). When large expanses of glass faced directions other than the south, few environmental problems arose. For walls exposed to the sun throughout the day, the *mur neutralisant* was supposed to handle unwanted heat gain.[10] The idea was that hot or cold air circulating in the cavity of double glazing would mediate temperature differences between the inside and outside. When this proved to be unworkable, sometimes for nontechnical reasons, another device was necessary—assuming that a return to thick-wall construction and "punched windows" was not an option. That other device was the external sunscreen, which was to compensate for the window wall's miserable thermal performance.

Two decades after Le Corbusier first struggled with this, Marcel Breuer confidently asserted that external screening was the only sensible solution to the heat gain problem of window walls, for the sun had to be "reflected before it [was] trapped behind the glass and fill[ed] the inside with radiant heat."[11] Curtains, blinds, shades, and moveable panels in the interior were sufficient for altering the amount of light entering the building, but sun control devices on the exterior were the

Henry Klumb, College of Law, UPR, Río Piedras, Puerto Rico, 1969–81; entry court and stairway

only instruments that could be effective against the heat that resulted from solar gain. Breuer's argument was furthered by Aladar Olgyay and Victor Olgyay in their comprehensive study of solar control and sunshading devices. Le Corbusier's solution in the Marseilles Block was, they thought, "fundamentally sound." Because it was opaque, the sun breaker intercepted both the direct and the diffused types of solar radiation. Correct sizing allowed heat to be excluded in the summer and admitted in the winter. Le Corbusier's design was also praised because it expressed "a strong spatial character," adding "new elements to the architectural vocabulary."[12] This suggests thermal or environmental performance was not all that the sun breaker allowed. Equally significant was its expressive or aesthetic performance.

This point can be extended. Clearly, in Le Corbusier's postwar projects the *brise-soleil* was as much an instrument of expression as of climate control. In the Maison Curutchet in Argentina (1952), the Millowners' Building in Ahmadabad (1954), the Secretariat at Chandigarh (1958), or the Carpenter Center in Cambridge, Massachusetts (1964), thermal control is achieved by devices that also have aesthetic, even monumental, expression. Alan Colquhoun observed that the sun breaker "was more than a technical device; it introduced a new architectural element in the form of a thick, permeable wall, whose depth and subdivisions gave the facade the modeling and aedicular expression that had been lost with the suppression of the window and the pilaster."[13] Expression, however, is not the same as representation—let alone symbolization. I will return to this distinction in a later section in this chapter, "Legible operations."

Continuity through resistance

Le Corbusier, Breuer, and the Olgyay brothers concentrated on the ways screening devices combat the harmful effects of sunshine. Resistance is only half the work of these elements, how-

Le Corbusier, Lucio Costa, et al., Ministry of Education and Health, Rio de Janeiro, 1937–42; sun screen from outside and inside

ever. The same devices that restrict heat penetration allow the free entry of fresh air—in fact, they do more than allow it, they work to accelerate it. One of the facades of Klumb's IBM building in Santurce exemplifies this yielding type of external screen: the full-height louver. A similar device can also be seen on the side wings of his Medical Services building at the University of Puerto Rico, where it encloses hallways that connect examination and treatment rooms. These elements also exist at the side of the University Museum entry portico and on other Klumb buildings; the Student Center on the Mayagüez campus is a very good example. In some instances the louvers were fixed in position, standing ready to admit fresh air while counteracting the sun's familiar lines of attack. In other places they could be moved manually, and in still others they were rotated electrically, as on the IBM building. Not only operation but vantage was key, as is clear from a sketch for the louvers on an apartment building, also in Santurce. This was important to Le Corbusier too, as can be seen in a plan for his Millowners' Building. And as with Klumb's use of the sunscreen, Le Corbusier's buildings provided ample precedent for the louver wall: La Tourette and the Carpenter Center, for example. Other architects were equally inventive: Neutra in the United States; Villanueva in Venezuela; Niemeyer, Costa, Reidy, and the Roberto brothers in Brazil.[14]

Klumb's Church of San Martín de Porres presents a subtle variation on the theme, however, for in that building there is not a single but a double row of filters: the fixed vertical louvers that line the parts of outer walls, allowing air and light to pass through the church, and affording a view; and the much larger fins that (in plan) limit the lateral extent of the nave, providing it with enclosure and defining its atmosphere.

Depending on one's position and vantage point, the louvered walls approximate the continuous planarity of solid partitions. One's view is, indeed, obstructed along such a wall's entire length, but not uniformly so, for darks contrast with

TOP LEFT Oscar Niemeyer, Hall of Industry, Parque Ibirapuéra, São Paulo, 1953; facade. ABOVE RIGHT Marcelo, Milton, and Mauricio Roberto, Brazilian Press Association Building (ABI), Rio de Janeiro, 1938; facade. BOTTOM LEFT Lucio Costa, Parque Guinle, Rio de Janeiro, 1947–53; facade

lights at each panel's edge, leaving the midsections to mediate the opposition. As this rhythmic play of bright against dark
spreads its effects laterally, a parallel space at the wall's edges
is created—basically a walkway on either side. A precedent for
this solution is the famous ABI building (1938) in Rio by the
Roberto brothers, with its passageway between the outer enclosure of the offices and the inner face of the sun breaker. Other
elegant examples in Rio are the apartment buildings in Guinle
Park by Lucio Costa (1947–53).

Because of the church's plan geometry, the wall in San
Martín de Porres adds to the room's orthogonality an oblique
orientation toward settings outside or beyond it. Both orienta-
tions increase the depth of the building, in the first instance by
layering, in the second by opening. As Father Maas observed,
depending on where one is standing in the church, the margins
of the setting become more marginal or less so—more interconnected with the interior they surround or less a part of it. Thus,
they introduce both frontality and obliquity into the building,
the latter by placing at an angle the openings of their continuous
planarity, which concentrates attention at one end of the hall or
room (here, toward the altar) and releases it at the other (into
the building's surrounds or adjoining rooms). The louver wall
is partition-like but wider than the typical "space-dividing element," and it is directional. It is more ample because it projects
a shadow space and is directional because it alternately concentrates and expands space, like a lens at one end and a manifold
at the other.

Here I would like to make a general observation: architecture such as this can be called *productive*, because its settings supply what the given location is unable to give on its
own. Ambient light, for instance, is made more intense when
reflected off the surfaces of the *quiebra sol*—brights are bright-
ened. Shadows are cast and cooled by these same devices. One

should not say architecture is the sole source of these conditions, for its real accomplishment is the alteration or adjustment of phenomena that are already there. Its work could be described as a crystallizing or cultivating sort of productivity; this is what makes architectural elements metaphorical. Speaking broadly of fiction, Paul Ricoeur used the term "iconic augmentation" to describe artistic productivity.[15] A key to this "augmentation" in architecture is the relationship between the building and the "pre-given" milieu. Klumb called prevailing conditions *latent*. He took great pains to understand what was *given* in each location his buildings were to occupy. Evidence of this concern appears in his attempt to diagram the movement of air across the sites on which he built (percentages and line weights on plan drawings showing the intensity of breezes coming from different directions).

Perhaps a building's productivity should be described as adjunctive or adjectival, since its chief role is to modify what it inherits. But this is acceptable only if the modification that is envisaged is understood to include taking a stand against what the natural world offers, discovering in what is not given what might be. Put differently, there would be no continuity if there were no resistance. Modern architecture did not eliminate the separation between inside and outside, so that the space of the one could flow into the other; it made that separation much more subtle than it had been in previous architectures. Boundaries between spatial interiors and exteriors are not overcome with the adoption of the structural frame, but thickened. Certainly the elements set up within the edge thickness of a structural frame are less weighty and visible than their load-bearing anteced-ents, but this is because they approximate themselves so closely to the potentials (not the results) of the world that surrounds them—its latencies. Klumb's buildings work with manifesta-tions of climate and culture by variously resisting and admitting their forces, with no less insistence than intelligence. Although a modest solution, Klumb's Serra Office Building in Santurce shows very clearly how resisting and admitting both climate and culture can be accomplished on the streets of a modern city. The case is helpful because much modern architecture that was designed to be "environmentally responsive" was also antiurban, which is to say culturally inadequate.

Anterior indivision

The idea of a building as an ensemble of devices that perform movements counter to the actions of the environment is not completely satisfactory, because it preserves a dichotomy that is a result of analysis, not experience. When one is drawn into some event inside the nave of Klumb's San Martín de Porres, it is hardly necessary—barely sensible—to differentiate which aspects of its "atmosphere" result from the building and which from its climate and culture, neither of which the architect designed. Only designers and theorists puzzle over these distinctions, in ill-considered attempts to grant primary causality to one or another. Children reading in a classroom, friends telling stories in the afternoon shadows of a plaza, or believers with heads bowed before an altar do not discriminate between the "natural and artificial elements" of their surroundings. Outside of professional interests, or prior to disciplinary deliberation and reflection, there is no uncertainty about what exists and unfolds in these settings, and participation does not require an intellectual summation of their constitutive conditions. In the church the light is less bright, the temperature is cooler, and the hum of activities is quieter than outside. Moreover, the setting has been prepared for particular performances that could not occur outdoors: the altar ahead, the ambo pulpit at the front left, the baptistery and shrine to the sides, confessionals front and back, the organ behind, and so on—each thing at the right distance and in the right position for the enactment of the institution's several services, as church, sanctuary, and pilgrimage chapel. While the separation between built and unbuilt conditions seems so obvious, it is in fact a product of analysis, an outcome of reflection that narrows a fuller and more basic grasp of the situation. If we try to catch a building's events as they actually unfold—reading, talking, or praying—there is no separation of the aspects of the setting's *mood* that result from the architect's provisions from those aspects of mood that are the gift of its unbuilt surround and everyday affairs, together with the historical grounds on which both are established.

When pointing to the relationship between the interior and exterior, Klumb spoke of their "fusion"; as he wrote, "architecture fuses man with his environment."[16] One way to think of this condition is to imagine a connection that is so tight that separation is impossible, like an amalgamation that results from intense heat and melting. Yet this image, too, is misleading, because it preserves traces of each element's "original" separateness. The concept of "fusion" must be interpreted differently if the actuality and metaphorical substance of the building are to be adequately described—in this instance, its *respiration*.

Father Maas observed that the interior of San Martín de Porres "has a deep religious and quite Catholic atmosphere." This was apparent, he said, in the "air of freshness and originality" it breathed. How is this atmosphere to be understood? From what does it arise, and what puts it at risk? We are presented, it seems to me, with a condition or quality that unmistakably imposes itself on experience but arises from a source that cannot be clearly identified. An atmosphere, like a mood, impresses itself on experience because it is global or oceanic: it envelops, surrounds, and entirely encloses the events and institutions of our lives. The meanings Martin Heidegger attached to the word *Stimmung* express this very well.[17] While a room's atmosphere is unmistakable and overpowering, all attempts to explain its several sources or causes are defeated by the unity, or *indivi-sion*, of the total circumstance. Describing the church's Catholic atmosphere, Father Maas did not individuate its several components; he treated the distinctions between architectural, social, or natural conditions as if they really did not matter, as if attending to them would have distracted him from what he was trying to express. Likewise, Klumb's notion of "fusion" referred not to the blending together, crossover, or integration of previously separate elements but to *a prior state of indistinctness*, a state that was not only energetic and creative, as he said, but too comprehensive to be seen or treated objectively.

If not as an object, or composition of several distinct things, how can architecture contribute to such an "atmosphere"? How can a building *discover and disclose similarities* in the elements that make up a given situation? An answer to this question will, I think, help us see the connections between a building's practical and metaphorical dimensions. In a book titled *Rhetoric as Philosophy*, the philosopher Ernesto Grassi described the logic of metaphor as "a capacity to see the similar." In explanation of what is involved in the "vision of the common," he cited Aristotle: "Transferal [*metapherein*] must be completed on the basis of similarity."[18]

In Klumb's architecture the breathing wall led to certain effects, it *produced* cool shadows, together with a measured supply of fresh air—donations for which all who use his buildings remain grateful. Certainly the building's elements are passive—they do not move or change position—but they can also be seen to be active if their "behavior" is seen to result in the creation of qualities the world lacks. This is to say, architectural elements are *passively active*. Seemingly at rest, they are secretly at work. The key is this: in their labor, architectural elements fuse themselves into the latencies of the ambient environment, adopting their capacity for change or *movement*. Obviously, this fusion is fictional; but in the events that define the setting, it is entirely believable.

To work or be active in this way, the building must accept the fact that its effects are codependent on the potentialities of a given situation. When the building operates as it should, the environment is not external to it but internal. If we insist on saying it is part of the landscape, we must also admit that it is also the terrain's *counterpart*, that the two are sides of one coin. Brighter light and cooler shadow both depend on the sunscreen. Similarly, the animation of Klumb's sanctuary depends on the breathing wall. More particularly, prayer, in Klumb's account, depends on breathing; the measured supply of its source is granted by the louver walls. Yet when the building produces light and life, it demonstrates qualities it does not possess on its own, qualities it was not given *by design*, for it acts as if it were all of a piece with its milieu, disposing itself into an interenvironmental system of correspondences. Father Maas praised Klumb's church for being "perfectly matched to the surrounding neighborhood."[19] But this "matching" is precisely what is difficult to understand, despite the fact that it is exceedingly obvious.

In unreflective experience, neither Klumb's church nor the milieu obtrude themselves into one's awareness. During the liturgy, the service, not the setting, occupies one's attention; the latter is the material and durable aspect of the former. Focus on the service in its setting does not eliminate the presence of the architecture and landscape, but only treats them as topics of marginal awareness. The decisive characteristic of these margins is their indistinctness or seamlessness. This unity is a condition that *seems* to exist, for architecture can only act *as if* it were part of the natural world. As noted above, the vertical fins are the means by which this is accomplished. While the building is not part of the environment—no one can sensibly deny that it was added to it—it presents itself as though it were coextensive with it. What Ricoeur described as the "paradox of fiction"[20] (a productive reference to a world that does not in fact exist) has its parallel in this paradox of productive fusion, *an antecedent indivision disclosed by the building.*[21] In its workings the building is what it was designed to be, but it acts as if it were part of a world that was never designed. This is how architecture creates the "atmosphere" of a situation, through its enactments, operations, or performances. Already in its mere functionality, then, the building finds itself taking on a role, acting a part that is not its own. This theatrical role is as much a metaphorical as a practical performance.

Legible operations

The building is thus already a symbolism, already a system of references beyond itself. This is by virtue of the metaphorical nature of some of its elements: in the case of the Church of San Martín de Porres, the breathing wall, in which both measure and rhythm are key. Imagine, one more time, a parishioner at prayer inside this building. The bench on which he or she sits is one of many that are spaced parallel to the regular intervals of the room's floor pattern. These intervals, in turn, are based on the repetitive spacing and geometry of the vertical fins. Their configuration regulates the infiltration of light and air, which obviously have their source outside the building, even beyond the surrounding gardens, in the open expanse of the Bay of San Juan or at least the line of its shore. The sound of the surf is too distant to be heard inside the building, but the force of its breeze is strong enough to be felt. Just as trees and dust give shape to the wind, the building's louvered walls measure its flow. And they give it scale; what wind is for the world, breath is for the person. Breathing, in most religions, is the foundation of prayer, because it is the cradle of rhythm or discipline. Klumb said as much when he observed that prayer depends on measured in- and exhalation.

Despite all its provisions, no building is sufficient for our expectations. Every architectural work suffers a constitutive and intolerable weakness at its core—no natural light, no fresh air, no views, and no real basis for renewal of its cultural heritage. Because of what it lacks, the building cannot escape behaving as if it were something other than it is, behaving as though it were part of the world around it, joined to what sustains and surpasses it. Klumb knew this, for he saw that care for the latent and inherited conditions of building would be necessary for architecture to "express a way of life." He once observed that beauty can be found in common things. He referred to this as an "aesthetics of what there is."[22]

Klumb worked in collaboration with local artists: a painter, a sculptor, and Maas himself. Relief sculpture can be seen behind the altar and above the choir; and a statue of San Martín de Porres stands in the shrine, mediating the nave and the landscape, or the church and the world. In postwar architectural debates in the United States and Europe, monumental expression was thought to result from the combination of artistic and functional elements; representational works were to be added to functional solutions as a supplementary form of compensation. Klumb's works cannot be identified with this notion of representation, because they are inherently metaphorical. They express not themselves but "a way of life"—the latencies and cultural inheritance, the content of which always exceeds every showing, hence the inadequacy of merely functional solutions. Insofar as the building's performances call for it to act as if it were something it is not, part of the natural world and social milieu, the functional solution inaugurates representation. Metaphorical articulation is not supplementary to the enclosure of events; it is their visible face, an outward demonstration of the ways the building conditions, limits, or resists the energies of those events. The problem with twentieth-century functionalism is that it neglected the potential for metaphorical and symbolic meaning within the subject matter that is proper to architectural articulation. Representation in Klumb's work is not grafted onto the accommodation of pedestrian necessities; it is their legible aspect. Speaking more broadly, metaphor in architecture is neither optional nor conventional. It is a way of showing—articulating—what the building does, how it behaves in contrast to itself, as if it were part of the world it finds itself within but was added to. The building's investment in the unseen fullness of what "there is" sets the stage for its situations to live and breathe as if they had arisen by virtue of nature itself.

Endnotes

1   Robert Rauschenberg, in *Sixteen Americans*, ed. Dorothy C. Miller (New York: Museum of Modern Art, 1959), 58.

2   As characterized by Martin Heidegger in his *Nietzsche: Volume One, The Will to Power as Art* (New York: Harper & Row, 1979). Quoted in David Farrell Krell, "Art and Truth in Raging Discord: Heidegger and Nietzsche on the Will to Power," *boundary 2*, 4, no. 2 (Winter 1976): 378–92.

3   Recent scholarship is beginning to give Henry Klumb his due. The most thorough study to date is one edited by Enrique Vivone, who also directs the archive at the University of Puerto Rico (AACUPR), where the Klumb materials are preserved. See Enrique Vivone, ed., *Henry Klumb and the Poetic Exuberance of Architecture* (San Juan, Puerto Rico: AACUPR, 2006). See also the recent (unpublished) doctoral dissertation by Rosa Otero, *Permeable Walls and Place Recognition in Henry Klumb's Architecture of Social Concern* (University of Pennsylvania, 2005).

4   Le Corbusier, *Précisions* (Paris: Crès et Cie, 1930), 64.

5   Henry Klumb, cited in "Iglesia moderna: arquitectura funcional avanca in PR," *Vision 3* (August 22, 1952): 30. Translation by Juan Manuel Heredia.

6   Gen. 2:7.

7   Acts 2:2–6.

8   Marcolino Maas, "The Sanctuary of Blessed Martín de Porres at Bayview, Puerto Rico," *Liturgical Arts* (November 1952): 5–6.

9   Reyner Banham, *The Architecture of the Well-tempered Environment* (Chicago: University of Chicago Press, 1969), 158.

10   Le Corbusier, 66.

11   Marcel Breuer, *Sun and Shadow* (New York: Dodd, Mead & Company, 1955), 117.

12   Aladar and Victor Olgyay, *Solar Control and Shading Devices* (Princeton: Princeton University Press, 1957), 7.

13   Alan Colquhoun, "The Significance of Le Corbusier," in *Modernity and the Classical Tradition* (Cambridge, Mass.: MIT Press, 1989), 187.

14   That early modern architects in Brazil were key in the development of this solution has been persuasively demonstrated by Carlos Eduard Comas in "Modern Architecture: Brazilian Corollary," *AA Files* 36 (Summer 1998): 3–13. Another Brazilian scholar, Margareth Campos da Silva Pereira, has shown how important a brief communication from Lucio Costa to Le Corbusier was in the very early history of the sun breaker. When advising Le Corbusier on the subject matter of his conferences for Brazilian architects, Costa suggested that he not spend too much time discussing light, for the Brazilians had quite enough of that and were wondering what to do with it—which is to say, how to reduce it and its negative effects: "Não falar muito de *Sol!* Temos sol até demais, e não sabemos o que fazer com ele." Cited in Campos da Silva Pereira, *Le Corbusier e o Brasil* (São Paulo: Tessela, Projeto Editora, 1987), 146.

15   Paul Ricoeur, "The Function of Fiction in Shaping Reality," in *A Ricoeur Reader* (Toronto: University of Toronto Press, 1991), 130.

16   Klumb, "My Architectural Design Philosophy." Talk presented at the 65th annual FAIA convention, Oct. 2, 1979. Quoted in Otero dissertation, 322.

17   Heidegger examined the phenomenon of "being attuned" in many texts, but perhaps most famously in *Being and Time* as part of his study of the spatial dimension of being in the world; see Martin Heidegger, *Being and Time* (New York: Harper & Row, 1962), 172ff.

18   Ernesto Grassi, *Rhetoric as Philosophy* (University Park: Pennsylvania State University Press, 1980), 94ff.

19   Maas, "Sanctuary of Blessed Martín," 5.

20   Ricoeur, "Function of Fiction," 129.

21   "Indivision" here follows the usage of the painter Georges Braque. He wrote: "*Je ne cherche pas la définition. Je tends vers l'infinition.*" Georges Braque, *Le Jour et la Nuit Cahiers 1917–52* (Paris: Gallimard, 1952), 30. Although intelligible in French, "infinition" is obsolete in English. What is more, it strongly conveys infinity. My concern, like Braque's, is to bridge the gaps between things. Among the English alternatives to "infinition"—infinition, indefinition, and indivision—I chose the last because it indicates a prior state of undivided continuity, as does Braque's description of "tactile space."

22   Klumb, "My Architectural Design Philosophy," 322.

CHAPTER 2

Unscripted Performances

The world is not an object such that
I have in my possession the law of its
making.

—Maurice Merleau-Ponty, *Phenomenology of Perception*

I think that in every building, every
street, there is something that creates
an event, and whatever creates an
event, is unintelligible.

—Jean Baudrillard and Jean Nouvel, *The Singular Objects of Architecture*

This study argues for a shift of orientation in architectural theory
and practice, from what the building is to what it does, defining the first by means of the second. Broadly speaking, there
are two ways designers and critics tend to view buildings: (1) as
objects that result from design and construction *techniques*, and
(2) as objects that *represent* various practices and ideas. Although
these accounts seem to explain fully the building's origin and
destination, technological and aesthetic styles of thought reduce
architecture to our concepts and experiences of it. Other and
essential aspects of buildings come into view if one supposes
that the actuality of the building consists largely in its acts, its
performances.

My aim is to outline how the building discloses content through its operations. For this to be apparent, technological and aesthetic explanations must be temporarily suspended. This means subordinating, at least for a while, the questions about experience, meaning, and production that normally occupy our attention. This methodological premise allows us to consider briefly the building as autonomous or independent from constructional and perceptual intentionalities. Such an approach challenges the notion of architecture's perfect rationality, for it will be seen that its performances depend in part on conditions that cannot be rationalized. This does not mean they cannot be understood, just that they must be understood differently.

Before proceeding, a certain assumption needs to be rejected, namely that the development of new instruments and methods of predicting the building's structural or environmental behavior will radically redefine the discipline's practice and theory. Perhaps attention to the ways buildings act will contribute to a new understanding of the manner in which they are imagined, made, and experienced. But this new understanding will not result from the development and deployment of new techniques alone. Continued dedication to a technical interpretation of performance will lead to nothing more than an uncritical reaffirmation of old-style functionalist thinking—a kind of thinking that is both reductive and inadequate because it recognizes only what it can predict. I will return to this point in the section under the heading "Effects, actions, and events."

Architectural performance

What is meant by "architectural performance"? The term is not new in professional discourse, but current usage draws upon nonarchitectural linguistic traditions. Is the performance envisaged for the building like that of a machine or engine, or is it closer to what might be seen on a theatrical stage or heard in a concert hall? This inquiry's central question can be stated simply: In what ways does the building act; what, in other words, does the architectural work actually do?

One way of resolving these questions rather quickly is to say that the building acts to "house" activities and experiences. An auditorium, for example, houses lectures; likewise a kitchen, cooking; a courtroom, trials; and so on. This answer contains a germ of truth—buildings do accommodate practical purposes—yet if we predicate the life of buildings on use, we assign to them a borrowed existence, for we then assume that the room or street's recognizable profile conforms to our expectations of it.[1] For the premise of predicated meaning to be sustained, we must take the side of the perceiving subject and must implicitly consider experience to be the light that illuminates the building's performance. Now what seems eminently sensible from a pragmatic and pedestrian point of view has been shown to be naive by Aldo Rossi in his critique of functionalism.[2] Uses, he points out, often change throughout the life of the building—private houses become clinics, theaters are turned into apartment blocks, and so on. Such an inconstant criterion as functional use cannot, he suggests, be applied to define the building itself. Decisive instead, for Rossi, is type. For me, it is operation or performance.

Thus, a basic question presents itself: Must the side of the subject be taken when an account of specifically architectural modes of behavior is given? Might this not leave something out, perhaps something essential? Certainly buildings are designed and built "for us": a farmhouse for farm life, a schoolhouse for schooling, for example. A definition derived from Aristotle, that architecture imitates human action and life, may be ancient but is still largely true. Granting this, cannot the building or some of its key aspects also be understood apart from us and its use, irrespective of programmatic requirements, individual desires, and cultural expectations? If not fully, can it be understood at least in part, without turning to ourselves as the benefactors of its identity? If we slacken the threads of intention that bind us to objects, what will appear?

The question seems worth pursuing, because it is undeniable that rooms predate our use of them. They also remain as they were once we have finished with them, at least basically the same. With just this single and simple observation about the building's extended temporality in mind, it seems fair to observe that architecture exists quite happily and completely without us. If that seems an unwarranted conclusion, I think one can affirm without demonstration that no building is entirely determined by "anthropological predicates"; instead, each is, in some measure, articulate on its own terms, each is to some degree unpredicated, even auto-predicated. The concern for "experience" in architectural discourse, often announced with all good intentions, is generally a secret concern for design and production insofar as what is "perceived" is taken to be what is offered in designed perspectives. While congenial to technical or professional interests, this trend might well cause us to miss the reality of the building itself—especially that architectural reality that exists regardless of my interests or yours. My working hypothesis is that the theme of performance is a key to the building's internal definition or pre-predicated existence.

Again, there are two common ways of missing the reality of the architectural work: one is to see the building as nothing but a system of components intended in design and realized by construction; the other is to view the building as a system of representations outlined in composition and experienced in perception. Both viewpoints make the building into an object bound to intentionalities, either a result of technical reason or a confirmation of aesthetic expectations. This is precisely what happened in modernist functionalism, especially in the version

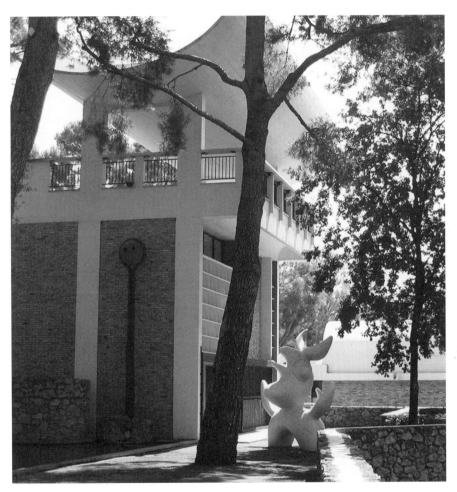

José Luis Sert, Maeght Foundation, Saint Paul-de-Vence, France, 1958–71; facade

advanced in the post–World War II period, after modernism's narrow determinism had revealed its incapacity for providing a plausible and legible urban architecture. The debates on monumentality, for example, clearly testify to widespread recognition of the poverty of functionalist solutions in their call for new alliances with art practices in the formation of urban centers. José Luis Sert's theory[3] and work exemplify this stance very well, as they demonstrate the desire to couple technical and aesthetic concerns in the formation of new civic institutions. Marcel Breuer's writings[4] and buildings demonstrate a similar thesis. Midcentury publications that address technical problems also assert the limited significance of functional concerns. The works of Olgyay and Olgyay,[5] which I mentioned in Chapter 1, are a good case in point, as are those of Max Fry and Jane Drew,[6] for both pairs of architects suggested that art could compensate for the cultural sterility of functionally determined buildings. The widely celebrated architects of our time no longer *insert* art into functional solutions, but use it to drape or cover them; yet here, too, sculptural form is essentially a compensation for the inadequacy of functionalist solutions.

Rather than rehearse this old debate between works that are useful and those that are beautiful, seeking new answers to questions that were poorly formulated in the first place, it may be helpful to ask not about the work, but about the way the work *works*. Is there "action" in architecture's apparent passivity, in its steady and static permanence? Is the application of the term "behavior" to architectural elements anything more than a pathetic fallacy, or do buildings really perform in some way? Compared to dance and musical expression, the building seems to be resolutely—even embarrassingly—inert and inactive: "frozen music," indeed. Compared to film, architecture seems positively motionless, about as animated as a stop sign. The house, theater, and museum sit where they have been planted, patiently awaiting a visitor's arrival and experience, as if they could only glow with life when ignited by interests you and I bring into them when we walk through their front doors. But is the building only what we make of it? One suspects there must be something more to this, because if it were only the consequence of an inhabitant's intentions, it would be impossible to understand why we often feel the need to habituate ourselves to buildings, and why they can alternately depress and delight us.

Effects, actions, and events

No doubt the building is, indeed, a technical and aesthetic work, but it is known as such through its workings, through its instruments and equipment (broadly conceived). Stated more strongly, the building *is* its effects and is known primarily through them, through its actions or performances. What is true for people is also true for buildings; character shows itself in what they do, in the decisions, choices, or actions they take. The real locus and realization of character is in action, not in signs of identity added onto surfaces. The difficult point is that these workings do not arise from capacities and conditions produced by technical reason or aesthetic intentionality alone. One could assume these operations intend the building to work "for us," but insofar as we will be followed by others who will have different expectations, this must be a very generalized "us." The generality of this determination is so great that it is insufficient to understand the building's full actuality. To grasp that, other kinds of performance must be described—not performances *in* architecture, but performances *of* architecture.

For example, imagine a lecture hall. Certainly such a setting can be described objectively: the four walls, the false ceiling that conceals air-handling equipment, the sloped floor, the seats arranged for the auditors, the lectern for the speaker, the gathering space on the other side of the doors that benefits from natural lighting, and so on. All of it exists in indisputable factuality, all of it stands within the building on its site in the city with impressive permanence and stability, waiting for events with unequaled patience. But is this availability, this "permanence in waiting" objective or objectlike in the way we commonly assume? Can such a room's performance be measured like other objects in the world, will it yield itself to techniques of sizing, weighing, and computing? Is the room a "machine for living in"?

The inadequacy of this conception can be seen if the room's performance over time is considered. Jean-Luc Marion, whose arguments on the "eventmental" character of given conditions I will summarize, elaborated the extended spectrum of performance temporality.

Consider first the room's prehistory. Insofar as the lecture hall was arranged for the uses we intend, we can assume that it existed before we walked through its doors. Otherwise it could not impose itself on experience. Taking an abstract view of the situation, one can say some of its characteristics could have been foreseen. But in its concrete actuality, every room is encountered as something donated to us from a past into which we have no real insight and over which we have absolutely no control. Of rooms, we commonly say they are given, but we generally have no knowledge of the people responsible for the gift, or of their specific intentions, desires, and expectations for the use of their gift. Once seen, a room might be judged marvelous, singularly depressing, or largely insignificant because so typical; but until it is observed in its concrete actuality, it is unknown and (in its specific qualities) unexpected. Whether great or small, there is always some surprise when buildings are entered, mostly because the particularity of each comes from a past about which we are largely uninformed; each is "charged with a history exceeding memory,"[7] the result of unknown and unknowable initiatives.

In truth, we do not so much enter rooms, but rooms, so to speak, *happen* to us. One way to begin thinking about what might be called the "event-character" of a setting is to consider its emergence out of a causality that no one understands very fully. Here we touch on an aspect of events that is essential— their mysterious beginnings and unexpected occurrence. When we use the expression "That was some event!" we acknowledge the unanticipated quality of what occurred. We give such an experience the name "event" precisely because of the unforeseen character of what happened; real events are always more than what was expected of them. Operations can indeed be managed, functions can, likewise, be scripted, but the events we take as important cannot be—or else what is planned is not what makes them important. Similarly, events do not result from technique or technical knowledge. This is because foresight is essential to technological thought.[8] Technique is always anticipatory; it is a form of knowledge that leads to preconceived results. Because events arise out of a past that we do not know, they cannot be produced technically. Putting the matter more forcefully, per-formative architecture is not the outcome of building or design technology, even up-to-the-minute digital technology. All that technique can give architecture is enhanced functionality.

Considering not the room's past but its present, what Marion called its "eventmental"[9] nature is perhaps even clearer. Viewing the way an auditorium presents itself on a given occa-sion, one could—speaking in generalities or broad abstrac-tions—imagine the ways it exists in its "indifferent emptiness" between various events. If the room's actuality is important, however, a wiser procedure would be to observe and describe its particularity on a given afternoon, filled for a particular cir-cumstance, such as a lecture on an announced topic. The set-ting stages an event, the success of which at any given moment is unknown. Is the room working? Are its provisions serving the aims of the speakers and of the audience? One could cer-

tainly say the room is generally adequate; but not until the event
unfolds—in its unparalleled particularity—will anyone be able
to say whether or not the room and the event were successes
or failures. Both the singularity of the occasion—the working
of the room on a specific occasion—and its undecidability in
the present must be stressed. Even if inherited factors confer
orientation, they offer no guarantees. As with its past, Marion
observed, the room's present condition is unknowable, but also
unrepeatable, and cannot be constituted as such by any explicit
intention. The event, as we say, is or is not happening. No single
contribution, no matter how well planned or thought out, can
control its unfolding: not the schedule of the presentations, the
refreshments provided for the breaks, the equipment provided,
or the soundproofing of the room will allow one to fully anticipate the outcome. If the event is only what was anticipated it
will have been both uneventful and unmemorable. Viewing the
way an event unfolds in the present, we can discern an essential
aspect of settings: place-bound events that truly merit the name
arise out of themselves, despite my interests or yours, as if they
were indifferent to them.

　　Lastly, in this little sketch of the auditorium's temporality, its future requires attention. How will a given event—a
conference, for example—play itself out? How will the room
perform for a speaker later in the afternoon when the time after
lunch brings a little sluggishness? Can one say that a listener's
inattention during that speaker's talk will have resulted from
the quality of the argument, the heaviness of the meal, or the
way the room's atmosphere blankets a person's awareness? And
what about one's understanding of the talks themselves (the differences between what the speakers will want to say and what
each of us will hear); what about all the disagreements, distor-
tions, silent understandings, exaggerations, and so on? Can any
of that be known objectively? To provide an adequate account of

what will have occurred, Marion suggested, one would need an unending hermeneutic. The event in and of a particular room is a phenomenon without a clearly known or knowable boundary, end, or identity. What objects possess in abundance—sharp definition—events lack almost entirely. That is to say, the performance of a setting can only be known on its own terms or, as I suggested earlier, pre-predicatively. Events cannot be defined, organized, or scripted because their beginning, middle, and end resist objective comprehension. This leads to a first conclusion: to understand architecture's performative character, we cannot rely on transparent and objective description alone, or on techniques of quantification and measurement.

The device paradigm

In what types of places do architectural operations unfold? Where are architecture's unscripted performances typically staged? One obvious answer is the building's moving or (more exactly) moveable mechanisms. This is an undeniable kind of "action" in architecture, for some of the building's parts literally move or allow themselves to be moved: apertures, screens, furnishings, for example, each of which has its own "range of motion," its stops, levels, intervals, which anticipate and regulate its shifts and repositionings. Movements of this kind are variously initiated by human or environmental prompts and controlled by manual, electrical, or digital mechanisms. Their tasks, in general, are the modification and mediation of the environment in its widest sense, from climate to human behavior. The work of Renzo Piano—Aurora Place (1996–2000) in Sydney, Australia, for example—could be used to illustrate this aspect of architectural performance. Each of its exterior surfaces, and each of their elements, consists of moving and moveable mechanisms. Perhaps the most famous early-twentieth-century example of a building that presents itself as an ensemble of adjustable equipment is Paris' Maison Dalsace (1928–31) by Pierre Chareau, with its exceedingly elaborate apparatus of ladders, screens, shades, and so on. Roughly contemporary with it, and offering equivalent devices on the building's exterior, is Giuseppe Terragni's Casa del Fascio (1932–36) in Como, Italy.

Design of elements of this sort follows what might be called the device paradigm.[10] The positions each element can take—the stops, levels, and intervals—script the device's performance. Typically, these positions outline or frame a range of movement, normally between the open and closed extremes. The intelligence of a device is measured not by the breadth of this range or the number of intermediate positions, but by its capacity to adjust itself to foreseen and unforeseen conditions. An analogy that may be useful here is with musical or theatrical improvisation, as if the stops and positions of the building's elements did nothing more than sketch out the guidelines of a performance, allowing for spontaneous changes that attune the ensemble to particular conditions and interests, as they vary over time. Approximate movements can be intended, but settings can also yield, respond, or react to unforeseen events. The architectural drama, then, comes alive through the building's performances. The first step in the development of a performative architecture is to outline strategies of adjustment.

Economy of performance

There is another site of architectural action in which performance is less obvious but no less determining: those parts of the building that give it its apparently static equilibrium, its structural, thermal, material stability. When discussing these elements (columns and beams, retaining walls, and foundations, but also cladding and roofing systems), it is common to talk of their "behavior"—and not only talk of it but anticipate, even predict it. Obviously, talk of this sort is metaphorical, but in

LEFT Mies van der Rohe, Tugendhat House, Brno, 1928–30; window mechanisms. RIGHT Herzog and de Meuron, Suva Office Building, Basel, 1991–93; adjustable windows

Tod Williams and Billie Tsien, Neurosciences Institute, La Jolla, California, 1996; auditorium retaining wall

truth the building must work at staying as it is. It must work with ambient conditions, such as gravity, winds, sunlight, and so on. It must also work *against* these forces. And it must suffer their effects. No actor on stage ever suffered as much as buildings do, whether one thinks of use and misuse, weathering, or additions and alterations.

The economy of performance—on a site, as on a stage—is always an exchange between forces and counterforces. To act is to counteract. The building's labor is quite simply the amount of effort it takes to sustain this economy, to keep up or play its part. The term we use most frequently for this labor is *resistance*. The buildings of Tod Williams and Billie Tsien, especially the Neurosciences Institute (1992–95) in La Jolla, California, demonstrate awareness of this kind of performance. The NSI works with and against its site and much more locally, with and against the pressure of human touch, which it both resists and welcomes with its variously rough and smooth surfaces. A similar well-known case from the twentieth century is Mies's Tugendhat House (1928–30) in Brno, Czechoslovakia. Somewhat less well known, but even more elaborately engaged with its site, is his Wolf House (1925–26) in Guben, Germany.

A building's capacities and identity become apparent through resistance. The facade, in fact, is the site of precisely this resistance, offered by the latent qualities of materials against ambient forces. Should one state, as I did above, that the building's destiny is to suffer? Is its work passive? That depends entirely on what is meant by the terms. Is it fair to say that the sprinter poised for the start of a race is passive? Isn't it more accurate to observe that the explosion ignited by the starter's pistol presupposes a coiled potential that can only be constituted and maintained through strenuous effort? Is the building's action against the steady pressure of the hillside into which it is cut any different? In both there is force and counterforce, which suggests an inevitable contextuality of the building's performative elements, by which its equipment transcends itself into a range of spaces and regions, in the same way that it transcends itself into several temporalities, disavowing, again, its status as an object, or a phenomenon, that can be objectively defined.

The topography paradigm

Design for performance of this sort is based not on a device paradigm but on a *topography* paradigm. Movement here is not change of position, but of state. The force–counterforce relationship results in alterations to the building's physical body that demonstrate its ability to respond to ambient conditions. Stains on the building are evidence of its capacity for resistance. Cracks in the wall indicate limited success on this front.

The obverse of cracking and staining is shaping and finishing—whether that of construction technology, environmental influence, or everyday use. This kind of suffering (architectural *pathos*) was described by Peter Zumthor as a process of enrichment.[11] Buildings, he said, take on a beautiful and specific richness when traces of life are sedimented onto their surfaces. Movement, action, or performance in the so-called static permanence of buildings or elements is toward or away from the fullness of their potential—movement typically described as development or deterioration. Because not one of these kinds of movement can be precisely predicted, architectural performance such as this can be described as *unscripted.*

Operations in and outside the building are dependent on several contingencies: those of the inhabitants' interests and habitual practices, or of the climate, the seasons, and the times. The building's workings are also dependent on changes to those parts that have been joined together to form the work. No doubt it is obvious to state that over time the building's materials eventually fail; but we rarely think seriously enough about this

Peter Zumthor, Caplutta Sogn Benedetg, Sumvitg, Switzerland, 1985–88; entrance door

inevitable or essential contingency. Materials suffer and vary at different rates. Some parts of the structure settle and move, others do not—or not much—while still others undergo a range of surface variations. In the face of these alterations, maintaining equilibrium among the building's parts is a task that cannot in principle be completed. Nor can its difficulties be foreseen. In the unfolding of the operations that sustain a dwelling situation, architectural elements constitute themselves into something of a stable ensemble that possesses a comprehensible but provisional finality, for such a configuration is always and only temporary.

Concerning the changes the building suffers as a result of "external" contingencies, there is some degree of predictability of developments, resulting from past experiences, but never certainty. Some locations—such as the Caribbean—show greater constancy of climatic conditions, or less seasonal change, while in others, like Canada, there is continual alteration. But even in moderate zones, the environment sometimes acts in ways it is not supposed to, as the history of tropical disasters proves. Were the ambient environment steadier in its offerings, the building could assure itself of the adequacy of its provisioning and would not need to continually adjust itself. In such circumstances (which are really those of the laboratory), performances could be scripted. But the world in which buildings actually exist is hardly so lawful.

The true measure of a building's preparedness is its capacity to respond to both foreseen and unforeseen developments. Stated in reverse, bad buildings are those that cannot respond to unexpected circumstances, because they have been so rigidly attuned to preestablished norms. Our tendency to think of environmental conditions as external or extrinsic contingencies should be resisted, for no building operates without or apart from them. Jean Nouvel claims to put nature to work in his architecture; the beauty and richness of his buildings' sur-

Jean Nouvel, Guthrie Theater, Minneapolis, 2005; café facade

faces do not result from design or construction technique alone but also from the action of ambient lighting, which variously and wonderfully saturates the skins with fluctuating qualities. The environment—in this case, natural light—must therefore be seen as intrinsic to the building. Workings of this sort are evidences of engagement between what was and what was not constructed, of the building's willingness (or need) to interact with what it is not. Here again, nonobjectivity, as contingency, enters the heart of the work, through its operations. Here, also, there emerges the possibility of a form of representation intrinsic to architecture rather than superimposed upon it, for when the building identifies itself with its milieu, it becomes something it is not, and hence *represents*. Put differently, the building's performance is the key to its inherent (unimposed) symbolism, because when the building defines itself in terms of what it is not, it inaugurates precisely the sort of self-negation that is necessary for representation to occur.

When the building is freed from technological and aesthetic intentionalities, we discover its lateral connections to an environmental and social milieu that are not of anyone's making, still less designed or planned. And it is precisely these connections that animate its "performativity," even if they cause the building's work to resist both conceptual mastery and exhaustive description. The point to be stressed is the building's *eccentricity*, its existence outside itself, for its behavior testifies to a constitutional weakness at its center, a negativity at its heart, because it must wait for its circumstances to give it what it lacks—light, air, human events. Still, what the environment offers is always somewhat different from what was expected. The building's internal disequilibrium obliges it to accept into its makeup conditions over which it has no control.

With the different dimensions of the building's contingency in mind, a second conclusion can be proposed: architecture's performative labor has no end, for it is a task that continually presents itself anew.

Topographies of performance

The milieu within which performance in architecture unfolds may be called *topography*, indicating neither the built nor the unbuilt world, but both.[12] Three characteristics of topography sustain the building's performativity: its wide extensity, its mosaic heterogeneity, and its capacity to disclose previously latent potentials. There is always more to topography than what may be viewed at any given moment. Excess is implied in its ambience, for what constitutes the margins of perceptual concentration always exceeds the expectations of that focus. But this "still more" is not more of the same. Differences are always discovered in the spread of topography; contrast and complementarity structure relationships among its several situations and sites.

In modernist theory, space was presented as the all-embracing framework of every particular circumstance, the unlimited container of all possible contents. In modern science, too, continuous space was understood to be isotropic and homogenous, possessing a selfsameness congenial to intellectual mastery because of the conceptual character of its attributes. The topography in which buildings perform is just the opposite of space. Polytropic, heterogeneous, and concrete, its regions contrast, conflict, and sometimes converse with one another. Yet it is not a field of infinite difference either, for it continually offers to experience both unexpected and familiar situations. If space advances its array all at once (in simultaneity), actual topography gives its locations through time. In any given site, at any given moment, its structure requires that some places be recalled, others anticipated.

Topography's latency is apparent if one considers the way it gives itself to experience. Like events, landscapes—whether urban or not—contain unforeseen potentials, and show these potentials in the various ways they offer themselves to perception. The word "capacity," applied to physical things, indicates similarly unseen possibilities. Capacities cannot be (fully) discerned, because they keep themselves recessive—like the reverse side of an object one is looking at or the inside of something whose surface is shaped or polished. Construction finishing aims to cultivate the potential of things. Because it, too, is material and can be cultivated, topography is not what physically appears in a given place—built or unbuilt—or not only that. Sites are surveyed in the early stages of design so that given conditions can be described and understood. While this seems obvious, the phrase "given conditions" is far from clear. We tend to assume that the place exhibits "its intentions" the way designs present theirs; in both, intentions are shown, and givenness, we believe, offers expressive display. But this again confuses the ways that figures and grounds are perceived, for the topography in which architecture performs is not composed of prominent figures or objects; it does not expose the intentionality of its formation, but serves as the basis *for* that formation.

If topography's potentials exceed one's grasp and remain unforeseen to some degree, they can also be said to be unreasonable, at least in some measure. If, as argued previously, the building is always, or necessarily, engaged with topography by virtue of its inevitable contextuality and contingency, its performances, too, will be (to some degree) unplanned or will arise from "causes" that are unassignable.

This suggests a different understanding of the building. It is not a technical preparation, or not that chiefly; nor is it primarily a representation of such a preparation. Instead, it is a nontechnical and nonaesthetic performance, the designer's comprehension of which acknowledges its continual need for readjustments in order to reclaim its own equilibrium and sus-

tain its engagement with unbuilt or previously built contingencies. Put more simply, the building's approximate disequilibrium
animates a life and a history of ever-new performances.

Aristotle once advised that the mark of a wise individual
is to strive for the degree of exactitude in descriptions that is
appropriate for the given subject. The same exactness, he said,
must not be sought in all departments of philosophy alike, any
more than in all the products of the arts and crafts. Let me
quote him: "[I]t is the mark of an educated mind to expect that
amount of exactness in kind which the nature of the particular
subject admits." Accordingly, it is equally unreasonable to accept
merely probable conclusions from a mathematician and to
demand strict demonstrations from an orator. In a similar vein,
Aristotle recommended that when building a house, sketches of
basic (configurational) principles be made in outline form only,
so that they can be gradually filled in as unforeseen exigencies
and opportunities arise. The carpenter and geometrician both
seek after the right angle, he said, but in different ways: "[T]he
former is content with an approximation to it which satisfies the
purpose of the work, the latter looks for the essence or essential
attributes."[13]

Instrumentality plus

At the outset of this book I distinguished between two kinds of
understanding in the theory of architectural performance: the
kind that can be exact and unfailing in its prediction of outcomes,
and a kind that anticipates what is likely, given the circumstantial contingencies of built work. The first sort is technical and
productive, the second, contextual and projective. There is no
need to rank these two in a theory of architectural performance;
important instead is grasping their reciprocity and their joint
necessity. If acceptance of an uncertain foundation for performance seems to plunge practice into irrationalism, we need only

remember that most of the decisions we make in our daily lives rest on a foundation that is just as uncertain. The cultural norms that serve as the horizon of unreflective existence will not stand up to rational scrutiny, but are not for that reason nonsense, nor are they opaque to understanding. They are certainly transparent enough to sustain debate, the result of which is adjustment or alteration. For a theory of performativity, we should seek nothing more and nothing less: instrumental reason and the rationality on which it depends, plus situated understanding that discovers in the particulars of a place, people, and purpose the unfounded conditions that actually prompt, animate, and conclude a building's performances.

Endnotes

Epigraph 1 Maurice Merleau-Ponty, Phenomenology of Perception (New York: Humanities Press, 1962), xi.

Epigraph 2 Jean Baudrillard and Jean Nouvel, The Singular Objects of Architecture (Minneapolis: University of Minnesota Press, 2002), 16.

1   The term "borrowed existence" is derived from Jean-Luc Marion's In Excess: Studies of Saturated Phenomena (New York: Fordham University Press, 2002). While my argument is indebted to his entire account of "givenness," his description of borrowed existence can be found in chapter 2, "The Event or the Happening Phenomenon." In what follows I paraphrase, but also elaborate on, his account of the event structure of the lecture hall.

2   Aldo Rossi, The Architecture of the City (Cambridge, Mass.: MIT Press, 1982), esp. "Critique of Naïve Functionalism," 46–48, and "How Urban Elements Become Defined," 114–19.

3   See, for example, Sert's contribution to the CIAM 8 conference: "Centres of Community Life," in CIAM 8: The Heart of the City: Towards the Humanisation of Urban Life, ed. J. Tyrwhitt, J. L. Sert, and E. N. Rogers (New York: Pellegrini and Cudahy, 1952), 3–16. While Sert's work is also documented in this publication, for a more comprehensive account see Knud Bastlund, ed., José Luis Sert, Architecture, City Planning, Urban Design, (New York: Frederick A. Praeger, 1967).

4   See Marcel Breuer, Sun and Shadow, The Philosophy of an Architect (New York: Dodd, Mead & Company, 1955).

5   Most helpful among their writings on this particular topic is Aladar and Victor Olgyay, Solar Control & Shading Devices (Princeton: Princeton University Press, 1957).

6   See, for example, Maxwell Fry and Jane Drew, Tropical Architecture in the Dry and Humid Zones, (Malabar, Fl.: Robert E. Krieger, 1964).

7   Marion, In Excess, 32.

8   This point is elaborated in David Leatherbarrow and Mohsen Mostafavi, Surface

Architecture (Cambridge, Mass.: MIT Press, 2002), Postscript.

9   See Marion, *In Excess*, 32.

10 This term, used more expansively, can be found in Albert Borgmann, *Technology and the Character of Contemporary Life* (Chicago: University of Chicago Press, 1984), esp. chap. 9.

11 Peter Zumthor, "A Way of Looking at Things," (1988), in *Thinking Architecture* (Baden, Switzerland: Lars Müller, 1998), 24.

12 For more on topography in this sense see my *Uncommon Ground: Topography, Technology, and Architecture* (Cambridge, Mass.: MIT Press, 2000), and *Topographical Stories: Studies in Landscape and Architecture* (Philadelphia: University of Pennsylvania Press, 2004), esp. the conclusion, "Ethics of the Dust," which elaborates the points summarized here.

13 Aristotle's text, *Nichomachean Ethics*, 1.3.

CHAPTER 3

Materials Matter

Then along came those nasty English and spoiled the game for our knights of the drawing board. They said, "Don't design, make. Go out into the world and see what is wanted. And when you have fully grasped that, go and work at the forge or the potter's wheel."

—Adolf Loos, "Glass and Clay"

Few would deny that individual buildings help shape and signify human settlements. Together with law, language, and customs, architecture contributes both to the formation of towns and cities and to their capacity for expression. Some architects, however, see the building as more than this; they have convinced themselves that the built work and its designer have a more determining role, that their task is to provide entire settlements—villages, towns, and cities—with their basic order, and that the individual and social patterns that settlements accommodate and represent follow from this. This is no small claim. This ambition can be seen in the work of designers who blur the distinction between urban and architectural design in order to see the city or its parts as susceptible to substitution by "big architecture." Rem Koolhaas, to name only the most famous of

Rem Koolhaas, Seattle Public Library, Seattle, 2004; interior

Street view

this group, has asserted that the building's "bigness" alone can constitute the urban character of our time: "Bigness no longer needs the city: it competes with the city; it represents the city; it preempts the city; or better still, it *is* the city."[1]

There are two obvious ways of reading this statement. One is that Koolhaas intended it to be less prescriptive than polemical, that his aim was to challenge basic assumptions and disabuse us of our presumed certainties so that new possibilities of urban order could come into view. Another way to read the text is to consider its hyperbole as a way of diverting attention from the somewhat discouraging fact that many of the cities and urban areas that have yielded to oversized insertions in the recent past are far from satisfactory. In many cases they are plainly miserable. In the last couple of decades, nearly every major city in the United States has demolished one or another of the "big" projects of the postwar years. When not demolished, these projects have been retrofitted with imagery of earlier architectures. Past failures do not exactly inspire confidence in renewed claims for architecture *as* the city.

Faced with this realization, it might seem wise for architects to retreat from the city and concern themselves solely with the individual building: its interiors, external appearance, and immediate vicinity—extending their interest no farther than the adjacent sidewalk, forecourt, yard, or garden. Retrenchment of this sort has the double appeal of limited exposure and greater control. It signals a retreat nonetheless. A better alternative involves differentiating types of concern an architect can have for the city and embracing a distinction between awareness of the city and responsibility for the building.[2] Neither hesitancy nor conservatism would be required for the adoption of this two-part premise, for understanding could certainly include criticism. Indeed, it should. Quite possibly, it must. It is hard to imagine how a design could be developed in the absence of judgments that are critical of existing conditions; that is, if the project's aspirations were restricted to accepting and affirming what predates it. Moreover, once it is granted that no city or urban district lacks problems, it becomes clear that all sites can be imagined otherwise. This means that the architect's recognition of the need for change, when taking contemporary interests into account, does not necessarily arise from unbounded ambition but from awareness of the inadequacy of the status quo.

Seen in this light, project making could be defined as a limited means of *approximating* a condition that ought to be. Approximation is implicit in the process of understanding, for every description, interpretation, and evaluation invokes a particular point of view that not only prompts but orients project proposals, each moving toward (approximating) a desired condition. Yet while they testify to both local and contemporary interests, survey work and design differ insofar as the former derives from an awareness of the city and the latter expresses responsibility for the building. Attentive surveying results in descriptions that can be verified, while design produces proposals that are more or less persuasive.

In the past few decades, arguments for the importance of urban understanding in architecture were often developed out of criticism of the modern movement, especially the so-called International Style architecture of the middle decades of the twentieth century. This style was frequently described as antiurban because its prejudice in favor of freestanding objects led to the disruption of existing patterns. Many buildings from that period give vivid evidence of this sentiment.

Even more forceful were the polemical writings of figures such as Le Corbusier and Frank Lloyd Wright, whose comments on the traditional city never involved ringing endorsement. Their writings should not be taken at face value, however. Like Koolhaas (and providing him with a rhetorical model), they overstated the problems they faced and the originality (epochal significance) of their solutions. Moreover, their dismissive statements conceal levels of understanding and engagement that are remarkably discerning—much more so than recent attempts to "recover," "restore," or "renew" the traditional town through the appropriation and imitation of its familiar patterns and motifs (as in postmodern projects). Urban understanding is apparent in the built work not only of the first-generation modernists, Le Corbusier, Wright, Mies van der Rohe, and Richard Neutra, for example, but also in that of a number of those who followed. Eero Saarinen, José Luis Sert, and the Smithsons come immediately to mind. Forgetting for a minute what these architects wrote, looking carefully at their ways of working with the city, one can discover that their projects accepted a double constraint: acknowledging what remained relevant from the past and imagining what would be required for the future because circumstances would have changed. This approach parallels the awareness–responsibility division introduced above, suggesting that the urban understanding many seek in current practice has antecedents in the modern tradition.

Is it true, then, that architects who endeavor to see and use the city as the framework for their projects must choose between an apocalyptic and a nostalgic vision, between the final substitution of "big architecture" for the city, and the restitution of the city's familiar forms through the strategies of "new [old] urbanism"? If we refuse the choice between a city that is unlike any that has ever been and one that reminds us of what we have always known, we will need to find another horizon of reference for contemporary architecture. My suggestion rests upon a simple observation: cities and buildings are not only spatial, geometric, and dimensional (patterns), but also *material*. Might the material aspect of cities and architecture clarify their relationships to one another? What is the connection between city form and architectural construction?

Glass and clay

In 1998, during his presentation at the Jerusalem Seminar in Architecture, Jean Nouvel argued for architecture's "non-image," proposing that our "extreme aspiration is that of [the] human as conjurer, who can make anything appear or disappear at will according to need or desire; who can travel instantly to any location by lighting up windows on the world, or by even-faster self-propulsion."[3] To substantiate, or at least buttress, his claim, Nouvel repeated Paul Virilio's observations on contemporary technology: "Speed and technology eliminate barriers between people and nature, between the world and the universe." Prompting these comments on technology and place were references both to the diaphanous works of James Turrell and to Nouvel's own recent projects in Paris: the Fondation Cartier (1991–94) and the Institut du Monde Arabe (1981–87). In all of these, there was a severe reduction—near elimination—of the separation between people (the "world") and nature that architecture had traditionally instituted. This was because "people want there to be nothing—nothing at all—between the heavens and us...we want an absence of materiality to put us in touch again with the non-synthetic world," by which, I gather, Nouvel meant nature. He did not assume that this new or newly close connection would require retreat from the city, for not only was a new contact with nature to result from the elimination of matter, but also a new form of engagement with the city, one of connectivity, flow, and immediacy. Glass, the most immaterial of materials, would be the key to restoring the links between architecture and both natural and urban life, as if the world–nature linkage were to occur within the world of the city.

The same year that Nouvel offered these comments, Peter Zumthor proposed an interpretation of the relationship between the building and its milieu that seems radically opposed to Nouvel's. Writing about his Thermal Baths at Vals,

Jean Nouvel, Musée du Quai Branly, Paris, 2001–2006; garden wall

Switzerland, he explained that "the building takes the form of a large, grass-covered stone object set deep into the mountain and dovetailed into its flank.... Mountain, stone, water, building in stone, building with stone, building into the mountain, building out of the mountain, being inside the mountain—our attempts to give this chain of words an architectural interpretation... guided our design for the building and step by step gave it form."[4] Instead of the absence of materiality proposed by Nouvel, here we have palpability in abundance, materials in their full concreteness—mountain, stone, water—as if architectural space resulted from the hollowing out of preexisting substances; it is not a light, but a solid, weighty, thick, and heavy architecture. Whereas Nouvel's work proposes pure passage from the building's interiors to its environment, because virtually nothing divides them, Zumthor's approximates pure connectivity by virtue of the absence of any gap between them: *substantive* spaces and situations, rather than what Virilio and Nouvel call "trajective" ones.

While this pairing would seem to present us with yet another opposition and choice, the fact that both Nouvel and Zumthor argued for continuity—through transparency in the first case and materiality in the second—suggests that when the two are seen as similarly dedicated to interconnectivity, they offer a more subtle understanding of the relationship between the building and its environment. I will introduce three terms to elaborate what is common in their understanding of the city–architecture relationship: "sedimentation," "saturation," and "surplus." The first two terms contribute differently to the constitution of the third, which measures the cultural content that the city and its buildings have to offer. My working premise is that materials matter no less in cities than in buildings. The key difference is that they are often *shown* in buildings and only *given* in cities.

Peter Zumthor, Thermal Baths, Vals, 1990–96; terrace

Traces of life

"I am convinced," Zumthor wrote, "that a good building must be capable of absorbing the traces of human life and thus of taking on a specific richness."[5] This passage implies, but it does not explicitly state, that the building's materials (more than its dimensions and geometries) allow this absorption. Architectural richness results from stone, steel, timber, and glass taking on "traces of human life." The passage also suggests that the building, or its materials, would not possess this richness were this deposit not to occur. That is a sobering thought for architects, for the basic ambition of design is to arrange and schedule all the techniques that will give the building its meaning, quality, and substance. Zumthor's statement makes room for the contribution of other, nontechnical or nonprofessional, agencies of enrichment and articulation. One way to form a fuller understanding of what he suggests is to think about the issue negatively, to ask what might prevent or retard the accumulation that defines a good building. What kind of architecture averts absorption or resists sedimentation? What inhibits construction materials from overcoming their preoccupancy poverty?

The opposite of receptivity is expressivity. Against an architecture that tolerates additions to its finished surfaces, one could posit buildings that insist on the adequacy and fullness of their *own* expression. Zumthor is sharply critical of garrulous architecture. "I frequently come across buildings that have been designed with a good deal of effort and a will to find a special form, and I am put off by them. The architect responsible for the building is not present, but he talks to me unceasingly from every detail, he keeps on saying the same thing, and I quickly lose interest." Good architecture should not constantly talk, it should keep itself silent, for only then will it "receive the human visitor."[6]

Zumthor is not the first architect to argue for semantic restraint in design, nor is he the only one to fault "chatty"

Peter Zumthor, Caplutta Sogn Benedegt, Sumtvig, 1985–88; entry door handle designs. In 1924, Le Corbusier famously criticized the excesses of French decorative art, rejecting chairs that were "too talkative."[7] A decade earlier, Adolf Loos had argued for the reticence (*Verschwiegenheit*) of urban images, suggesting instead the "unveiling" of the house's "richness" within.[8] More recently, Tadao Ando echoed these arguments in advocating a taciturn architecture: "My aim is to limit materials, simplify expression to the maximum, eliminate all non-essentials, and in the process interweave in my spaces the totality of the human being."[9] In different ways, and in consideration of furniture, facades, and other architectural forms, Le Corbusier, Loos, and Ando recommended an architecture that silences itself in deference to the sorts of articulation that result from the impress of practical affairs. Settings that are talkative, chatty, noisy are the ones that are incapable of absorbing the specific richness Zumthor sees in good buildings, because they are so fully dedicated to declaring their designer's message and meanings.

Zumthor's opposition to excessively communicative designs does not preclude expression altogether; his desire for moderation would seem to recommend instead an architecture of *expressive materiality*. If this is indeed the case, he appears to be adopting a familiar position once again. As long ago as the seventeenth century, architects argued that the beauty of the building could be positively determined by the "richness" of its materials, as in Claude Perrault's celebrated distinction between positive and arbitrary beauties, his demotion of proportions to the latter category, and advancement of *la richesse de la matière* to the former. Since that time many other architects have sought to derive significance and beauty for their buildings through the selection and refined treatment of materials, especially those that were rare, vividly qualitative, or unusual. In this tradition Loos represents something of an exceptional figure, for while his buildings are clad in strikingly beautiful materials (mainly on the inside), he asserted with great insistence that "all materials are equally valuable." In his account, only the merchant, not the architect, sees a kilogram of gold as worth more than a kilogram of stone.[10] If we feel awe before a granite wall, the sentiment that overwhelms us arises from our estimation of the labor required for the wall's construction and finishing, not from valuation of the material itself. Value or significance arises not from things, but from the ways they are handled, worked, or treated. Loos, like Ruskin, saw in the architectural surface the marks of human hands. Both judged beautiful those works that revealed evidence of uncoerced craft in their production. Architecture can be eloquent if the designer first recognizes the preliminary poverty (thus also the potentials) of unfinished materials—not their (natural) richness. If a preconception of quality prevents the free exercise of finishing, the result will lack the rich specificity that makes a work wonderful. Here, by an indirect route, we return to Zumthor's argument for "traces." Zumthor once asked if the effort and skill put into the construction of a building were not inherent parts of the thing itself. His answer was yes, or, in reverse, that in the world of artifacts, there is really no "thing in itself." In a work of architecture, nothing exists apart from the efforts and intentions that brought it into being and visibility. "The notion that our work is an integral part of what we accomplish takes us to the very limits of our musings about the value of a work of art, a work of architecture."[11]

But traces of labor are not all that the materials of the building were meant and seen to absorb. When he imagined "architecture exposed to life," Zumthor also envisaged prosaic and pedestrian affairs as the subject matter inscribed onto the pages and chapters of the building's history. Patina is both a physical deposit and a narrative composed through the use and misuse of settings: "[The] innumerable small scratches on surfaces, of varnish that has grown dull and brittle, and of edges polished by use" bear witness to the lives lived within specific settings.[12] Here, too, Zumthor echoes Loos's comments: "I did not grow up, thank God, in a stylish home...there was the writing table! There was an ink stain on it; my sister Hermine had knocked over the inkwell when she was a little baby...Every piece of furniture, every thing, every object had a story to tell, a family history. The house was never finished; it grew along with us and we grew within it."[13]

The finishes and forms specified in design and realized in construction are undone in life, but the result is not only deformation, not only negative. Although wear and tear result in subtraction, they also allow for a significant sort of addition. Over time and through use, architectural settings accrue legibility as they chronicle the patterns of life they accommodate. Time does not pass in architecture, it accumulates. If it passed, it would leave no trace—but the reverse is true. Everything around us exhibits signs of its history, its development or deterioration. All physical things, especially bodies and buildings, offer themselves to visual experience as sedimentations of actions and behaviors. If a face is recognizable, it is because time has written onto its skin, or surface, signs of the ways it has conducted itself in the world. In a famous passage from *The Notebooks of Malte Laurids Brigge*, Rainer Maria Rilke observed this kind of record on the inner wall of a Parisian building that had been brought to light by the collapse of the other sides of the structure. Between the supporting timbers that had been "rammed slantwise" against the bared wall, he could see vivid, if torn and fragmented, traces of the lives that had been lived within:

> ...the stubborn life of these rooms had not let itself be
> trampled out. It was still there, it clung to the nails that
> had been left, it stood on the remaining handsbreadth of
> flooring, it crouched under the corner joints where there

was still a little bit of interior. One could see that it was
in the paint, which, year by year, it had slowly altered....
But it was also in the spots that had kept fresher, behind
mirrors, pictures, and wardrobes; for it had drawn and
redrawn their contours.... It was in every flayed strip, it
was in the damp blisters at the lower edges of the wallpa-
pers.... And from these walls... the breath of these lives
stood out.... There stood the middays and the sicknesses
and the exhaled breath and the smoke of years.... The
sweet and lingering smell of neglected infants was there,
and the fearsmell of children who go to school, and the
sultriness out of the beds of nubile youths. To these was
added much that had come from below, from the abyss
of the street.... And much the feeble, tamed domestic
winds, that always stay in the same street, brought along;
and much more was there, the source of which one did
not know.[14]

The "it" to which Rilke refers in this passage is the life
that was lived in these apartments. *It* is generally apparent in the
materials but is made particular in their specific qualities, their
dulled, frayed, and blistered qualities, "drawn and redrawn"
by the behavior of those who tenanted the rooms, and by the
influences from the street below, and more besides. It—life—is
inseparable from the things against which its movements are
played out.

As Zumthor suggested, events and settings are not two
aspects of a place, the first performed and the second planned,
the one resulting from practical considerations, the other from
professional decision making. Instead, they are bound together
in reciprocal dependence, for without the resistance offered by
things, life would have no way of making itself apparent, of making itself present, of occurring. Zumthor uses the word "resis-

tance" in two senses. The first indicates the critical posture taken by architects and architecture; it points to the building's standing against the corrosive tendencies of contemporary culture, the "waste of forms and meanings." Zumthor's second sense of the term is more difficult to grasp, because it is paradoxical: resistance is also the means through which buildings, or their materials, make life visible (even possible) by offering obstacles to unbounded and unstructured motion or flow. Architecture reveals life to itself by giving it limits and resisting its forces. Absorption or sedimentation is the process whereby the movements and energy of everyday existence encounter, and come to rest in, the spaces and surfaces of a setting. Thanks to the building and its capacity for resistance, patterns of occupation that would otherwise remain inconspicuous obtain both definition and legibility. The wall's readiness to serve as a counterforce to all kinds of movement in the environment is also its potential for articulation and expression.

Events and their effects

Jean Nouvel, unlike Peter Zumthor, proposes an architecture for our time that is light, not heavy; changeable, not permanent; dematerialized, not matter-bound. The proposal was not offered ideologically but in recognition of cultural and professional history. "Today," Nouvel observed, "we can produce a single sheet of glass which is ten meters long and three meters wide. We enter into a kind of architectural Darwinism in which our knowledge is used to eliminate useless matter and to increase performance in the areas of loading, lightness, and insulation."[15] To ignore this fact and the possibilities it suggests is to retreat from the reality of the current condition. But an ethics of contemporaneity was not all that prompted Nouvel's turn toward a dematerialized architecture, toward ephemeral effects. Technical progress leads toward a nontechnical goal: renewed contact with nature. This progressive reductionism is supposed to bring us back in touch with the natural world, for the absence of "things" means the unobstructed presence of the environment.

An oft-repeated truism of architectural history holds that the use of glass in modern architecture established a new connection between inside and outside. The window wall is the most conspicuous and frequently discussed evidence of this achievement.[16] When José Luis Sert addressed the problem in a short text called "On Windows and Walls," he saw the development of new modes of construction as an opportunity to rethink the ancient tradition of joining exterior to interior through openings in the wall: "For thousands of years, from the doors of the caves until recently, all windows...served the triple function of providing light, ventilation, and view. It was only with the lightening of structures...that the window could be radically transformed and its triple function re-examined....Large sheets of glass gave birth to the 'picture' window....This established a partial separation of the functions of view and light from that of ventilation."[17]

What might have been seen as an achievement—"the all glass front"—was for Sert the beginning of a serious problem. As curtain walls for office buildings gained wide acceptance, "facades of anonymity" started appearing throughout the world. No city these days is without an entire crowd of them. But Sert never advocated abandoning curtain wall construction. The task was to use the new materials and methods but also to recognize the long-standing desire for identity through difference. "We still need walls and windows of some kind," he observed, but "can we not find an architectural vocabulary that will permit greater variety?"[18] His solution was to reintroduce the differentiations that existed before the window wall, distinguishing elements that accommodate views from those that modulate the intensity of light (or create shadow) and from those that regulate the flow of air into the interior. This meant treating the glass wall as if it were not all of a piece, but as if it were instead aggregate or composite, as if—ironically—it presented apertures, as in traditional masonry construction.

There are other ways of achieving variety, however. Nouvel, for example, has sought to assimilate the window wall into the natural world so that the (environmental) changes of the latter would give animation to the former. He calls this "putting nature to work."[19]

Nature, for Nouvel, is not an object to be viewed, but an element that can "structure" the building. He wants the pane of glass to be more than a picture of the landscape. The metaphorical "interpenetration" of inside and outside is also inadequate to his sense of contact with nature. His aim is to have the building and the environment work together, operate as one, and perform their task jointly. This intimately links metaphor to performance; the building's task is to bring architecture to life. Nouvel's strategy is to let the qualities of the ambient landscape saturate the building's surfaces so completely that they become the qualities of the building itself. For this to happen, two types of change must occur: first, the building must be dematerialized; and second, light must be seen and treated as if it were matter.

In an interview with Jean Baudrillard, Nouvel outlined a new sense of transparency. He said he is less interested in spatial continuities and unimpeded views than in the play of ephemeral effects. Traditional architecture always played with permanent effects. Now, impermanent effects are possible: "[W]orking with transparency involves nothing more than working with matter to give a building different appearances."[20] It is not clear in this passage if the matter to which Nouvel refers is light or glass. His aim, I take it, is to see the two as one. Transparency is a kind of evaporation, it is the means by which the building allows itself to be absorbed into the atmosphere or, in reverse, the means by

Jean Nouvel, Guthrie Theater, Minneapolis, 2006; interior

which the atmosphere completely saturates the building's surfaces, making them coextensive with its unbounded expanse.

With reference to the same effect in the canvases of
Georges Seurat and Paul Signac, Nouvel described this architecture as a kind of "cosmic pointillism." From the earliest years
of the movement, neoimpressionist painters demonstrated a
strong interest in industrial imagery, particularly surfaces of
steel and glass near bodies of water. Signac asserted that the
urban world was his central preoccupation. An example of his
interest might be *Gas Tanks at Clichy* (1886). He was not alone;
in fact, a number of painters focused on the industrial zones
at the city's periphery. Bleakness characterizes these scenes,
for they are often empty landscapes, without focus or hierarchy. Typically, the terrain is rendered in blue, gray, and white.
Regardless of the colors used, however, light suffuses everything
seen. Describing Seurat's Conté crayon drawing *Scaffolding*
(1887), Robert Herbert observed that light mediated between
the construction's geometry and the space's "mysterious layers
of depth." Patches and patterns of shadow and light fluctuate
from foreground to background in the compressed depth of the
image, so that "the play of light and dark threatens to push us...
into a realm of enigma."[21]

It is precisely this unstable or enigmatic quality of surfaces saturated with light that Nouvel has sought to achieve in
architecture. The capacity of glass to mirror its surroundings
was just as important as its transparency. Speaking of his Arab
Institute in Paris, he stressed the ephemerality of its appearance; its image, he said, changes under different conditions:
rain, fog, cloud cover. Architects of our time are trying to capture "variations in time, the seasons, the movements of visitors,
etc."[22] This effort is not for the sake of novelty but of relevance.
Once the building and its materials transcend themselves into
the atmosphere, the old deadening permanence of architecture

is abandoned, and the building joins step with the pace of contemporary life.

Architecture exceeding itself

While the areas of difference between Zumthor's and Nouvel's conceptions of architectural materiality are obvious and undeniable, points of convergence also exist.

One similarity between their approaches concerns architecture's relationship to its ambient surroundings, although at first sight neither architect appears to underscore the necessity of an interconnection between the building and its milieu. Zumthor's advocacy of the "completeness" of the architectural object, for example, would seem to make a case against engagement and for independence; when defined as whole and entire unto itself, the building is free from entanglements with its location. Similarly, Nouvel seems to be arguing for the autonomy of the architectural object. His emphasis on the contemporaneity of the building might suggest an essential separation from contexts that date from earlier times. He has frequently claimed that the traditional city has been "blown apart" in the modern world. Demographic shifts, technological change, and globalization have contributed to the disintegration of traditional patterns; a radical break with past forms would therefore seem to be inevitable. Further, Nouvel sees himself as heir to the tradition Le Corbusier inaugurated: the traditional city represents the "pack-donkey's way."[23] Nevertheless, both Zumthor and Nouvel envisage the constitution of the part (the building) as a condensation or crystallization of salient aspects of the whole (the environment). Where these architects differ is only in the aspects of the environment they choose to stress.

Zumthor views the surrounding milieu as a pattern or framework of practical affairs. The city is an ensemble of life's typical situations. His short text "The Body of Architecture" narrates his participation in a number of these: observing others in a hotel lobby, feeling isolated on the streets of a nineteenth-century suburb, wandering through a museum, and so on. His fragments allude to the different ways these situations are structured: socially, linguistically, topographically, and architecturally. Although architecture is one of the most permanent of these structures, all of them have the same subject matter, which Zumthor calls "life." His argument about "traces" takes this "context" as the building's primary horizon of reference. It is also the source of the building's more legible articulation, its richness.

Nouvel, by contrast, views the surrounding milieu as the natural world, as the play and variation of environmental phenomena, wind, rain, and, most importantly, light. His use of glass and his treatment of other materials are always in the service of reducing the separation between what has been built and what precedes and follows all constructive acts—nature. The capacity of materials to receive, reflect, and modulate light is so significant that it determines the building's dimensions and geometries. A theater built out of metal, plastic, and glass, he said, cannot be the same as one built out of stone. The ways in which these materials catch light and orchestrate its effects redefine our conception of theatricality. Were the landscape not "put to work" in the project, these changes would not be so dramatic; but once the building is codetermined by forces outside itself, its essential character results from something other than just design intentionality.

Zumthor's horizon of reference is practical, Nouvel's is physical. The first finds richness in the sedimentation of prosaic affairs; the second looks for qualities that result from the saturation of surfaces by natural light. Zumthor's frequent use of stone and Nouvel's of glass would seem to reinforce this opposition.

That the matter is not so simple becomes clear when one realizes that neither architect really narrowed his choices in this way, nor did either dogmatically abbreviate the full spectrum of materials. Zumthor's Kunsthaus in Bregenz, Austria, for example, has all the materials and many of the qualities one might find in a building by Nouvel. Likewise, Nouvel's use of wood in the Genoscope in Lanaud, France, or Les Thermes project in Dax, France, develops the very same qualities Zumthor achieved in his timber-clad buildings at the Archaeological Museum in Chur, Switzerland, for example, or in his own studio. Materials matter to these architects because of the ways they can be treated. Neither stone nor glass possesses any essence or "truth," nor is one or the other singularly apposite to our time. The whole matter rests on the ways the materials are shaped and transformed, the ways they become what they had not been before, the ways they exceed themselves.

Both architects argue for materials becoming more than they were and for an architecture that offers experience much more than the architects themselves could have designed—more perhaps than they could have foreseen. In the same way that Baudrillard underscores the "unintelligible" foundation for events and effects,[24] Nouvel recognizes the significance of aspects of the project that were never rationalized: "[W]hen you talk to a developer... [there are] a ton of questions.... And then there are those things that remain unsaid.... [W]hat remains unsaid... signifies something vital."[25] Zumthor, for his part, observed that "the most important things are often those one doesn't see."[26] Further elaborating on this idea, he also stated that "when we look at buildings which seem to be at peace within themselves, they seem empty.... It is as if we could see something on which we cannot focus our consciousness."[27]

Perhaps something of this understanding of architecture as exceeding itself was implied in Koolhaas's statements, for instance when he claimed that "[b]igness transforms the city from a summation of certainties into an accumulation of mysteries."[28] Such mystery has potential that is analogous to the capacity of materials: "if urbanism generates potential and architecture exploits it, Bigness enlists the generosity of urbanism against the meanness of architecture."[29] Both the generosity of the town and the yielding readiness of materials give the architectural work opportunities to surpass its motivating intentions and constructive techniques.

Both Zumthor and Nouvel also subject architectural space to the order of historical time. This has already been implied in the observation about the limits of design's foresight: if the building is enriched by agencies outside the specifications of the project, this occurs after the completion of the construction. To put it differently, as agencies of articulation outside the compass of professional instrumentality, both sedimentation and saturation accomplish their results in the building's open and extended history. Construction does not end the process of articulation; it is its beginning. Rilke's phrase is apposite here; surfaces that we find legible are "drawn and redrawn" over time. Once taken up in the adventure of construction and use, the materials of a building invite modes of behavior and environmental influence that, as they recur over time, are registered onto the building's surfaces in the form of traces constituting the memory of those events. This makes each surface something of a clock, calendar, and chronicle. Space in architecture is not measured in inches, feet, and yards alone, but also in minutes, days, months, and years. The (temporal) processes of sedimentation and saturation bring surfaces into visibility. But the vectors of architectural time do not only point toward the past; each trace also prompts or invites subsequent events. The chronology that is particular to urban architecture allows its heritage to be renewed through acts of appropriation that obey no obligation to the past other than its use for purposes of redefinition. In the built world, past, present, and future do not line up one after the other like soldiers in formation, but bend that line back onto and out from itself so that both directions overlap *in the present.* While it may seem sensible to distinguish two agencies at work in the process of sedimentation whereby architecture accrues and extends history—human and environmental forces—only their compounded effects give it its proper voice.

Architecture's debt to the city

The difference between figure and ground, or outlay and sup-ply, is not absolute. Not only can one easily become the other, but they coexist. In many paintings traces of background color can be seen *through* the foreground figures. The sedimentation to which Zumthor referred and the saturation sought by Nouvel never fully conceal the materials of the building; their assimila-tion into the life of the milieu is always incomplete. As long as it stands, the building resists the environment. In urban archi-tecture those materials that are seen (the figures) and those that remain unseen (the background) interpenetrate one another; however, the background always surpasses the limits defined by the figures, for otherwise it could not continually serve as their supply. Viewing the city as a big building, or as the outcome of design work, is akin to seeing the background as if *it* were the figure. From this angle, its withdrawing character is ignored and its capacity to fund the project's visible richness is wasted. The city and the environment exceed design intention and produce effects that cannot be foreseen, but they enrich intuition and experience in the process.

Urban and natural phenomena act in ways that run counter to received wisdom, but at the same time, they grant to both expectation and understanding their greatest reward. Despite their differences, the materials that make up the build-ings of both Zumthor and Nouvel come to life by drawing from a territorial source that is as abundant as it is nonarchitectural.

Endnotes

Epigraph Adolf Loos, "Glass and Clay," in *Spoken into the Void* (Cambridge, Mass: MIT Press, 1982), 36. I have adapted the translation.

1 Rem Koolhaas, "Bigness or the Problem of Large," in *S,M,L,XL* (New York: Monacelli, 1995), 515.
2 David Leatherbarrow, *Uncommon Ground: Architecture, Technology, and Topography* (Cambridge, Mass.: MIT Press, 2000), 170ff.
3 Jean Nouvel, "Presentation," in *The Jerusalem Seminar in Architecture*, ed. Kenneth Frampton (New York: Rizzoli, 1998), 83. Nouvel's reference to Paul Virilio in this text probably points toward Paul Virilio, *Speed and Politics* (New York: Semiotext(2), 1986), first pub. as *Vitesse et politique* (Paris: Galilée, 1977).
4 Peter Zumthor, "Stone and Water," in *Thermal Bath at Vals* (London: The Architectural Association, 1996), 9–10.
5 Zumthor, "A Way of Looking at Things"(1988), in *Thinking Architecture* (Baden, Switzerland: Lars Müller, 1998), 24.
6 Zumthor, "The Hard Core of Beauty" (1991), in *Thinking Architecture*, 32.
7 Paul Boulard [pseud. of Le Corbusier], "Le Salon de l'Art Décoratif au Grand Palais," in *L'Esprit nouveau* 24 (June 1924), cited and trans. in Caroline Constant, *Eileen Gray* (New York: Phaidon, 2001), 63. I discuss Le Corbusier's remark more fully in Chapter 5, "Table Talk."
8 Adolf Loos, "Heimatkunst" (1914), in *Trotzdem* (Vienna: Prachner, 1982), 129. A more detailed analysis of Loos's idea of "reticence" may be found in my Chapter 6, "Sitting in the City."
9 Tadao Ando, "Light, Shadow, and Form," in *Tadao Ando Complete Works*, ed. Francesco Dal Co (New York: Phaidon, 1996), 458.
10 Loos, "Building Materials," in *Spoken into the Void*, 63.
11 Zumthor, "A Way of Looking at Things," 12. I developed a similar argument against the notion of materials as "things in themselves" in *The Roots of Architectural Invention* (Cambridge: Cambridge Univ. Press, 1993), particularly sections 23 and 24.
12 Zumthor, "A Way of Looking at Things," 24.
13 Loos, "Interiors in the Rotunda," in *Spoken into the Void*, 23–24.
14 Rainer Maria Rilke, *The Notebooks of Malte Laurids Brigge* (New York: Norton, 1949), 46ff.
15 Nouvel, "Presentation," 76.
16 See David Leatherbarrow and Mohsen Mostafavi, *Surface Architecture* (Cambridge, Mass.: MIT Press, 2002), 39–78.
17 José Luis Sert, "On Windows and Walls," in *José Luis Sert*, ed. Knud Bastlund (New York: Praeger, 1967), 192.
18 Ibid., 193.
19 Nouvel, *Presentation*, 78.
20 Jean Baudrillard and Jean Nouvel, *The Singular Objects of Architecture* (Minneapolis: University of Minnesota Press, 2002), 61–62.
21 Robert Herbert, *Georges Seurat 1859–1891* (New York: Harry N. Abrams, 1991), 261–62.
22 Nouvel, *Presentation*, 86.
23 See Le Corbusier, "The Pack-Donkey's Way and Man's Way," in *The City of Tomorrow* (London: The Architectural Press, 1929), 23–30; first pub. as *Urbanisme* (Paris: Editions Crès, 1924).
24 This is discussed more fully in my Chapter 2, "Unscripted Performances."
25 Baudrillard and Nouvel, 8.
26 Zumthor, "I Build on My Experience of the World," *Detail*, 41, no. 1 (2001): 25.
27 Zumthor, "A Way of Looking at Things," 17.
28 Koolhaas, *S,M,L,XL*, 501.
29 Ibid, 515.

CHAPTER 4

Roughness

Below us the roaring city lies like a great animal on the prairies, but we do not run out to the prairies. We stay in our rooms and talk... of beauty and subtlety...[but] I grow weary of talk and walk in the streets.
—Sherwood Anderson, "An Apology for Crudity"

This study of roughness in architecture, gardens, and cities is structured in three parts, each a different dimension of a single argument. The opening section examines historical materials in order to define terms and pose the central difficulty of the concept. That review is followed by a descriptive section, which considers landscapes and buildings from the eighteenth, nineteenth, and twentieth centuries. These examples are adduced to exemplify the continuity of concern for picturesque roughness from the time of its historical emergence to the present. Lastly, I present rather more philosophical considerations under three headings: temporality, practicality, and situatedness. In this section, too, I try to describe the contemporary relevance of roughness, even though this potential resists conceptual mastery. Far from being a historical curiosity, this topic occupies a central place in current considerations of the limits of design understanding and authority.

William Shenstone, Leasowes, near Dudley, West Midlands,
England, 1743–1763; river view

Picturesque roughness

For Uvedale Price, one of the main landscape theorists of
the late eighteenth and early nineteenth centuries, the picturesque represented a third type of expression, distinct from
representations that were either beautiful or sublime. In his
1794 *Essay on the Picturesque*, he offered the following definition: "[P]icturesqueness...holds a station between beauty and
sublimity...[and is] perfectly distinct from either," because
it is founded on qualities neither of them possesses."[1] Beauty
is characterized by smoothness, apparent in easy and gradual
transitions; sublimity is characterized by roughness, apparent
in abrupt alterations. Landscape elements served as the subject matter of Price's characterization of the picturesque. The
paths of some gardens, for example, demonstrated intricacy of
composition through multiple and surprising deviations. Also
picturesque were topographical sequences that demonstrated a
variety of forms, tints, lights, or shadows. But Price observed
analogous attributes in other forms of expression, rhetoric,
for example. Ancient writers, he noted, thought that striking
passages and sudden changes of topic characterized sublime
speeches. Longinus famously argued that sublime rhetoric is
evident in "the vigorous and spirited treatment of the passions."[2]
Distinguishing the roughness of Demosthenes from the grandeur of Cicero, he said that the speeches of the Greek contained
passages that were "vehement, rapid, vigorous [and] terrible; he
burns and sweeps away all before him; and hence we may liken
him to a whirlwind or a thunderbolt."[3] Such presentations had
considerable effect on listeners; their turbulence roused violent
emotions. Intensity was key, intensity of delivery and of reaction.
But ancient writers were not the only ones to whom Price could
turn for an account of the differences between sublimity and
beauty. In fact, he openly acknowledged an eighteenth-century
source for the first two of his three concepts, the *Philosophical*

Enquiry into the Origin of our Ideas of the Sublime and Beautiful by Edmund Burke, published in 1757.[4]

As indicated by his title, Burke concentrated on the sublime and the beautiful, not the picturesque. Yet many of Price's arguments about the latter were fully anticipated by Burke. Smoothness is a case in point; it was, Burke said, "a quality so essential to beauty, that I do not now recollect any thing beautiful that is not smooth."[5] Although Burke claimed originality for this observation, it had been set out in antiquity by Plato, but less dogmatically. Comparing beauty to both friendship and the good, Plato wrote in *Lysis* that "[b]eauty is a soft, smooth, slippery thing... which easily slips into and permeates our souls."[6] Sublimity contrasts with this; "take any beautiful object," asserted Burke, "and give it a broken and rugged surface, and however well-formed it may be in other respects, it pleases no longer... any ruggedness, and sudden projection, any sharp angle, is in the highest degree contrary to that idea."[7] Obviously, a name for that contrary is the sublime.

Between the time of the ancients and that of Burke and Price, there were many writers who also attempted to define sublimity. I will not relate that history in any detail, only mention that influential figures included Nicolas Boileau in France, and John Dennis and Joseph Addison in England. But there is another English writer whose texts merit close attention, Anthony Ashley Cooper, the third Earl of Shaftesbury. Not only did he have new things to say about the sublime and beautiful, but his hymn to the natural landscape set the stage for the historical emergence of the picturesque garden. *The Moralists, a Philosophical Rhapsody* also indicates why roughness is key in the picturesque and why it is more than a problem of appearances—smooth, rough, or some combination of the two.[8]

Many, if not most, accounts of the origin of the informal, later the picturesque, garden cite the following passage from Shaftesbury as a sign of a new conception of natural order:

> I shall no longer resist the passion growing in me for
> things of a natural kind, where neither art nor the conceit
> or caprice of man has spoiled their genuine order by
> breaking in upon that primitive state. Even the rude
> rocks, the mossy caverns, the irregular unwrought grottos
> and broken falls of waters, with all the horrid graces of
> the wilderness itself, as representing Nature more, will
> be the more engaging, and appear with a magnificence
> beyond the formal mockery of princely gardens...[9]

That this primitive state is hard to apprehend is obvious, for Shaftesbury defined it several times. Consider, for example, the passage's ending: "princely gardens" were rejected because they conceal nature's genuine order. Their formality results from human conceit and caprice, not nature itself. Earlier in the passage, he seems to have opposed this uncultivated state to anything produced by art. I state that he *seems* to have rejected art in favor of unfashioned or rough forms, because in fact he did not; elsewhere in the same essay he praised both technique and execution. What is more, he supervised the construction of an extensive garden on his own estate, one that was not "informal." The difficulty of his position is apparent in the following quotation: "In medals, coins...statues, and well-fabricated pieces... you can discover beauty...but not for the metal's sake. 'Tis not the metal...but the art [which is beautiful]...So that the beautifying, not the beautified, is really the beautiful...the beautiful [was] never in the matter, but in the art and design...never in the body itself, but the...forming power."[10] The *forming power* that beautifies the beautiful is what Shaftesbury thought essential. Forms that have been overly wrought conceal it; others that are rude, unwrought, or rough, do not. Coarse figures are preferred because of what they reveal; each is an evidence, sign, or trace of the energy, force, or power that gives rise to representations of nature's unreasonable power. Burke thought similarly;

William Kent, Rousham Gardens, Oxfordshire, c.1740; faun

he wrote that "the rudeness of the work increases this cause of grandeur, as it excludes the idea of art and contrivance; for dexterity produces another sort of effect…" But again, it is not roughness per se that is important, rather its cause. Stonehenge, Burke argued, is not admirable for its ornament or disposition. What makes it awesome is its roughness; "those huge rude masses of stone, set on end, and piled each on other…turn the mind [to] the immense force necessary for such a work." [11]

Before and after finishing

The forces that partly form and then inevitably re-form artistic works show their effects over time. There would seem to be three chapters in this story: before, while, and after a work has been finished. In the passages I have cited, both Burke and Shaftesbury concentrate on the early period of a work's chronology. The terms they used need some clarification because art theory since the eighteenth century has burdened their vocabulary with many levels of meaning. The word "primitive," for example, does not mean for Shaftesbury non-Western or exotic, but rather what is unfinished in its development. Similarly, "rude" means neither impolite nor unformed. "Unwrought" figures are not lacking in shape or profile, only final form, because they are still being shaped, still becoming something other than they have been, quite possibly something other than what was expected. "Rough" means not yet fully formed, approximately finished. Forms of this kind, or at this stage of their formation, are genuine, because each has arisen out of an intrinsic law of development. "Mocking forms," by contrast, are those that have resulted from constraints being applied to the figures' native or local potential, in order to ensure conformity to familiar profiles, assuming that the end was known at the beginning. Roughness is prized because it bears witness to creative energy. Burke confused his account somewhat when he listed the sublime's telltale signs—broken edges, abrasive textures, or irregularity. These are only important when they disclose a tendency toward some identifiable figure, one still approximated. Roughness, then, is significant when it reveals recondite or implicit powers of change. In those instances or moments, a form shows its own possibilities for development, as if it were a sketch.

Roughness can also appear at the opposite end of the temporal spectrum. Complementing figures that are unwrought are those that are undone. Stonehenge, Burke's example, was a ruin. Over centuries, some of its elements and all of its edges had suffered the effects of the ambient environment, leaving its geometry confused (at least confusing to interpreters), the rhythm of its elements interrupted, and the profiles of its individual stones dulled. In Burke's time this incompleteness gave rise to considerable speculation about its so-called original form. Twenty-five years before his *Philosophical Enquiry*, for example, John Wood (who had such an important role in the architectural history of Bath) had interpreted the ancient stones as the remnants of a Druidic temple dedicated to the moon.[12] But his account—speculative as it was—had many rivals. Despite their differences, all of the interpretations read ruins as traces, remnants, or vestiges of antecedent intentions. The work's roughness was not, then, an indication of development but of deterioration. Yet the monument's end was no less significant than its beginning, for on its broken edges and uneven surfaces could be discovered sediments of all the forces it had suffered since construction. This is to say that the ancient stones chronicled their past. Once worked by design, then reworked by the environment, rough forms voiced a history of alterations, each of the recent alterations no less significant than the ancient ones despite coming late in the process of definition. If unwrought forms show possibilities, those that are undone testify also to the work's resilience in the face of forces that would undo it.

Roughness at a work's beginning and end would then seem to be categorically distinct from the form intended in design and realized in construction. Caught up in the time of their unfolding, unwrought and undone figures appear to be just the opposite of those defined by sharp profiles or clearly apparent shapes. Thus, an important question arises: If rough forms precede and follow those that have been finished, can picturesque roughness be the outcome of art, can it be designed? Shaftesbury's account of the grotto and Burke's of the ruin suggest that roughness results from agencies other than art. Can this quality, can this emblem of natural development and deterioration, of unauthored power, be the object of creative making, or is it, when designed, the result of mere simulation, a representation of a representation?

Throughout the history of architecture and gardens from the eighteenth century to the present, there have been many attempts to find a place for rough among smooth or highly finished forms. Solutions that are wonderfully lyrical are not difficult to find. Consider first, eighteenth-century garden *fabriques*.

About midway along the circular route through one of the most important eighteenth-century English gardens, that at Stourhead House in Wiltshire, the path begins a slight descent. As the level drops, the plantings at the path's margins become increasingly dense. The sense of enclosure is heightened still further by the arching of tall trees over the path, forming an arboreal vault. An important change occurs when the path passes through an archway. From this point onward, there are no more evidences of horticultural intent or of layout design; in fact, the threshold to the grotto itself is less a doorway than a break in a stone outcropping. This apparently "rude and unwrought grotto" perfectly represents Shaftesbury's sense of nature's primitive state. Certainly, much of the construction is "man-made," but it

Henry Flitcroft, Stourhead Grotto, Wiltshire, 1748; view onto lake

was not meant to appear so. Arrival at the cave's center involves a surprise, however, for set within its back wall, cresting the fall of an underground stream, is a statue of a nymph, not black like the stones but white, not rough but smooth and highly finished, possessing, therefore, all the qualities Burke associated with the beautiful. And this coupling of contrasting qualities does not end there. Turning one's back on the nymph, a similar mixing appears on the cave's other side, looking outward. In place of the statue is the lake, perfectly placid and unbroken in its horizontal expanse. Instead of a niche is a window that is similarly rough, broken, and irregular. The combination of rough and smooth at the garden's lowest level also occurs at it highest. A prospect across the lake opens toward the so-called Temple of Apollo. No view of the whole of this very refined building can be taken that frees it from its landscape base, a topography with all the opposite characteristics of the temple: irregularly sloped, heterogeneous in its makeup, alternately growing and deteriorating in its several parts.

Pavilions in later French gardens show much the same thing. Consider, for example, the famous Queen's Dairy at the Château Rambouillet. Quite apart from the oddity of Marie Antoinette drinking fresh milk in the environs of an experimental farm, the interior is a stunning juxtaposition: a rather severe classical portico on the entry side and a rough stone fountain at the rear. Astride the roughly hewn rock work sits the statue of a nymph (white, smooth, polished), who could also be a shepherdess poised to supply a nutritional source. The horizontal relationships between these extremes had a vertical equivalent in a project by Hubert Robert, the famous Apollo Baths at Versailles. Claude-Nicolas Ledoux posed the same relationship in an urban setting, where the main salon of his Hôtel de Thélusson in Paris sat above a grotto that ended a sunken garden. His buildings at the Saline du Chaux at Arc-et-Senans are

Frank Lloyd Wright, Fallingwater,
Bear Run, Pennsylvania, 1935; detail

Oscar Niemeyer, Canoas House, Rio de Janeiro, 1953; interior

similar, although rough and smooth elements are not stacked vertically or laid out horizontally but compressed together in the thickness of a facade.

The juxtaposition of rough and smooth forms also occurs in some of the best-known projects of the early twentieth century. In fact, this conjunction appears to be a central theme of one of the century's greatest monuments, Wright's Fallingwater. As in the Temple of Apollo at Stourhead, here smooth, highly refined, and vividly artificial forms have been seated on top of elements with all the opposite characteristics. As a whole and in its parts, the building conjoins things that are dry with those that are wet, light with dark, planar with faceted, simple with aggregate, fixed with changing, unblemished with marked, and—of course—smooth with rough. The junctions are always difficult, but the contrasts serve the function of emphasizing the qualities of each form. Perhaps the most lyrical details are those that join the elements that differ most: glass and stone. A perfectly equivalent case, albeit smaller, is Oscar Niemeyer's famous Canoas House (1953) in Rio de Janeiro.

Nor were Wright and Niemeyer the only prominent modernists to present this picturesque juxtaposition. Instances of *coincidentia oppositorum* are exceedingly common in the work of Le Corbusier. Many historians have suggested that his preoccupation with rough finishes began at the time of his famous turning toward the organic, his turning away from objects of mechanical selection to those of poetic reaction. The Villa Mandrot is often taken as a sign of this course correction. Three years after it was finished, the architect described its prominent material as follows: "This fine stone from Provence, orange and pearly with crystals, will be highlighted by the quality of the joints. This plan will become the lord of the whole landscape, from inside to out."[13] A few lines later, he repeated his principle of topographical continuity, "every inside is an outside." But his praise of stone tells only half the story; the building's apertures, wall coverings, and furnishings made use of the most contemporary industrialized products, making the entire building no less hybrid than any of the other examples I have mentioned. The same can be seen in the project that served as the villa's precedent, the Maisons Loucher (1928). Here the stone wall, to be made with local materials by local craftsmen, was to support a metal skeleton clad in materials Le Corbusier proudly called "dry." Other projects from these years showed the same dedication to juxtaposition—particularly the studio in his own apartment, the Errazuris House in Chile, and the Villa Félix outside Paris. Perhaps the most stunning instance of his coordination of earthwork and framework is the Swiss Pavilion. The Brazil Pavilion is still another variation on the theme.

Between the time of these designs and contemporary architecture, a number of designers experimented with the same issue. Two of the most interesting are José Luis Sert and Marcel Breuer. For each, the coupling of elements that might be called raw and cooked became highly rhetorical. In their work, rough and smooth elements were often used as cladding, which is to say used for their representational value as much as for their functionality. A fascinating example of this same tendency in still more recent work is the so-called Stone House in Tavole, Italy, by Jacques Herzog and Pierre de Meuron, finished in 1988.[14] On each elevation a concrete frame subdivides, but does not contain, stacked limestone. I say the frame does not contain the stone, because at the corners the concrete columns have been recessed. Because of the apparent instability of this mode of construction, the building cannot be called traditional, despite its use of local materials. Rather than structural, the stone is surficial. Yet as a cladding material, stone also acts as the building's environmental barrier. Similar ambiguity can be seen in the later projects of these architects, the Dominus Winery in California,

Herzog and de Meuron, Stone House, Tavole, 1985–88; facade

for example, finished in 1998. From a distance, it appears to be a solid block—green-gray basalt. Yet as one approaches, an opposite sense of the building appears, an aggregate quality, resulting from two sorts of assembly: small pieces of stone in wire baskets and wire baskets in walls. What initially appeared to be monolithic and massive is revealed to be doubly composite. Moreover, the first impression of solidity is disavowed by the penetration of light through the gaps between the stones. Stone, then, is not monolithic but aggregate, not broken but regular (at least when caged). Likewise, light, ordinarily limpid and clear, is broken by the surfaces of the stones, showing itself in highlights, flashes, or local intensities, no less irregular and rough than the hard surfaces it variously illuminates.

In these last two buildings, single elements are alternately structural and surficial, monolithic and aggregate, regular and irregular, and smooth and rough. This suggests that single materials can be used in different ways, depending on how they have been prepared, assembled, finished, and (later) refinished. This range of possibilities makes the determination of the "right" use or "essential" character of a material impossible. No material is essentially rough or smooth; these qualities depend as much on the way the material is treated or finished as on so-called inherent qualities. This means that concern for a material's quality—let's say its roughness—is less important than interest in the conditions under which that quality becomes apparent. Shaftesbury seems to have made the same point when he asserted that the beautifying, not the beautified, is really the beautiful. Here, then, is the key question: Under what sorts of conditions does a work's roughness appear? Put more simply, what forces roughness into visibility? In my concluding arguments, I will address this question under three topics: first, I will return to the problem of a work's temporality, then its practicality, and lastly its orientation. In each case, roughness will be seen to show itself as a sign of the work's resistance to the ambient forces that would soften, discipline, or rationalize it.

Latent roughness: not a quality but a tendency

"From the time a building is completed its destruction begins."[15] So wrote Frederick Gutheim in a melancholic reminiscence about one of modernism's greatest works, the Philadelphia Saving Fund Society (PSFS) building. Once begun, the process of destruction can be retarded through periodic maintenance, but never abated. While they generally outlive their designers, buildings do not last forever. For Gutheim, this conclusion called for a shift of focus, from preserving the look of the new to understanding the ways that a work could remain significant, even graceful, as it aged. He was not the first to think this way. Early moderns also wondered about the continuity of architectural quality. Gutheim mentioned, but did not cite, Auguste Perret on this topic. "The Palace of Versailles," Perret observed, "is badly built; the vault above the Hall of Mirrors is made of a thick layer of rubble, attached to an inferior framework, and in the course of time, what will remain of the palace will not be a ruin, but an anonymous heap of debris. This is not architecture; *architecture is what leaves beautiful ruins.*"[16] Perret's position also had antecedents. My concern, however, is not with the notion's early history, but rather with its echoes in the late twentieth century, for the continued interest in ruins shows a steady preoccupation with architectural temporality. This is important, because it indicates sustained interest in the problem of finishing, and therefore roughness, an aspect of the picturesque.

In 1975, the Greek architect Aris Konstantinidis offered the following explanation of Perret's assertion: "'True architecture makes beautiful ruins,' said Auguste Perret. This happens when the material (whether natural or artificial) used in making a certain structure grows beautiful with the passing of time, and also when a structure is well and truly built from the beginning. In which case, even when it falls into ruin...it allows its initial complete form to appear through its deterioration or mutilation."[17] Ruined works can allow complete forms to appear, not despite but by means of deterioration. How is this possible? How is it that something that exists no longer, the finished work, remains present when its finishes are gone? Obviously, in its ruined state the work is not what it was, but neither is it something entirely different; it shows the present form of what once was, because every single moment's passing draws those preceding it in its wake. Continuity of this sort allows the past to abide in the present. Imagine fragments of a massive stone column resting on the ground—a broken shaft, patchy surfaces—no longer serving its intended purpose, the life it lived over. But there on the ground, the column's bulk, finish, and endurance still testify to what it once was, to its former standing, capacity, and radiance. This testimony allows for the abiding of what is no longer.

Another way the past can be discovered within the present is through acts of renewal. Konstantinidis reported that across the Greek lands, there was a long-standing practice of whitewashing rough stone walls. While this happened throughout the year, the practice was particularly common at Easter time. Konstantinidis stressed the fact that, calendar aside, this process was without end, that renewal was a task that lasted as long as the building did. "Love of life is nourished and sustained," he said, "by the continuous motions of the human hand as it whitewashes, day after day, the walls and the doorsteps and window-sills of buildings. And gradually, day by day, as each new coat of white-wash covers the previous one, these surfaces seem to acquire a soft, warm, human like skin..."[18] Presumably, the building's first finish was smooth. But over time, through the corrosive action of environmental forces, pristine finishes got roughened. Whitewashing restored smoothness. Time was not annulled through this practice; its layers accumulated. Here, too, as with abiding temporality, the past was condensed into the present. Rather than being set apart, now and then coexist through renewal, the several ages of what once was stack themselves up to support the qualitative richness of what is now.

The third instance of continuity that can be discovered in Konstantinidis's writings, buildings, and photographs is a time of sedimentation. Distinguishing this from the time of renewal, one could say this is not a now *as* then, but a now *plus* then. He developed his argument in favor of sedimentation while discussing architecture's social dimension. Great works do not result from the inspiration or creativity of a single genius but from collective endeavor, from many contributions building on one another over time. To strengthen his claim, he cited a passage from Victor Hugo's great chapter on architecture, "This Will Kill That," in *Notre Dame de Paris*: "The greatest works of architecture are not so much individual as social achievements... the heritage bequeathed by a nation... the residue of successive emanations... each [depositing] its own alluvium... its own layer."[19] If one thinks about the building mathematically, it might seem that historical action subtracts the building's smooth finishes, resulting in a loss—the loss of clear evidence concerning the designer's intentions. Konstandinidis, however, following Hugo, introduces the opposite sign, a plus: when finishes are roughened over time, the marks thus added enrich the building's surface by chronicling a family of related efforts, a community of effects that attests to a people's action and creativity.

The last kind of continuity I want to adduce from Konstantinidis's writing conflates the work's beginning with its future. In this case, the present neither sediments, renews, nor recalls earlier times but reaches toward those yet to come. As with the first three instances, however, temporal extension in architecture involves finishing rough forms, not those that have become but those that remain approximate. Konstantinidis wrote: "A true work of architecture will become more effective...the less finished it is, in other words more easily shaped and converted, not completed once and for all." To explain himself further, he cited Bertold Brecht: "Whatever is destined to be perfect presents deficiencies—Whatever is long-lasting—Continuously comes from some sudden occurrence—Whatever is truly nobly conceived—Remains unfinished."[20] Unfinished forms invite creative responses. Rough situations occasion new beginnings. Because of this, they are also the means by which time is measured. Smoothness, by contrast, allows time to be lost, because it evens out the moments of its flow. Picturesque space, shaped by the broken surfaces of its forms, is incidental. Some early gardens were criticized for being episodic, which is to say, lacking in narrative structure. This was a risk designers were willing to take to avoid landscapes like those designed by Capability Brown that were "dull, vapid, unvaried, and smooth."[21] Perhaps one reason for the contemporary relevance of the picturesque is that it allows us to rediscover—or to name—the temporal fullness and creative potential that arises out of discordant situations.

Whitewashing, according to Konstantinidis's account, is a practical response to the roughness of a building's surfaces. When first built, the walls were uneven. The first coat (like all those that followed) reduced irregularities, approximating smooth planarity. Smoothness does not seem to have been desired, or thought to be equally important, in all situations, only those in which the building came into contact with the human body. Smoothness, Konstantinidis said, leaves a trace of the human hand, allowing the architectural body to take on something like a human skin. If we focus not on the beauty or on the temperature of these surfaces, but on their need for peri-

odic renewal, we see that the roughness to which they respond
indicates a dimension of the building's inexhaustible potential.
Over time, which is to say through use, the unevenness of the
entry step becomes apparent once again; also, the door frame's
abrasiveness, the shutter's graininess, and the wall's cracks.
Roughness returns because it had only been covered over. This
is significant, for the reemergence of irregularity—irregularity
itself—is a sign that local conditions remain forceful, that the
energies, capacities, or power that made the work possible have
not been dissipated. Practical affairs allow a building's local
strengths to reassert themselves, thereby individuating the work
and, as I argued earlier, measuring time's passing.

Just as rough edges are smoothed by the foot and hand,
they are softened by the forces of the environment. This soften-
ing cannot be avoided. The realization of an architectural project
involves construction in a location. Once built, the work suffers
the effects of that location, effects I earlier described as corrosive—meaning that wind, water, and sun destroy the building's
finishes, the lines and angles intended in design. Konstantinidis
called this process "mutilation." Yet the destruction of a work's
finishes also allows it to articulate another dimension of its nature.
Over years of exposure to the sun, the building's surfaces show
what strengthens their makeup. Although covered over when the
building was first finished, these strengths show themselves to
be the means by which the work continues to stand where it is,
as it is. Facing south, the timber wall is bleached white; to the
north, the moisture sheltered in its shadows deepens its colors.
Certainly these changes give voice to the building's orientation,
but they also show its capacities, strengths possessed by it alone,
local capacities of resistance. Here again we see that roughness individuates works; it shows the building's resolve to stand
against the flows of the environment, and this resolve endows it
with particularity.

When a building is finished according to well-conceived designs and carefully controlled construction practices, the potentials, strengths, or capacities I've tried to describe are unapparent. The rough surfaces that particularize a project and give voice to ways of living and patterns of the environment emerge now and then. They appear in acts of resistance to the varying flow of ambient conditions. Although unplanned, even unthought, their appearance is significant, for they not only attest to a work's real strengths but also give measure to the life it sustains.

Endnotes

Epigraph Sherwood Anderson, "An Apology for Crudity (1916)," in *Sherwood Anderson's Notebook* (New York: Boni and Liveright, 1936), 196.

1   Uvedale Price, *An Essay on the Picturesque, as compared with the sublime and the beautiful; and, on the use of studying pictures, for the purpose of improving real landscape* (London, 1796); cited in John Dixon Hunt and Peter Willis, eds., *The Genius of the Place* (London: Paul Elek, 1975), 354–55.

2   Longinus, *On the Sublime*, trans. A. O. Prickard (Oxford: Oxford University Press, 1949), 144. The best study of the history of this idea is still Samuel Holt Monk, *The Sublime; a Study of Critical Theories in XVIII-Century England* (New York: Modern Language Association of America, 1935). A more recent and philosophical study is that by Jean-François Lyotard, *Lessons on the Analytic of the Sublime* (Stanford: Stanford University Press, 1994).

3   Longinus, *On the Sublime*, 155.

4   Edmund Burke, *A Philosophical Enquiry into the Origin of our Ideas of the Sublime and Beautiful* (1757), ed. J. T. Boulton (London: Routledge & Kegan Paul, 1967).

5   Ibid., 114.

6   Plato, *Lysis*. 216d. Trans. J. Wright in *Plato: The Collected Dialogues* (Princeton: Princeton University Press, 1963), 160.

7   Burke, *Origin of our Ideas*, 114.

8   Anthony Ashley Cooper, third Earl of Shaftesbury, *The Moralists, a Philosophical Rhapsody*, in *Characteristicks of Men, Manners, Opinions, Times*, vol. 2 (1711), ed. John M. Robertson (Indianapolis: Bobbs-Merrill, 1964).

9   Ibid., 125.

10   Ibid., 131. As for the problem of his garden's "formality," see David Leatherbarrow, "Character, Geometry, and Perspective," in *Topographical Stories: Studies in Landscape and Architecture* (Philadelphia: University of Pennsylvania Press, 2004), 131–68.

11   Burke, *Origin of our Ideas*, 77.

12   John Wood, *A Description of Bath, wherein the antiquity of the city, as well as the eminence of its founder,...are respectively treated of,...illustrated with the figure of King Bladud* (London: W. Bathoe and T. Lownds, 1765).

13   Le Corbusier, *Croisade ou le crépuscule des académies* (Paris: G. Crès et Cie, 1932), 63. My translation.

14   A brief description and set of drawings of this house can be found in Gerhard Mack,
      Herzog & de Meuron 1978–1988, The Complete Works, vol. 1 (Basel: Birkhäuser Verlag,
      1997), 56–67. I have written briefly about this house in the Conclusion to my *Topographical
      Stories*, 242–46. Also brief, but very useful, is Alan Colquhoun, "The Concept of
      Regionalism," in *postcolonial space(s)*, ed. G. B. Nalbantoglu and C. T. Wong (Princeton:
      Princeton Architectural Press, 1997), 13–24.

15   Frederick Gutheim, "Saving Fund Society Building: A Re-appraisal of the Old Beauty,"
      Architectural Record (October 1949): 88–95.

16   Auguste Perret, "Architecture," *Revue d'art et d'esthétique*, 1–2 (1935): 41–50; trans. Karla
      Britton, in *Auguste Perret* (London: Phaidon Press, 2001), 238–43.

17   Aris Konstantinidis, *Elements for Self-Knowledge* (Athens: American School of Classical
      Studies, 1975), 301–02.

18   Ibid., 305.

19   Quoted in ibid., 308.

20   Ibid., 321. Source not indicated.

21   The assessment is from Richard Payne Knight, "The Landscape," cited in John Dixon Hunt,
      The Picturesque Garden in Europe (London: Thames & Hudson, 2002), 72.

Part 2

Situations

CHAPTER 5

Table Talk

Although architects are responsible for the design of spatial settings, the measure of their success depends on the adequacy of those settings with respect to patterns of behavior no one has designed, the situations and institutions of contemporary culture. Adequacy in this formulation includes two kinds of performance, practical and figurative, for settings must accommodate and express the patterns of our lives. The question this chapter takes up is the relationship between these two. Perceptual issues enter into the question, for both accommodation and expression are known in concrete experience. But a more radical question is implicit in this first one about the relationship between the practical and figurative aspects of rooms or buildings. What is it that settings give to perception? Do places offer objects, signs, types or traces? And according to what schedule are the setting's provisions offered: all at once, or over time, according to the pace of passage or of viewing, or to that of memory and anticipation? The advance into and retreat from perceptual prominence will be described, as well as the instruments and evidences of those movements. Rather than considering these questions generally, though, I will focus on a familiar and representative situation.

Imagine returning to a restaurant in which you have just finished a meal—assume you went back for your keys. Before leaving a second time, you take a minute to notice the way the table looks after everyone has gone.

Inscribed onto the table's surfaces are traces of what just occurred, in much of its particularity. Like the clothes of a laborer at the end of the day, this tablecloth, china, and cutlery vividly attest to the ways they were just used. "Service" is a term we sometimes use for tableware; two things, the physical premises of a meal and their readiness to assist those who want to eat, are meant by this term. Surface stains result from the table's voluntary subjection, because the contents each receptacle receives—hardly ever dry—leave telltale marks. But to notice these traces only is to neglect a different way the elements that make up the table perform and present themselves. Let me say a little more about this presentation and performance, for the first largely depends on the second.

Before the meal occurred, the table and its more permanent preparations displayed themselves as just the sort of setting we were looking for, as if by some miracle of foresight they had anticipated this all the time. "Presaturated" with indications of possibilities, the setting proposed a possible meal, because it had been prescribed for typical or customary ways of dining. If the tabletop is particular once we have finished, because now marked with traces of our food and drink, it was general (generally okay) before we began. To describe a table—or for that matter a room, sidewalk, or garden—as a trace or chronicle is to recognize that it also served once as a prescription. Thus, a symmetry: inscription after the meal, prescription before it; the reply the table gave to our "orders" was written on the back of its invitation.

But that is not all the setting had to say, or to imply. The enjoyment of a meal hardly requires steady attention to the chairs, glasses, and napkins that allow it to take place. The "service" they perform involves not only subjection and anticipation but a particular kind of recession, a retreat or withdrawal from perceptual prominence. That they allow themselves to be overlooked during the meal is not a fault of their "form"; actually it is the reverse, its relative perfection. During a meal, the serving, not the setting, sustains one's interest. Good service tends to be quiet; good tables, tacit. At the center of a meal experience is thus a blind spot with respect to its instruments, as is true for furnishings and equipment of all sorts. Elements in service forego conspicuousness once they commit themselves to sustaining events. Although silent, they are not inarticulate.

Before, after, and during the meal, then, the table gives itself in different ways: as a trace once eating is over, as a type before one sits down, and tacitly while dining is occurring. While architects often concern themselves with the first two of these modes of articulation, trace and type, the third, the tacit voice, is equally important in what I would like to describe as "table talk."[1]

Familiar in experience but often neglected in architectural study, the everyday meal is a particularly instructive example of how spatial settings make sense in different ways. The meal's diversity or spectrum of articulation probably results from the fact that each meal is one among many that over time and through memory accrue a history endowed with richly stratified meanings. Prosaic habits are not rituals, for they lack a mythical substrate, but in the case of a meal, ordinary practice may transcend itself into a rite. Each serving spreads itself out over memories of antecedent practices, the historical accumulation of which saturate the situation with content that can be called symbolic, for its foundation, or presumed origin, is believed to be "right." Christianity has a sacramental history because a particular Passover meal was preceded by the emphatically prospective injunction: "Do this in remembrance of me," demanding of each follower a performative mimesis. Comparable commands exist in other traditions, often involving sharing and sacrifice. But often the meal is only understood prosaically. Though shorter than sleep and longer than a shower, most servings are similarly matter-of-fact. Whether seen as a reenactment or repetition, each lunch or supper is both a recall and a prompt of others. The meal's extended temporality complements its levels of disclosure, from tacit to outspoken.

While we tend to think of architectural settings as essentially spatial configurations, in what follows I would like to focus instead on their temporal character. I will use the meal as an analogue in order to describe the ways in which spaces not only accommodate the patterns of our lives but also provoke reflection on their implications. My argument unfolds in three stages. The first, "Time tables," describes the ways that settings—meals—allow one to remember and anticipate similar performances. Next, "Tables and terraces" shows that these settings adhere to and crystallize latent characteristics of their vicinity, making the meal situation *topographical*. Finally, under the heading "Table talk," I consider the spectrum, dimensions, or levels of articulation in the setting, from those that are understated to those that give rise to thought.

Time tables

As a site, the dining table offers relative stability to the many positionings and repositionings that occur across its surface. From meals eaten "on the run," to lunch on a park bench, hors d'oeuvres at a party, or a full course meal at a wedding banquet, there is generally some horizontal surface on which the stages of the meal succeed one another. Such a surface may be as immediate as the palm of your hand, as expedient as a molded plastic tray, or as refined as bone china on black lacquer. The stages that follow one another on these surfaces are not necessarily the meal's courses, ranging from soup to sweets.

Adolf Loos, Loos apartment, Vienna, 1903; dining room

A meal's steps can also result from practical requirements, each with its own priority and timing. First comes the clearing and cleaning, then the "setting" of the surface. After this follows the sharing of the several courses, which are variously interwoven with periods of rest and talk for those around the table, giving rhythm and amplitude to the meal's social dimension. Finally, there is a second round of clearing and cleaning. Not only the table's surface, but its interior space and outer edge center and organize these stages and their configuration. Anthropological studies such as Mary Douglas's "Deciphering a Meal" map this geometry, and describe the moral and religious injunctions that govern the layout. Manuals of domestic protocol—such as Mrs. Beeton's *Household Management* or the *Better Homes and Gardens Cookbook*—provide rule and pattern for this layout and its sequences.[2] In no two cultures are these positions and protocols precisely the same, but in each they are taken to be correct and taught to children at an early age. The dining setup is a particularly clear indication of the cultural specificity of spatial situations.

Through the meal's several courses, some things or objects—such as the centerpiece—hold their position, as if permanent, while others—such as the basket of bread, bottle of wine, salt and pepper—migrate. The elements of a "place setting" may not be anchored to a specific spot, but the relationships between them are relatively stable. This is true no matter what instruments are used; each item has its proper distance from others. But permanence of place is not permanence in time, for some things appear at different stages and then linger, others disappear, while still others are ever present—for instance, the tablecloth, whether it has been spread out on the small table in the kitchen or on the ground during a picnic. These comings and goings are governed by relationships between the several elements of the situation. Some elements belong to "sets," others remain essentially isolated. Further, some are shared, others not, for the dining table also configures public and private spaces. The steps that pace the meal's schedule are instances of change in which elements assumed to be long-standing play against those that are not.

Yet the stability of the situation is not guaranteed by objects alone, for the most durable aspects of the layout are the (implied) positions of things that answer to the reach and habits of the bodies around the table, as they variously but systematically follow and diverge from traditional protocols. While these positions include plan locations with objects located at the right or left, center or margin, they also relate to sectional strata. Some items may occupy the horizon of the tabletop, which is stratified according to surfaces that are variously clean and polished. Other items may occupy the horizon of conversation, normally at eye level, a horizon of glances toward other diners, pictures on the walls, mirrors, and so on. And still other items occupy even higher or lower levels in the room. Horizons below integrate the darkest and most recessive elements of the setting; those above gather together the lightest and most ambient of elements. Objects (food, people, utensils) may occupy these positions in section and in plan, but not one of them is more enduring than the horizon itself, for it antecedes and follows the arrival of each object, serving as the (ideal) place in which objects will have been positioned—an a priori of dining. If one can say that such a framework for positioning is "there," it is so as a result of the meal's typicality, "sedimented" in embodiments that range from stains on the table, to the habits of the body, to memories. While paradoxical, this means that the meal's uniqueness is conditioned by the frequency with which other meals like it pass. Put categorically, the particularity of an instance presupposes a history of repetitive performances.

A pair of drawings that explore this delicate choreography of a meal in time can be used to exemplify these observations.[3] In the first, Nicole La Rossa superimposes a number

Nicole La Rossa, *Three @ Kisso*, 2001

Ariane Sphikas, *Meal Time*, 2001

of perimeter frames, recalling the table's ambient conditions, through which people find their bearings. A horizontal band runs through the drawing and the meal, guiding and tracing the arrival and departure of items to and from the surface. The waiter begins and ends this series of movements. As the meal unfolds (from right to left in this drawing), objects come into sharper focus, while ambient conditions recede. They come back into view when the plates are cleared, thus the vertical break in the drawing and the reorientation (reconnection) to the perimeter. The lateral drift of elements continues beyond this line or break, departing from the table at the left. This edge at the "end" of the lateral transit, like that at the "beginning," is black, which is to say, capable of absorbing into its darkness all objectlike definition. But this is temporary or provisional, for the blacks and whites at the edges are also the means by which the meal "finds its place" and attains its definition. The singularity of the event repeats others that have been occasioned by these premises, just as it anticipates those that will follow.

Time marked by transits across a surface is also what appears in a second meal drawing, by Ariane Sphikas. The argument here, however, is that once the setting—the table setting—has been used for its specific purposes, the notion one has of its permanence or fixity is replaced by a more accurate idea of change or shifting positions. On the lower part of the drawing, a filmlike band charts the progressive disappearance of the elements that make up the meal, steadily dissolving the integrity of the "set." The elements and objects one handles during the meal are scheduled by this band (contained within the drawing's verticals), variously apparent on the table, but not offering themselves for attention for very long. This advance into prominence and retreat begins when the food arrives, shown in this drawing by the strong vertical that edges the drawing's left quarter, which distinguishes the table set before the meal (in dark tones) from the table appropriated into use (lighter tones and disconnected figures). With this sequence of movements, this chronology of positions in mind, it would seem possible to call the surface of the table a clock; but the comparison is inexact, because the intervals derived from the lateral drift of objects are also the means by which they lose their definition—into a set at the meal's beginning and into the background at its end. The duration of the meal is no more regular than its ambient context is uniformly apparent, which is almost never the case, given the shifting interests that characterize this (and any other) situation.

Tables and terraces

When I sit down to order a meal, in the restaurant of a hotel, for example, the chalkboard menu on the wall interests me greatly, my table just a little, and the wall behind the menu or the light above it barely at all. I am not alone in this respect; everyone in the restaurant who wants to eat looks at the menu as I do, for a while, taking for granted the quiet suitability of the furniture and the room. But prominence, in each of its degrees, is never permanent, the freedom natural to perception allows for reversals in the figure–background structure. A shadow on the wall, next to the menu, may divert my attention, similarly, someone passing on the street. This suggests that "withdrawal" is as much a possibility of an element as is prominence. When I pick up a book, its printed words immediately stand out; yet, as soon as I begin to read through the lines, paragraphs, and pages of the text, they begin to efface themselves so that the sense of the text can fully occupy my attention. Once I'm engrossed or absorbed in the book, the print and pages are not *not* there, but their manner of being there has changed. Maurice Merleau-Ponty has observed in his paper on the experience of expression that the perfection of language lies in its capacity to pass unno-

ticed: "[O]ne of the effects of language is to efface itself to the
extent that its expression comes across."[4] What is true for the
experience of facial and textual expression is also true for a kind
of articulation that occurs in architecture: its forms and figures
efface themselves as they accomplish their practical purposes,
their service.

The reversal of figures and grounds assumes a *field* or
horizon structure of elements within a setting. Before any figure
emerges as the object of thematic attention, it is "pre-given"
as part of a wide context of interdependent components, each
materially and practically relevant to the others. With the table
come not only the chairs, but also the bar, the menu on the wall,
the windowsill, the garden terrace, and much more, each poten-
tially conspicuous but all "tending toward" the others, somewhat
horizontal because "horizonal." When I am eating (not thinking
architecture) the "near" and "far" elements of the setting release
themselves from the places they had been assigned in perspective
space and commingle with one another in a way that is "impos-
sibly" congruent. Modern painting, particularly the cubism of
Juan Gris, brought this "congruence" to light. The "service" of
a setting's elements is to wait within their milieu until targeted
by practical interests and their associated perceptual structures.
Traditional discourse, and the design techniques it sustains, has
nothing to say about this thicker space; in fact, it conceals it.
The light and shadows on the dining table are as much a part
(a property) of the linen cloth as they are of the window looking
onto the café at the front and the trees in the garden at the rear.
Without the cloth, the window glass, and the leaves, the play
of shadows would never appear. Considering food, the meal's
dependence on the remote landscape is recalled by flowers at
the table's center, testifying to the interdependence of sun and
soil, grasses, grain, and grazing. The table—much like a building site or even a city—concentrates (incorporates) the field in

Juan Gris, *Le Canigou*, 1921; Albright Knox Gallery, Buffalo

relationships that bear upon the person having the meal. Once I saw someone take a little bite out of a flower from his lover's place setting, as though appetite were desire. Downcast eyes and a blush answered the advance. Now what is true of a flower and friend, terrace and table—anterior continuity and implied consubstantiality—holds for all of the setting's elements and platforms; each reciprocates the others until some local interest (yours or mine) rewrites the agreements they had established among themselves. All together and latent, they constitute something like an atmosphere, a disposition, or mood that is not easy to describe but is never unclear. This "character" is often what is memorable about settings.

Let me try to elaborate this atmosphere in view of a specific setting. A man and a woman face each other over a table at the edge of a restaurant interior painted by Edward Hopper in 1930.[5] Neither the pair in conversation nor any of the other figures in the interior is distinctly prominent in the painting. In part, the painting's diagonal composition causes this, with the line of lemons (grapefruit?) on display accelerating to the right, and the run of tabletops drifting to the left. In this weave no figure proposes itself as primary; the wine at the center of the "table talk"—if wine is what the carafe holds—is no more important than the instruments of its supply and cost: the staff in white and black, the kitchen, and the cash register.

Although unobtrusive, each of these figures is distinct. The woman in the foreground has the features of a Veronese contessa but adopts the posture of a Tintoretto saint. As an emblem she indicates abundance, much like the produce spread before her; but she also expresses hygiene, hence her unblemished apron, white like a tablecloth, the tidy row of produce she organizes, and so on. Her attention has two vectors, however: her hands toward the window display, her gaze beyond it, joining kitchen and street, as if the dining room were not there.

The waitress at the register is similarly specific. Her body trails behind her eyes like the tail of a comet. Flat black from the shoulders down, half hidden, she is entirely absorbed in counting. Although focused, she is not alone in her work; her stance and glance align three kinds of reckoning (counting, pricing, and timing) and their instruments (her gaze, the register, and the clock). This stance is also the most fixed point in the interior; the containers she oversees hold the cash and trinkets on display. If the first figure is an emblem of supply, the second exemplifies definition or restraint: white and black, giving and taking, substance and measure. The two of them, and their "performances," stand between the street and the table talk that is sheltered in the depth of the room.

If all of this seems beyond the border of the meal, it is because we tend to think of eating as a tabletop occurrence only. This painting shows, in contrast, that the simplest of meals depends on highly differentiated, even discordant, ambient conditions: on *topography*.[6] With this term I mean terrain that is endowed with implications of practice that extend beyond the edges of discrete objects and events. Such a structure integrates a vicinity, in this case an urban location. Lloyd Goodrich, commenting on Hopper's urban images, wrote:

> In many of his urban subjects, individual men and
> women do appear, but as parts of the whole scene rather
> than in leading roles. The woman undressing for bed,
> the diners in a restaurant, the bored couple seen through
> their apartment window, the solitary passerby in the
> street at night, are integral elements in his version of the
> city; but their environment is as important as they are.[7]

The compression of a figure (back) into its field proposes a unity that is not only pictorial or optical but also practical; thus, the

Edward Hopper, *Tables for Ladies,* 1930; Metropolitan Museum of Art, New York

Le Corbusier, Pavillon Suisse, Cité Internationale Universitaire de Paris, 1933; refectory lounge

positions of the figures and items at the room's center or perimeter, their role in support of the event, and so on. Although the "serviceable" elements that structure such a field are recessive, the topography is expressive, for it traces practices we know but normally neglect.

Table talk

Writing in *L'Esprit nouveau*, Le Corbusier once compared architectural settings to servants: both are best when unnoticed in the performance of their several tasks. He seems to have preferred interiors and arrangements of "equipment" that are discreet and self-effacing. Thus settings and servants are best when taken for granted, in much the same way as the human body at work in the world, because all—bodies, servants, settings—are "limb-objects." Operation, what something does, is important here, but even more so is recessiveness. Commenting on an exhibition of interiors and their furnishings, he criticized "chairs that are charming, intelligent, but perhaps too talkative...If chairs and armchairs extinguish Picasso, Léger, Derain, Utrillo, Lipchitz, then chairs and armchairs are insolent...are extremely loud. One thinks: To live here one must be damned distinguished—and without respite. Good manners are commendable and they embellish life—but only when one is least aware of them."[8] Hence his statement of principle: "The human-limb object [the chair or table] is a docile servant. A good servant is discreet and self-effacing, in order to leave his master free."[9] Does this silence the table's voice, or is there a kind of articulation that communicates implicitly? And what is the relationship between (self-effacing) furniture and (self-expressive) walls and windows, particularly when the former are conceived as "part of" the latter, built-in or not?

Le Corbusier was not the only twentieth-century architect to make this point about limb-objects effacing themselves.

Louis I. Kahn elaborated a similar concept of "servant" spaces. Before that, when Le Corbusier was still developing his arguments, Eileen Gray offered a comparable observation, without the analogy to servitude: "One must build for the human being, that he might rediscover in the architectural construction the joys of self-fulfillment in a whole that extends and completes him. Even the furnishings should lose their individuality by blending in with the architectural ensemble."[10] I take it that this loss of individuality allows the individual item to recede from one's awareness insofar as absorption into an ensemble means retreat into a context that serves as a background for "the joys of self-fulfillment."

Unobtrusiveness was also an aim of the architecture of Adolf Loos. His complaint against artistic furnishings in "Poor Little Rich Man" argues for this quality. So does the call for "reticent" architecture that he put forth in his essay on the vernacular idiom:

> In a few days' time, one of the last of the old Hietzing
> houses will be demolished...What culture was in these
> houses, what refinement! How Viennese, how Austrian,
> how human!...It is well known that such houses do
> not have a facade, and this is not liked [by the planning
> council]. It is preferred that one does the same as the
> other newcomers, the one is to outshout the other.[11]

The contrary stance, the one that Loos himself adopted, holds that the building, like its furnishings, should not proclaim prominence, but express its standing and history noiselessly, like a silent witness, not commanding attention, but—here is the difficulty—rewarding it when it is given.

One of Loos's students, Rudolph Schindler, also was concerned with architecture's inconspicuous standing. His

Rudolph Schindler, Schindler-Chace House, West Hollywood, 1921–22; interior

somewhat unusual application of the term "transparency" demonstrates this. For him, transparent figures are those that are unseen because unobtrusively present in a setting. One is reminded of Loos's quip about the best-dressed man being the one least noticed in public.[12] Schindler's interpretation, however, was developed with respect to metal furniture; "transparency" distinguished all deployable items from those that were built-in or immovable, the permanent furniture used to "define" the "space conception."[13]

One of the most celebrated aspects of the Schindler-Chace house is its use of exterior fireplaces as sites for the preparation of meals. The house's floor slabs comprise one level of a beautifully elaborated site section. The use of the slabs on the inside of the house is obvious, but they are not confined to its limits, to those of the thermal barrier. As if to serve as the basic premises of an "encampment," the slabs extend into the garden court and serve as the surface on which open-air fires could be ignited. Otherwise, cooking, Schindler said, was to be done "right on the table, making it more a social 'campfire' affair, than the disagreeable burden to one member of the family."[14] In fact, there was a central kitchen or "utility" room. Meals prepared in the kitchen seem to have been served on trays. In the absence of a dining room, or functionally specific rooms of just about any sort, the stratification of platforms remained dominant, whether concrete or grass, canvas or timber. Seating for meals seems to have migrated across these surfaces; sometimes "interior" furniture was brought to surround an outdoor fire.

Viewed in plan, the topography can be read as a mosaic of dwelling platforms, each offering no more than a setup for some practical purpose and preferred posture. Frequently they are not in typical locations. This is not to say that "outdoor dining" was atypical, but that meals were "set up" in different locations, thus instituting peripatetic dining—as if the Schindler and

Chace families envisaged eating as a sort of grazing, or cooking as a nomadic practice that resulted from hunting and gathering. The accent here is on the "primitive," which in California at that time might well have been described as the natural or authentic. One need not subscribe to this anthropology, nor to this version of the modern world, to recognize the expressive, even symbolic, aspirations of this outdoor dining. Obviously, this shift in domestic meal decorum has practical and material "premises," but it is also indicative of more than that, for it reveals what Schindler took to be new ways of living in a house and, more broadly, of modern existence. In this instance, the setup or topographical instruments of a specific situation give rise to thought about their wider implications: that modern life would usher in a new primitivism, that freedom from precedent would lead to more creativity, or that the traditional discord between art and life could thus be overcome.

Just as tables talk in different ways, settings articulate their sense variously. They can remain tacit while endowing experience with its instruments, its "limb-objects," and they can give experience its characteristic expression, narrating its history or symbolizing its foundation. The topography of the meal invites us to consider how settings have different ways of voicing their contents, sometimes by speaking and sometimes by keeping quiet.

Endnotes

1   This term is one way to translate the title given by Leon Battista Alberti to his
     Intercenales, a collection of moral tales or parables that were typical of Renaissance dinner
     conversation; see Leon Battista Alberti, *Dinner Pieces: A Translation of the Intercenales*,
     by David Marsh. Medieval & Renaissance Texts & Studies, vol. 45 (Binghamton, N.Y.: The
     Renaissance Society of America, 1987). Talk is what fills the gaps or pauses in the meal:
     inter cenales. Alberti's stories, many of which take the form of dialogue, are rhetorical,
     not philosophical. "Table Talks" is the translation of the title adopted by Mark Jarzombek
     in *On Leon Baptista Alberti: His Literary and Aesthetic Theories* (Cambridge, Mass.: MIT
     Press, 1989), 20ff. While a few of the stories refer to architecture, the dining table itself

does not come into focus. In this sense, Alberti's "table talk" exemplifies the architectural "oversight" I want to describe.

2   Mary Douglas, "Deciphering a Meal," in *Implicit Meanings* (London: Routledge & Kegan Paul, 1975), 249–75. The section in the *Better Homes and Gardens Cookbook* entitled "Table Settings and Entertainment" is devoted to this topic. Particularly interesting are the instructions listed under "More Table Talk—type of service and seating guests."

3   These drawings were completed by Nicole La Rossa and Ariane Sphikas, students in my first-year design studio in the Master of Architecture program at the University of Pennsylvania, in the spring of 2000. They were part of the preliminary work in the studio. I asked students to share a meal together and during its course "survey" its "premises" (material, metric, and spatial), paying particular attention to what developed over time. The approach in the studio was analogical; the meal survey was followed by the development of an architectural plan that was similarly sensitive to spatial and temporal conditions.

4   Maurice Merleau-Ponty, "Science and the Experience of Expression," in *The Prose of the World* (London: Heinemann, 1974), 9.

5   Edward Hopper, *Tables for Ladies*, 1930, Metropolitan Museum of Art, New York.

6   This topic is central in my book *Uncommon Ground: Architecture, Technology and Topography* (Cambridge, Mass.: MIT Press, 2000).

7   Lloyd Goodrich, *Edward Hopper* (New York: Abrandale Press, 1983), 69.

8   Paul Boulard [pseud. of Le Corbusier], "Le Salon de l'Art Décoratif au Grand Palais," *L'Esprit nouveau*, 24 (June 1924): n.p.; cited and trans. in Caroline Constant, *Eileen Gray* (New York: Phaidon, 2001), 63.

9   Le Corbusier, *The Decorative Art of Today* (Cambridge, Mass.: MIT Press, 1987), 79.

10   Eileen Gray and Jean Badovici, "From Eclecticism to Doubt," first pub. in *L'Architecture vivante* (Winter 1929): 17; trans. and repub. in Constant, *Eileen Gray*, 238–40.

11   Adolf Loos, "Vernacular Art," trans. and repub. in *The Architecture of Adolf Loos* (London: Arts Council of Great Britain, 1985), 112–13. I have modified the translation. I discuss another passage from the same essay in Chapter 6, "Sitting in the City."

12   Loos, "Men's Fashions," in *Spoken into the Void* (Cambridge, Mass: MIT Press, 1982), 11.

13   R. M. Schindler, "Furniture and the Modern House. A Theory of Interior Design," in *The Furniture of R. M. Schindler*, ed. Marla C. Berns (Santa Barbara, Calif.: University Art Museum, 1996), 49. I discuss this passage in more detail in the chapter "Sitting in the City."

14   "R. M. Schindler to Mr. and Mrs. Edmund J. Gibling, November 26, 1931." App. A, in Kathryn Smith, *Schindler House* (New York: Harry N. Abrams, 2001), 80.

CHAPTER 6

Sitting in the City

It seems reasonable to assume that conditions as distinct as being in and outside an architectural enclosure require equally distinct ways of thinking about the body and the settings it inhabits. However, Joseph Rykwert suggested at the end of his paper on "Meaning and Building" that the two conditions should be seen as one, that architects should think about the body within an interior in the same way that they imagine it within the environment.[1] Perhaps this suggestion, made some years ago now, seems uncontroversial, for widely shared notions about the unity and centrality of individual experience, the continuity of space, and the several scales of architectural design assume the indivisibility of the interior and exterior, and of our experience of them—even if most design projects focus on one scale and site or another, the room or the street. What is more, the central motif of modern architectural space—the building's inside connected to its outside—posits these two topics as part and counterpart. Yet aside from the suggestive elaborations of the concept of the environment in ecological theory (Max Oelschlaeger's writings for example) and the social science of everyday praxis (the texts of Pierre Bourdieu or Henri Lefebvre), architecture's role in establishing this connection remains rather unclear or not clearly discussed. Perhaps this is because the vocabulary we normally use to discuss the environment, the vocabulary of space, is conceptually vague and technically narrow. Further, and paradoxically, when architects concern themselves with the vicinity as well as the building, both tend to become objects of "design," as if the town or one of its neighborhoods were the outcome of project making, not the reverse. The aim of this chapter is to take up Rykwert's invitation to consider the designed interior as part of the environment, and to do so from an architectural point of view, intending to complement but not restate arguments made by others concerned with "material culture." To this end I will introduce and partly redefine the term "topography" to name a horizon of architectural work that is more inclusive than the outer walls of a building, and more indicative of the existence it sustains—a wider horizon of physical and spatial conditions that traces typical human affairs. Because I oppose totalizing design practices, I will also outline a kind of architectural work that recognizes its own limitations, not, however, territorial limitations—the edges of a parcel of land a client happens to own—but limitations on one's ability to envisage and project a "complete world." I will consider what Rykwert called the "semantic" aspects of the built world as well as the habits and histories of the human body within it; I mean that situated and ambulatory locus of the memories and anticipations through which each of us knows and lives in the world. Just as I want to observe the building being "occasioned" by its vicinity, I want to see the body emerging out of the lived world, but also disappearing into that world, testifying to the world's ontological priority. Rykwert's concluding passage still provokes reflection on the status of the body: "Every moment of perception contains a whole personal and collective past, our body is the incarnation of that past; and with every moment of perception this past is reordered and revalued."[2]

Organic unity

In the first years of the twentieth century, no architect was more insistent about the need to join the interior setting to the environment than Frank Lloyd Wright. Because he wrote so very much, it is risky to suggest that any single theme is primary in his texts, but this one, to which he returned repeatedly, must be seen as among his most important. The late, more or less midcareer, summary presented in *The Natural House* can be taken as an adequate account of his understanding of "organic unity." He explained that after the Winslow House of 1893, his conception of the wall changed; simply put, it was "no longer the side of a box." The wall was still a means of protection against environmental inclemencies, but it had become both less and more than that; after being reduced in length or interrupted in its perimeter continuity, it took on the role of bringing "the outside world into the house and let[ting] the inside of the house go outside." Obviously, doors and windows had done that before the "box" was broken, but not as fully. With this new development, the wall had become a screen, a means of spatial extension that would permit the "free use of the whole space without affecting the soundness of the structure." The milieu into which the interior was extended, or with which it was now connected, was not only the building's immediate vicinity, but also the greater region surrounding the site.[3]

The step was consequential, for the abbreviation of the wall led to changes in what was built on either side of it, in the building's furnishings and gardens. Not only were they reshaped in what was to become the Wrightian manner—extended and superimposed horizontal planes—but more basically they became subject to this reshaping, to design and construction technique, as if they, too, were permanent parts of the house, of the same fabric or weave, parts of a single, "simple," "integrated," and "organic" whole. "Breaking the box" thus extended not only the

Frank Lloyd Wright, Coonley House, Riverside, Illinois, 1908; plan

Frank Lloyd Wright, Robie House, Oak Park, Illinois, 1909; fireplace and seating

house but also the authority and responsibility of the designer. Wright intimated this in an account of the ruined finances of his early clients:

> The clients themselves usually stood by interested and excited, often way beyond their means. So, when they moved into their new house, quite frequently they had no money left...and had to drag their old furniture into their new world. Seldom could I *complete* an interior because the ideal of "organic simplicity" seen as the countenance of perfect integration...naturally abolished all fixtures, rejected the old furniture, all carpets and most hangings, declaring them to be irrelevant or superficial decoration. The new practice [of organic design] made all furnishings so far as possible...integral parts of the architecture.[4]

Similarly for the building's outward extension; "planting was [not] to be done about the houses without cooperating with the architect." Nor was a sculpture or painting to be "let in" unless approved by the architect. Whenever this restriction was ignored, there was "trouble." Clients, Wright wistfully noted, occasionally held onto furnishings and rearranged garden layouts, compromising unity for the sake of a few familiar forms. So did the sculptors, painters, and gardeners with whom he sometimes worked. At best, and "[o]nly in a grudging and dim way did most of them even understand" the idea of such a synthesis. But there was a way to avoid this sort of trouble; Wright would make designs for all of it—all of the furniture, the gardens, and applied art—on the assumption that it was better to "design *all* as integral features."[5] Thus, from lamp to table, table to room, room to room, and all of this to the site, he composed everything as if it were a single "world," each setting and scale verging toward others. And the verging went further. Just as the house was "integral" to its site, the site was to its region, and the region was to the nation, for his was an American architecture that expressed the essential characteristics of a people and place at all of its scales. Wright's project for The Living City, embodied in the Broadacre City model, elaborated this territorial claim.

The result of organic unity or "plasticity" would be harmony, he said, essentially the same as the harmony of nature, which is always selfsame throughout, purposeful and beautiful. This idea of harmony was clear to Wright even in his early years. Already in 1896 he observed that in nature all things "harmonize with the whole," never is one shown in relief at the expense of the rest; nature shows that "all arrangement is organic and therefore complete in itself." Accordingly, or analogously, architecture should have "the *repose* which only a sense of *completeness* can give."[6] He argued these points a few years later under the title "The Modern Home as a Work of Art," anticipating the totalizing authorship that was to become his practice in later years.

The house is not a work of art

In 1896, another architect concerned with "the home as a work of art" left America after a three-year stay and returned to Vienna, having visited not only Chicago, but also New York, Philadelphia, and St. Louis. Given this architect's great enthusiasm for America, it is important to stress that the "*abendländische Kultur*" to which he referred in the subtitle of his short-lived journal *Das Andere: Ein Blatt zur Einführung abendländischer Kultur in Österreich* was not the America of Frank Lloyd Wright, or that of "organic simplicity," a verging from the dining table toward the hillside. For Adolf Loos, "*abendländische*" meant not only the United States but also, and perhaps more largely, Britain. Loos infrequently mentioned architects in his writings; Wright's name is hardly prominent. Had he been discussed, Wright might well have been treated as a European, for his work clearly intended a domestic *Gesamtkunstwerk*—the sort of compositional synthesis that became the object of Loos's stinging critique. Does this mean that Loos, and those who saw architecture similarly, disavowed the interconnection between the interior and exterior?

"Completeness" is the central point of attack in Loos's "The Poor Little Rich Man."[7] Summarized briefly, the text presents a parable about total design, or the consequences of art governing the patterns and style of everyday affairs. Loos describes a client whose talented architect "had forgotten nothing, absolutely nothing. Cigar ashtrays, cutlery, light switches—everything, everything was made by him." Expressed in all of these artifacts, and the house itself, was not some vague or generalized local, regional, or national characteristic of Austria or America, but the character and personality of the owner. This made it familiar, intimately so, but also complete, completely new, so much so that the architect had to supervise the inhabitants during their first few weeks in the house in order to prevent the misplacement of or substitution for an object by accident or under the illusion of convenience. The architect's visits were, however, inadequately preventative: "trouble" occurred when the poor owner received and wanted to display a few birthday gifts. In reply to a request about their placement, the architect thundered: "How do you come to allow yourself to be given gifts! Did I not design *everything* for you? Did I not consider *everything*? You don't need anything more. You are complete."[8] There were to be no more gifts for the poor little rich man, nor were there to be painters, artists, or craftsmen, none of the desiring, striving, and developing that defines every individual's life. Thanks to the architect, the client was finished, *complete*. That the individual could be identified with his surroundings was by this time a familiar conceit; nineteenth-century writers in and outside the field of architecture, such

Charles Rennie Mackintosh, House of an Art Lover, reconstruction, Glasgow, 1901; interior

as César Daly and Edgar Allan Poe,[9] had argued for this identification; and impressionist and symbolist painters had developed it into the principal subject matter of turn-of-the-century portraiture (Vuillard, Degas, or Sargent, for example). In Loos's parable, the finality of the inventory of utensils was as important as its entirety; he ridiculed its once and for all, unchanging, or atemporal character, for the unhappy client soon discovered what it was like "to go about life with one's own corpse." At risk in totalizing or complete design is not only spontaneity and choice but freedom.

Perhaps I have been unfair to Frank Lloyd Wright in directing Loos's irony and invective toward him. The designer Loos actually seems to have targeted was Josef Hoffmann. But alternatives could also include Joseph Maria Olbrich or Henry van de Velde. Even architects from Britain, the pinnacle of "*Kultur*" that was to "guide" Austria, can be seen to have supplied targets for Loos's critique. An obvious case would be the works of Charles Rennie Mackintosh, which were shown in the eighth exhibition of the Wiener Secession in 1900 (the year of Loos's article). This exhibition attracted about 25,000 visitors, of whom Loos was most certainly one. In praise of the exhibition, *Ver Sacrum* announced: "Those who have attained the heights of civilized refinement in their daily life, even if they have otherwise little time for art, make certain demands upon the things which serve them, upon their whole environment, demands which can only be satisfied with art."[10] Two years after the exhibition, in a paper called "Seemliness," Mackintosh repeated this conclusion in his call for "improvement in the design of everything... [proposing that] artistic intention [be] evident in the making or adornment of each article of everyday use or requirement, [assuming] a discriminating thoughtfulness in the selection of appropriate shape—decoration—design for everything no matter how trivial."[11]

Given the irony of the "Poor Little Rich Man" text, it is hardly surprising to find Loos proposing just the reverse approach to residential furnishings: "I considered the design for a new dining room chair to be foolish, an utterly superfluous foolishness which entails a waste of time and effort. The dining room chair of the Chippendale period was perfect. It was the solution...just like our forks, swords, and screwdrivers."[12] Good solutions are inherited, tradition supplies the equipment of the domestic interior: "[T]he best form is always already given and no one should be afraid to use it, even though it may come almost entirely from someone else."[13] The best way to invent new solutions is to neglect this inheritance as well as the practices through which it renews itself; "those who have no table manners...find it easy to design new forks. This they do with artistic imagination." Does this sense of historical continuity isolate the interior from the exterior, insofar as the city, the modern metropolis, had in these years apparently dispensed with traditional patterns?

Reflexive spatiality

Loos's critique of artistic imagination weakens design, or at least abbreviates its need to originate the forms that will "guide" modern life. It also makes problematic the role of art in architecture, particularly in the typical settings of the house, their architectural (spatial) definition, and their equipment. Yet even more important for me is the fact that this sense of the interior also redefines the relationships between different settings, both in and outside the building. Against the ideal of uninterrupted continuity, or formal sameness among the parts of an ensemble, Loos proposed differentiation and complementarity: not a "verging" but a reflexive or reciprocating spatiality. This was to be accomplished in several ways. Differentiation was thought to be a matter of the physical body of the room: the "temperature,"

Adolf Loos, Moller House, Vienna, 1928; interior

Adolf Loos, Scheu House, Vienna, 1912; facade

dimension, and location of its materials within the extended topography. Loos's paper on the *Bekleidung* principle explained that different settings have different "effects"; each setting and associated effect is first envisaged by the architect and then realized through the selection, assembly, and finishing of materials. But the setting's temperature is not all that distinguishes it from other settings; equally important is size. Presupposed in the *Raumplan* configuration of settings is their dimensional differentiation: "[E]very room requires a specific height (the dining room needs one different from the larder) therefore ceilings must be arranged at different levels."[14] But the *Raumplan* also proposes the differentiation of volumes and their combination into one "unified" configuration.

Considering Loos's "distribution of volumes in space," many authors have described the *Raumplan* as a way of treating the architectural interior, a technique of structuring or ordering private settings.[15] The usual support for this interpretation is an isolated phrase from Loos's essay "Heimatkunst": *"Das haus sei nach aussen verschwiegen, im inneren offenbare es seinen ganzen reichtum."*[16] (The house should be reticent on the outside and unveil its entire richness on the inside.) That his buildings were rich on the inside cannot be denied; this is apparent in their cladding materials and their sectional geometry. But if the sophistication of Loos's three-dimensional configurations cannot be disputed, neither can their "integration" into the vicinity in which they were sited, for the *"miteinander verbinden"* (interlocking) of room to room in a "plan of volumes" was also a binding together of interior and exterior settings, even if openings of the sort Wright proposed are not in evidence. One cannot have reciprocity without distinct boundaries, without separation between the corresponding parts. The phrase I have quoted above was used in an argument that concerned not only facades, but also monuments and streets, in German and Italian cities,

with which Loos thought those of Vienna could be compared—
"reticence," or *Verschwiegenheit*, being the typical characteristic
of buildings in both the Austrian capital and Italian cities. Not
only a technique of interior design, the *Raumplan* was a mode
of interpreting the relationships or connections between settings
that were both enclosed and unenclosed, those that reciprocated
one another in a differentiated topography that tolerated both
consonance and dissonance. Every setting, interior or exterior,
was understood and conceived with respect to another; no room
or ensemble of rooms was seen "in itself."

Hermann Czech and Wolfgang Mistelbauer have shown
in their discerning study of Loos's building on Michaelerplatz
in Vienna that the building's site plan, section, and construction details were developed in dialogue with its ambient circumstances.[17] Loos himself prompted this interpretation, explaining,
for example, that the limewash of the upper floors was a way
of establishing continuity with Viennese street architecture:
"*Wien ist eine kalkputzstadt,*" he said.[18] Czech and Mistelbauer
have shown that spatial connections were also carefully structured. I believe the same reflexive relationships can be observed
in Loos's other urban projects, the American Bar on Kärtner
Strasse or the so-called Cafe Nihilismus. And I think his houses
were conceived similarly. Considering the Moller or Rufer
houses in Vienna or the Müller Villa in Prague, one could, I
think, "reconstruct" the distribution of settings inside their
walls by considering carefully the opportunities for repetition
and contrast latent in their sites, interpreting the vicinity as a set
of "predispositions" within which a "plan of volumes" could be
developed: entry at the front, service at the back, morning light
from one side, quiet on another, and so on. One could develop
such an interpretation, because one knows, without special
study, just from cultural experience, how rooms of various types
are typically oriented in typical sites, near to or far from this or

that ambient quality. This is not to say that design in this sense involves the comprehensive or uncritical duplication of models; instead, it develops systematic deviations from them, in recognition of or in response to the exact particulars of the project, particulars that derive partly from its modernity. A reconstruction of the building's section from an interpretation of its vicinity, such as I am proposing, would not be error-free, but it would not be impossible either. The *Raumplan* is as much a function of the opportunities of the building's surrounds as it is of internal relationships and dependencies, the latter being insufficient in themselves to determine any configuration. More emphatically, without the salient characteristics of the vicinity, Loos would have been at a loss to determine things as basic as window sizes and their placement, the orientation and extent of a terrace, and the location of an entry. In other words, he would have been lacking exactly half of what it takes to establish a configuration of rooms in a way that would make them not only useful but significantly or "semantically" so. I do not mean to say that the site, any more than the typical dining room, predetermines the solution simply because it has been "received via tradition." Rather, both "inheritances" (the site and the program) serve as predispositions, pretexts, or first premises for design, outlining or sketching the basic limits of a possible configuration, against which topographical invention works itself out through modification, contrast, and differentiation, to the degree design judgment determines is right. This decision making is where design technique (geometry) is guided by nontechnical and nonteachable forms of understanding, which in brief can be called practical or ethical understanding. The matrix of differently qualified settings that results from both kinds of understanding constitutes a legible terrain of affairs or topography that discloses the building's participation in a collective past through its modification of the forms in which that past had been known.

Adolf Loos, Scheu House, Vienna, 1912; interior

The aesthetic unity Loos criticized in "Poor Little Rich Man" was rejected by others in the period of early modern architecture, but on different grounds. The stylizing that typified late art nouveau or arts and crafts interiors was criticized by functionalist architects because it seemed to be insufficiently attentive to practical requirements. Moreover, from the functionalist point of view, Loos's work, too, was stylized—at least the Chippendale chairs he installed into his houses. The "tradition" to which he referred was that of the bourgeoisie. While it may seem sensible to challenge his work as the sort that uncritically affirms the status quo, I think it is more accurately seen as the result of an attempt to modify or "guide" the status quo, thus both a conservative *and* progressive attempt. Nevertheless, in place of what they saw as stylized "unity," functionalist architects seem to have substituted another form of compositional synthesis: images of functionality. At least that was the conclusion reached by one of Loos's near contemporaries in Vienna, Josef Frank.

As with Loos's criticism of aesthetic unity, the problem Frank had with functionalist compositions was their finality:

> ...the mad desire for the uniformity of form, for the
> endless set, the basis of the antiquated idea of applied
> art as *a closed system* is unchanged [in functionalism]
> and it cannot understand how many-sided our lives have
> become, how everything that exists must be a part of it.
> Our era is the whole known of historical time. This idea
> alone can be the basis of modern architecture.[19]

More aggressively, Frank wrote: "I am of the opinion that anyone who has the desire to rest his posterior on a rectangle is in the depth of his soul filled with totalitarian tendencies."[20] German architects associated with the Werkbund or participating in the

Weissenhof Siedlung, namely Mies van der Rohe and Walter Gropius, had these "tendencies." Frank's rejection of any kind of synthesis—organic, aesthetic, or functional—is even more apparent in the assertions he made about domestic interiors in his late and very provocative paper on "Accidentism": "The living room, where one can live and think freely, is neither attractive nor harmonic nor photogenic; it came about as the result of accidental events, which will never be finished, and by itself can absorb anything whatsoever to satisfy the owner's varying expectations."[21] This paper was written in Sweden, to which Frank had returned after his rather unsuccessful World War II years in the United States. His American period had ended with an exhibition of his furniture in Edgar Kaufmann's department store in Pittsburgh, an exhibition that seems to have led to the arrival of one his chairs at Fallingwater, no doubt despite Wright's desire for organic unity.

Unlike Loos, Frank designed a great deal of furniture, over two thousand pieces in fact. Nor did he advocate the use of forms "received via tradition"—or not these only. Just as the rooms of a house were to be furnished over time, they could incorporate examples from different periods. His arguments against unified interiors led him to reject the idea of a "system" or "synthesis" at the scale of the room and of the ensemble of elements. "[E]ach [piece] must be independent of the rest, obstructing nothing and only giving the impression of belonging together as a 'group' in this particular context. We no longer need 'sets' consisting of two inseparable easy chairs, a couch, and a table."[22] Thus, pieces from different periods could be arranged together. Having been so arranged, each could, in time, be replaced by some other. An architect could propose such a change, as could someone living in the house. Pieces were chosen, placed, and preserved as long as they accommodated and represented a "set" of practical affairs, the "unity" of which was not formal but *situational*. If a fabric metaphor is useful, the craft of room construction was no longer that of weaving but of stitching or sewing; it was the kind of assembly that brought together pieces that pre- and postdated the architect's project. This stance weakens the authority of the designer or transforms architectural invention from the discovery of new shapes into the interpretation of recurring and contemporary dwelling situations.

The most striking aspect of Frank's arguments about such a fabric is that the adjustable synthesis proposed for the living room was also to be found in the street, as if the architect were to consider the environment like the interior, as if both were designed and "undesigned"—which is to say, interpreted and acknowledged. "The conditions valid for making living rooms comfortable are likewise valid for houses, streets, and cities whose present rigid forms are making their inhabitants homeless [*Heimatlos*]."[23]

Josef Frank's doctoral dissertation examined the buildings and ideas of Leon Battista Alberti.[24] He focused on Alberti's churches, their motifs and typical forms. Apart from struggling with the "modernity" of Alberti's work, Frank drew comparisons between church and domestic architecture. This style of interpretation was not new; others had proposed these comparisons, and Alberti himself established analogies between different types, most famously between the house, the city, and the body, following ancient precedent. Frank's version of the analogy was set forth in a key article called "Das Haus als Weg und Platz."[25] Following other authors, he compared the center of the house to the piazza of the town, and domestic passages to streets: but for him all analogous forms—the living room, piazza, passage, and street—were incomplete or always capable of being rethought and reformed. Frank observed that the rules for a good house never change in principle, yet he argued they must be "continually considered anew." Such consideration would question the way the garden is entered, the layout of the entry sequence, the opening of the entry door, the passage from the vestibule to the living room, the configuration of seating with respect to the door and window, and so on. Questions such as these, of typical situations and practical affairs, must be asked anew because dwelling interests change, no matter whether one is considering the kitchen or boulevard. Asking and answering questions such as these is the basis for an architecture that would be "modern," and such architecture would be apparent both in and outside the house. Topography so conceived does not project settings that verge toward and diverge from one another, as do Wright's, or the reciprocities envisaged by Loos; instead, it is based on analogies, it projects a field of similarly structured (and unstructured) practical situations. Such an ensemble is neither continuous nor discontinuous, concordant nor discordant; it is a field in which reiterations play against one another, each inviting choice and sustaining both historical memory and contemporaneity.

Another architect who came under Loos's influence in Vienna merits consideration because he introduced yet another sense of the relationship between the interior of a building and the environment, one that echoes Josef Frank's sense of unity arising from the domestic *Lebensraum*, but also recalls the aesthetic or compositional synthesis of Wright's work. After studying with Adolf Loos for one year, Rudolph Schindler left Vienna in 1914 for the United States, traveling from New York to Chicago and working there, eventually joining Wright's office in 1917. Work for Wright took him to California in 1920, where he later set up his own office, although he continued to work for Wright until 1923. But before then, while still in Chicago, Schindler designed the Buena Shore Club (1916–18), the only large building he completed. The building no longer stands and has been neglected in most Schindler scholarship, but it indicates themes that were to preoccupy him throughout his career.[26]

In his own account of the design, Schindler emphasized topographical concerns: "Right at the sandy beach [of Lake Michigan]—below street grade—the planning Architect began to start his building, growing gradually to higher levels, as it is stepping back from the border of the water. The beach and the sea wall, the sunken garden with its banks and walls, the walls, the terraces and roofs—up to the street grade and still higher— up to four floors."[27] Both this passage and Schindler's perspective drawings describe a stepping or stratified spatiality that links together by sectional increments the watery origins of the site, the surrounding city, and the remote (because elevated) recesses of the building (the private rooms above those for card playing and billiards). Precedents for this stepped section and configuration of gardens, courts, interiors, and terraces can be found in much of Wright's work, particularly the Midway Gardens of 1914. Wright's written works also seem to have anticipated Schindler's thinking. While still in Vienna, Schindler would have had access to Wright's introduction to the 1908 Wasmuth publication of his projects, in which he advocated horizontal extension, sectional stepping, and the assimilation of the building into the "prairie" horizon.[28] But the comparison with Wright is not the only one that demonstrates Schindler's interests and background. Considering the three-dimensional relationships of the Buena Shore Club—those between the beach, the gardens, the dance hall, the "living room" above it, the porch/dining room/ terrace, and the library—one can identify this configuration of volumes with the *Raumplan* spatiality of Loos. Moreover, each setting has its own "temperature," dimensions, and sectional position (between the water, the street, and the roof), and they are interlocked. The same concerns inform Schindler's design for the so-called Translucent House of 1927, a design of much more sophistication and subtlety than the Buena Shore Club, although he circumscribed its terrain by perimeter walls and dense planting.

Both "translucency" and "transparency" are indicative terms in Schindler's work. His usage invoked the customary sense of the words, meaning optical or visual conditions, the state of some material being impervious to or penetrable by light or air, allowing one to partially or completely "see through"; but for him transparency was also a quality of things that are familiar or habitually used, and this is an unusual sense of the word. Transparent figures are those that are unseen because inconspicuous or unobtrusively present in this or that setting. Within settings they are tacit; their significance, latent. He wrote: "The few places which are necessarily moveable (chairs, etc.), become so in an accentuated degree. Moving, they are unfit to define the space conception and must therefore be eliminated architecturally for the sake of clarity. They are either folded up and stored away or made transparent to become inconspicuous. This is the real meaning of the metal chair. Its essence is its transparency...."[29] This quality distinguishes all deployable items from those that are built-in or immovable, the permanent furniture used to "define" the "space conception." In fact, Schindler thought of built-in furniture and architecture as inseparable, for he saw the house as essentially a weave that includes walls and windows, beds and bookcases. His spatial ensembles, unlike Frank's, are not sewn but woven. This again repeats Wright, who had argued for the integration of furnishings into the permanent parts of the building. Wright also took up the issue of "unobtrusiveness" or "inconspicuousness." In the Wasmuth edition introduction, he suggested that the several parts of an interior should be designed to "wear well" and have "absolute repose," by which he meant they should make "no especial claim upon attention." For Wright, repose was also a quality of the prairie landscape, as already noted, and it assumed the completeness of an "organic" design. Similar but not identical arguments about a setting's background character were made by Schindler: "It must be the basic principle of all interior decoration that noth-ing which is permanent in appearance should be chosen for its individual charm or sentimental associations, but only for its possible contribution to the room conceived as an organic entity, and as a *background for human activity*."[30]

This last passage introduces an instructive contradiction. Both moveable *and* immovable furnishing were thought to serve as the "background for human activity," yet the first was to be "transparent" (unseen) and the second to be instrumental in the definition of the "space conception," definition that was surely meant as apparent, even prominent. In what ways can both fixed and deployable furnishings be inconspicuous and yet define a room, especially if they are designed as "background," not to be noticed or to obtrude into prominence? Can something built-in be transparent, in the sense of being "seen through" and yet still be significant, "semantically" so? Schindler does not say, but certainly implies two kinds of "seeing": a lateral sort that appre-hends configurations at the margins of a focused regard, and a perspectival sort that concentrates that same regard. Paintings, not furnishings, are seen in this latter sense. By contrast, the equipment of domestic life does not bring attention to itself continually or insistently. Yet somehow it can emerge (from the "transparent" fabric of practical affairs) in order to "define the space conception." Furnishings are sometimes figures, but most times they are background. Not only the "emergence" but the retreat of objects (the table or chair and the body they accom-modate) into their vicinity is what needs to be considered and clarified as much as possible.

The relationship between the room and the "world" outside it can help with these distinctions. Schindler's argu-ments about the interconnection between the building and its site are similar to Wright's in their emphasis on horizontality, but they are not identical. While Wright referred repeatedly to the "prairie" as a symbolism of the American landscape—platforms "fitting in" with the terrain—Schindler emphasized changes in the ways people had come to understand and use their houses. Perhaps the best outline of his ideas is contained in a short text entitled "Shelter or Playground," the last of a series of articles on "Care of the Body."[31]

As shelter or as playground are alternative ways of seeing the house, each relevant to a historical epoch. In the past, when "the earth, the sky, and the neighbor" were "frightful," the house was envisaged as a shelter, and "fear" dictated its form and spirit, hence the emphasis on safety, accomplished by and apparent in "heavy walls, small windows, ponderous grills, thick curtains, and dim light."[32] In the first decades of the twentieth century, this way of thinking about the house, and the anxiety implicit in it, was regrettably still common, despite the changes brought about by new construction technologies and new patterns of life. In the future, Schindler announced, the house would

> cease being one of dens, some larger for social effect, and a few smaller (bedrooms) in which to herd the family. Each individual will want [and should be given] a private room to gain a *background* for his life. He will sleep in the open. A work-and-play room, together with the garden, will satisfy the group needs. The bathroom will develop into a gymnasium and will become a social center.[33]

The site and style of cooking was predicted to change too; it was to become another setting for "group play." This account provides a fairly precise description of the Schindler-Chace house of 1921–22, to which I will return. The rooms in the house of the future will loose their autonomy, their compartmentalization, because they will merge or "melt" into a new "fluidity," as will the house itself, into the "flow" of the wider horizon. Situations previously located within the confines of the "shelter" will discover their furnishings and equipment in the garden, "in the open." I propose naming this lateral repositioning "displacement," intending to contrast it with the "verging," "reciprocating," and "analogous" settings of Wright, Loos, and Frank.

The framework for the displacement of settings and situations is a set of horizontal strata that extend from the recesses of the interior to the expanses of the building's vicinity. Three strata are prominent and recurrent: the horizon of the land, of social encounter, and of the sky. The emphasis on levels can be understood in contrast with earlier understandings of sectional topography: "[T]he stereotyped form-sentence of the conventional designer: base, body, cornice, crown—has now lost its meaning. The contemporary form-sentence may move horizontally, around the corner, or even downwards... [O]ur time, with a more democratic scheme, has discovered the meaning of the neighbor and allows us to stretch our hands out horizontally."[34] The origin of this lateral drift is not only social but postural, the traces of which are apparent in the furnishings we prefer. Schindler suggests but does not elaborate a history of postures. There was in these years, he said, a tendency to seek the horizontal as a more relaxed position. This was not so in the past; previously, furniture had leaned against the wall. Now it "merges with the floor." The carpets, pillows, and low benches shown in all the views of Schindler living rooms are receptacles and signs of this horizontal inclination. Likewise for the articulations at the midlevel of the room, from sill and table to typical shelf height: "[T]he imaginary horizon in the room has dropped from door to elbow height. This divides the room at a lower height and increases its spaciousness."[35] Similarly, the concentric arrangement of furnishings had given way to linear configurations not bounded by the house's thermal barrier. Schindler

Rudolph Schindler, Schindler-Chace House, West Hollywood, 1921–22; interior

invented storage "units" that could be deployed throughout his houses. Like a house, they were low and wide, not intended for an upright position against the wall. When placed above one another "they establish[ed] several horizontal planes throughout the room, giving the furniture the character of floor terraces."[36] The idea that a piece of furniture could be conceived of as a terrace suggests its potential for relocation or displacement; so too for other "permanent" fixtures in the house.

Both the exterior fireplaces and the rooftop "sleeping baskets" of the Schindler-Chace House exemplify the displacement of settings that are typically thought to be "interior." Both also demonstrate ways of interpreting the potentials of topographical strata. The floor slabs of the house comprise one level of an elaborate site section. Overhangs above some of these slab extensions annexed into the holdings of the house other stretches of the surrounding gardens, whereby patches of shadow cut out of the sun's brightness marked thresholds into and out of the interiors. Rooftop beds blanketed by canvas covers and the sky were not displaced laterally but vertically, defining levels within the sky horizon. Each level served as a setup for some practical purpose and preferred posture. Frequently they were not in typical positions. Nevertheless, the ensemble as a whole served as a "background for life," one that was meant to be unobtrusive in its presence and latent in its significance, marginally indicative of some situation.

Given Schindler's acceptance of the basic principles of much of Wright's built and written work, it is not surprising that he invokes the concept of the "organic" in explanation of his own buildings. What is more, the outcome of organic composition was described as a unified ensemble, a synthesis. Having circled back to this ambition, after considering the counterarguments of Loos and Frank, it is now possible to turn to the problem of unity, or wholeness, itself, in an attempt to indicate the ethical and philosophical implications of its different meanings.

At least two primary senses of *unity* can be discovered in the work of these architects: formal and practical unity. I propose this distinction even though much of the work I have considered resulted from efforts to make the first dependent on and expressive of the second. Wright's arguments in favor of plasticity and organic synthesis—verging spatiality—were based on his criticism of boxed-in enclosures. Schindler repeated this criticism and likewise proposed a "fluid" alternative, in which settings could be freed from their traditional moorings and allowed a striking degree of leeward drift. In both cases the "box" was a symbol for settings that were closed in on themselves, unified within perhaps, but isolated in their context—suffocatingly so. Both Loos and Frank also criticized closure, not in its spatial manifestation but instead in its effect on the inventory of domestic equipment, from the ashtray to the painting. Confined to surroundings in which everything had been designed, the life of the poor little rich man was not only "complete" (fully taken care of) but "finished" (over and done with). Josef Frank found the prejudice in favor of a "set" of "functional" furnishings evidence of totalitarian tendencies. Even more than Loos, he was against the atemporal or unchanging character of such a synthesis or "system"; thus the assimilation of ages in his modernity and his acceptance of "the occasion" and "accident" as part of project making. The complete set, like the box within which it was shelved, contained and constrained existence against the practices it sought to perform, those present in one's memory and anticipation. Thus the alternative: instead of a formal synthesis, each of these architects proposed a unity that somehow reflected the pattern of typical situations, in both spatial and temporal aspects. Yet Wright's articulation of this pattern also demonstrates his manner of stylizing, as did Schindler's to a lesser degree. Authorship was less in evidence in the work of Loos and Frank, particularly the latter, whose sense of "acci-

dent" emphatically disavowed representational synthesis, even
though he sometimes simulated chance encounters.

I have called the architectural setting a "trace." With this
term I mean the sediment of some usual practice and its indication. But no trace of this kind exists nowhere, even if its elements are moveable; each one is located somewhere, each one is
typically here or there. While the settings are always somewhere,
they also always invite or suggest typical forms of appropriation,
which means they are "there for that purpose"; elsewhere, their
capacity is lower, and less apparent. Nothing of this is lawful or
fixed; at best, one can say preferred positions are probable. The
likelihood of a setting's purpose depends on adjacent conditions,
what it is close to or what it is there *with*: the bookcase with the
desk, the desk with the window, the window with the street.
This suggests that definition is always regional. Each element
traces aspects of typical situations that are dependent on others,
no matter whether the dependency is approximate sameness or
difference, gradation or contrast. The topographies of reversal,
analogy, and displacement I have described enable and indicate
the occurrence of similar and different situations, only some of
which need to be constructed, resulting in the affirmation of
all the others that have not been designed. The task of topography, which is not that of design, is to posit probable sequences
through these relationships, some of which express sameness;
others, difference. The positive sense of difference is its evidence of the place's historicity. Disjunctions within the horizon
of typicalities demonstrate how times have changed and how the
inheritance has been recast in response to new interests.

Only in such a field can an event and its setting find a
place. In design we are always concerned with this or that single
setting. Consequently, we tend to see the field as a background,
the darkness needed in the theater to show up our performance.
Reflection on topography reorients design and thought to the

world that is there independent of my knowledge and experience of it, let alone my action within it. Were the "world" not largely indifferent to the body, there would be nothing like suffering. This prioritizing of the (undesigned) world, this reaffirmation of the town, no doubt weakens design as originating authorship. Nevertheless, the real prospect for an architecture of our time is still to be found within the horizon of the city, that spatial and material trace of reciprocal interests. The reverse, however, is not true.

Endnotes

1   Joseph Rykwert, "Meaning and Building," in *The Necessity of Artifice* (London: Academy Editions, 1982), 9–16; for an elaboration of parts of this article, see in the same book "The Sitting Position," 23–32.

2   Rykwert, "Meaning and Building," 16.

3   Frank Lloyd Wright, *The Natural House* (New York: The Horizon Press, 1954), 38.

4   Ibid, 28.

5   Ibid, 29, 43.

6   Wright, "Architect, Architecture, and the Client," (1896), in *Frank Lloyd Wright Collected Writings*, vol.1, ed. Bruce Brooks Pfeiffer (New York: Rizzoli, 1992), 31–32. Emphases added.

7   Adolf Loos, "Von einem armen, reichen Manne," (1900) in *Ins Leere Gesprochen* (Vienna: Georg Prachner, 1981), 198–203; trans. by Jane O. Newman and John H. Smith as "The Poor Little Rich Man," in *Spoken into the Void* (Cambridge Mass.: MIT Press, 1982), 124–27.

8   "Wie kommen sie dazu, sich etwas schenken zu lassen! Habe ich ihnen nicht alles gezeichnet? Habe ich nicht auf alles rücksicht genommen? Sie brauchen nichts mehr. Sie sind komplett!" In Loos, "Von einem armen, reichen Manne," 202. Loos did not observe the rules of capitalization of nouns in German, objecting to what he considered unnecessary "ornament."

9   César Daly addressed this topic repeatedly in his volumes on domestic architecture, the first of which was published in 1868 as *L'Architecture privée au XIXe siècle*. For Poe, see particularly his "Philosophy of Furniture" and the well-known story "The Fall of the House of Usher." I have addressed this problem in "Literature and the Poetics of the Architectural Setting," *Via* 8, (1986): 7–15.

10   *Ver Sacrum*, no. 3 (1900): 343.

11   Charles Rennie Mackintosh, "Seemliness," (1902) in *Charles Rennie Mackintosh: The Architectural Papers*, ed. Pamela Robertson (Cambridge, Mass.: MIT Press, 1990), 220–21.

12   Adolf Loos, "Josef Veillich," (1929), in *Trotzdem* (Vienna: Georg Prachner, 1982), 216. Except where otherwise indicated, all translations from the German given in this chapter are mine.

13   Adolf Loos, "Heimatkunst," (1914), in *Trotzdem*, 130.

14   Loos is quoted by Karel Lhota, in "Architekt A. Loos: Adolf Loos spricht," *Ausschnitte aus Aufzeichnungen*, in *Architekt SIA*, 8 (1933): 143.

15   Representative examples, in chronological order, are Benedetto Gravagnuolo, *Adolf Loos: Theory and Works*, trans. C. H. Evans (New York: Rizzoli, 1982), 50–51; Beatriz Colomina, *Privacy and Publicity* (Cambridge, Mass.: MIT Press, 1994), chap. 6, 233–82 esp.; and Hilde Heynen, *Architecture and Modernity* (Cambridge, Mass.: MIT Press, 1999), 75–94.

16   Loos, "Heimatkunst," 129.

17   Hermann Czech and Wolfgang Mistelbauer, *Das Looshaus* (Vienna: Löcker Verlag, 1984), esp. chap. 5. I have also commented on this building in my *Roots of Architectural Invention: Site, Enclosure, and Materials* (Cambridge: Cambridge University Press, 1993), 55–59.

18   Loos, "Wiener Architekturfragen," cited in Czech and Mistelbauer, 58.

19   Josef Frank, *Architectur als Symbol* (1931) (Vienna: Löcker Verlag, 1981), 166. My emphasis.

20   Frank, "Die Rolle der Architektur" (1948) in *Josef Frank 1885–1967*, ed. J. Spalt and H. Czech (Vienna: Hochschule für angewandte Kunst, 1981), 215.

21   Frank, "Accidentismus," (1958), in *Josef Frank*, 239–40.

22   Frank, "Einselmöbel und Kunsthandwerk," *Innen-Dekoration* 34 (1923): 338.

23   Frank, "Accidentismus," 240.

24   Frank, "Über die ursprüngliche Gestalt der kirchlichen Bauten des Leone Battista Alberti" (diss., Technische Hochschule, Vienna, 1910).

25   Frank, "Das Haus als Weg und Platz," (1931), in *Josef Frank*, 36–39.

26   The building has recently been studied at some length by Barbara Giella in "Buena Shore Club," in *RM Schindler Composition and Construction*, ed. Lionel March and Judith Sheine (London: Academy Editions, 1993), 38–47.

27   R. M. Schindler, letter of 21 April 1921, quoted in Giella, "Buena Shore Club," 41; exact citation not given.

28   Frank Lloyd Wright, Introduction to *Ausgeführte Bauten und Entwürfe von Frank Lloyd Wright*, repub. in *Frank Lloyd Wright Collected Writings*, vol. 1, 101–15.

29   Schindler, "Furniture and the Modern House: A Theory of Interior Design," in *The Furniture of R. M. Schindler*, ed. Marla C. Berns (Santa Barbara, Calif.: University Art Museum, 1996), 49–56.

30   Schindler, "About Furniture," in *The Furniture of R. M. Schindler*, 39–41. My italics.

31   Schindler, "Shelter or Playground," (2 May 1926) repub. in August Sarnitz, ed., *R. M. Schindler, Architect:1887–1953* (New York: Rizzoli, 1988), 46.

32   Schindler, "Furniture and the Modern House," 46–47.

33   Ibid., 46–47.

34   Schindler, "Furniture and the Modern House," 50.

35   Schindler, "About Furniture," 51.

36   Ibid., 53.

CHAPTER 7

Practically Primitive

Many recent texts argue that the building's material, constructed, or "tectonic" dimensions constitute its radical, irreducible, or "primitive" aspects. Contrast is often drawn between
this "reality" of the work and its functions, which are seen to be
contingent because they change over time. Uses come and go,
stone and steel do not. The title of this chapter indicates that I
want to try to overcome the conceptual separation between the
built object and its purpose. In point of fact, I think this division is false and debilitating. My aim is to discover something
"primitive" in praxis, in the actions, behaviors, or performances
that people and buildings enact together. Basically, I have two
aims: to introduce and critique a few common conceptions
of the "primitive" in art and architecture; and to propose an
alternative conception, one that admittedly diverges from common usage in art history writing and quite possibly exceeds the
term's proper application, but may for these very reasons avoid
its more disabling assumptions and more positively increase its
significance for contemporary architecture. I will begin somewhat obliquely.

Savage modernity
For Le Corbusier, the Philadelphia Saving Fund Society (PSFS)
building evoked the true splendor of the Cartesian skyscraper;
it was a "tonic spectacle, stimulating, cheering, radiant...."[1] This

Howe and Lescaze, PSFS Building, Philadelphia, 1931; exterior view

high praise was set out in *When the Cathedrals Were White*, Le Corbusier's report on "the land of timid people." He had used the last of these adjectives, *radiant*, a few years before to describe his new city. "Through transparent glass walls," its towers would reveal the greatest splendor of all, "space."[2] But in Philadelphia something else earned his admiration, something no unbuilt project could ever reveal: truly magnificent workmanship. Precise craft was present, he said, in the building's details and finishes to "an astonishing degree." The ventilators and bank vault doors, for example, were so well made that he noted in his travel log: "They are gods."[3] Hyperbole is not uncommon in Le Corbusier's writing. In this instance it seems extreme. The building's exemplary status becomes a little clearer when the "spiritual" consequences of radiant construction are described. Architectural transparency—the transparency of the PSFS solarium, for example—gives free range and full amplitude to a primitive human desire, the outpouring of the self, the heart, lungs, and eyes, into the vast, infinite, and unlimited expanse. Well-crafted materials disclose an equally primitive reality: the inner potential of things, their unforeseen possibilities and unspoiled clarity, no matter whether they are artificial or natural.

That Le Corbusier should witness an epiphany such as this in America is not entirely surprising. Reporting on his travels as if he were a modern Captain Cook, he described New York as a "savage city." From the first moments of his arrival, its uncivilized vitality was vividly apparent. "[W]hen my ship stopped at Quarantine, I saw a fantastic, almost mystic city rising up in the mist. But the ship move[d] forward and the apparition [was] transformed into an image of incredible brutality and savagery."[4] Like its skyline, the city's people expressed a primal energy all their own. "In the evening, on the avenues of the city, I began to appreciate the people who, by a law of life which is their own, have been able to create a race: handsome men,

PSFS Building; vaults

very beautiful women." "Aboriginal" beauties also attracted his attention at Vassar College a few weeks later. He compared the female students there to Amazons. Apparently, a fairly unruly band of the six hundred that had invaded his lecture that night reduced a large drawing he had made to confetti, wanting a signature on each of its torn fragments. At a buffet dinner that followed, "they did almost as much" to him. Their unbridled passion for cultural objects was not directed toward the architect alone; they also had a strong appetite for the paintings of Caravaggio.[5]

In 1929, William Lescaze, one of the two designers of the PSFS building, was described by a New York critic as the "Le Corbusier of America."[6] Given the somewhat eclectic and derivative character of much of Lescaze's work, it is obvious that this, too, is an instance of hyperbole, perhaps greater than Le Corbusier's. Still, the two architects did know one another. Lescaze had visited Le Corbusier in Paris in 1927. They had taken that opportunity to console one another about the conversion projects they had been given, jointly expressing confidence that meager work of that sort would lead to bigger and better opportunities. Lescaze had good reason to complain; by the mid-1920s he had designed just a few renovations, albeit for wealthy and forward-looking clients, including the great conductor of the Philadelphia orchestra, Leopold Stokowski.[7] After Paris, back in New York, Lescaze finished the renovation of his own apartment. For a self-appointed herald of *l'ésprit nouveau*, the elements of the interior are surprising: furniture from eighteenth-century France filled the bedroom, and ornaments from seventeenth-century Spain, the entry hall. Even more surprising, perhaps, is the mural Lescaze painted in his bathroom; resting on top of some rough stonework is a Chagall-like dream landscape that twists together emblems of the natural world and primitive culture. A contemporary journal described the experience of the space as "stepping into a pool in the heart of a jungle."[8] Here, as in so many instances of early modernism, the great step forward was meant to be accomplished by an even greater leap backward (skipping the present). The progressive aspect of the apartment was apparent, however, in other murals; a portrait hanging in the architect's professional office looks like a still from Fritz Lang's *Metropolis*, released the year before.

Emblems of remote cultures were not, of course, what Le Corbusier admired about the PSFS building. Nor were exotic peoples and places important to Lescaze when he worked with George Howe on the design of that building between 1929 and 1932. According to art historians, a different aspect of primitivism was important to them: the inner and native properties of things, *raw materiality*. The finishes of the building are, as Le Corbusier pointed out, remarkably beautiful, at once simple and eloquent. Frederick Gutheim found in its "boldness and rugged strength," a "curious, haunting, and distinctive kind of beauty."[9] This arose, he suggested, from a reduced palette of materials that possessed sharply contrasting qualities—black and white, hard and soft, opaque and transparent—that were inherent in the materials themselves. Under the cool glow of indirect lighting, marble, metal, timber, and fabric were allowed to speak for themselves, to say or show their most basic—which is to say "primitive"—capacities and characteristics. PSFS, then, does not display images but reveals qualities, not representations but properties. This made its settings somewhat uncanny, at least unfamiliar, because customary forms of articulation typically involved imitative shaping and inscribing. When their unfamiliarity or remoteness is taken into account, Le Corbusier's idolizing of stainless steel hinges becomes a little more intelligible, for remoteness or distance is the most basic attribute of the gods. Idols, of course, mediate this distance; I suppose his report was meant to recall archaic forms of worship. Mircea Eliade, in his

PSFS Building; banking hall

study of comparative religion, wrote that "the hardness, ruggedness, and permanence of matter was itself a hierophany in the
religious consciousness of the primitive." Speaking of rock and
stone in particular, he said that "in its grandeur, its hardness, its
shape and its color, man is faced with a reality and a force that
belong to some world other than the profane world of which he
is himself a part."[10]

Primitivism, then, would seem to be the key to this
wonderful building, primitivism in a number of senses. Like
American skylines, city streets, and college students, it shows a
savage sort of beauty. Like untamed animals and uncultivated
landscapes, it expresses undomesticated or native potential.
Its steel and stone offer to experience "a reality and force that
belong to some world other than [our own]," and "a curious,
haunting, and distinctive kind of beauty."[11]

Illusions of remoteness and immediacy

Attractive as it might be, two problems weaken this interpretation. The last passage from Eliade (quoted above) indicates the
first problem. If primitive materials belong to some world other
than our own, the steel and stone of the PSFS building cannot be described with that term, for they are—or the building
is—completely enmeshed in its surroundings, reciprocating by
contrast its geometries, distances, types of occupation, and construction, bound to its milieu like day is to night. I will further
develop this idea of reciprocity below. The second problem with
this reading is that it treats aspects of the building as objects,
assuming they have been independently conceived because they
can be distinctly experienced. Such a view reduces characteristics to caricatures by severing the links between explicit figures
and their tacit background, assuming that what is apparent on
the surface of things adequately represents what is latent within
them. These two problems, which I will call illusions of remote-

ness and immediacy, exist not only in most descriptions of the PSFS building, but also in many accounts of "the primitive" in modern art and architecture.

When thought of spatially or geographically, the primitive is normally imagined to exist in some other place, like the wilderness. Considered temporally or historically, it is also assumed to be very far from present circumstances, typically, the remote past. Similarly distant is its social reality; the primitive is generally taken to indicate a very basic cultural level, the style of societies we describe as "underdeveloped." Thus, the primitive is removed from the here and now in three ways: geographically, chronologically, and socially. Paradoxically, this primal state can also be understood as something uniquely immediate, particularly when physical concreteness is at issue. Architecture in its primitive state assembles raw materials. Beginning construction means beginning with *something*, something simple, which is to say unprepared and irreducible. Primitive is the presence of things in their uncultivated manifestation, undomesticated, self-determined, and brutally direct. Unblemished by mimetic intent, showing nothing but themselves, primitive materials have an immediate and undelayed manifestation, which means that they are rarely thought about, even if sometimes seen; normally, they are just felt. This explains why metaphors of temperature and touch so often come into play when primitive forms of experience are described.

Here is the core of the problem. Conceived of in these ways, the primitive is either so remote that it is inaccessible, or so close that it resists shared understanding, known only in intimate contact, as if it were an extension or modulation of one's own flesh and corporeality. Because they alternately make artifacts too far and too near, neither of these notions of the primitive helps describe the actuality of things, particularly that of architecture, and more narrowly, the Philadelphia building Le

PSFS Building; stairway

Corbusier admired so greatly. If the PSFS is to be understood as primitive, another sense of the term must be understood, one that avoids the illusions of remoteness and immediacy. To work toward another sense of the primitive, I will change my approach.

Pedestrian beauty

Were we to accept the account offered by the building's architects, the PSFS would have to be seen as a work designed to be ultra-practical. According to this thesis, what is basic in the building is not something distant from prosaic affairs but dependent on them. The term "ultrapractical" was not coined by Howe and Lescaze, however, but by the bank's president.[12] While its meaning is not immediately clear, two senses seem obvious: programmatic and technological practicality. Considering the building's program, much has been written about the novelty and foresight of placing the banking facilities on the building's second floor, above street level, reached by a stairway, elevator, or the famous escalator.[13] While unusual and controversial, this solution—which may have been proposed by the architects and in any event was reluctantly accepted by the bankers[14]—proved to have a great practical advantage. The ground level was thus freed for retail activities, which attracted potential customers into the bank, customers who might not have entered it otherwise. Before this design, bank buildings were basically fortified strongholds, designed to resist, not invite, pedestrian and public activities. The Philadelphia Saving Fund Society was not, however, an ordinary commercial bank, but a depository for savings, especially those of the working poor (the first institution of this kind in the United States). During the most desperate years of the Great Depression, under- or unemployed Philadelphians used its vaults to hold whatever savings they could collect. Imagine someone without a job sliding a quarter across the marble of a teller's countertop. Put differently, the bank's

PSFS Building; mezzanine landing

doors, windows, and repositories received all that the city was able
to give. This receptiveness could be described as practical urbanism. Its practicality was also technological. This is clear in both
the interior settings and the elements that particularized their use,
providing for daylighting, for example, or for thermal comfort.
The PSFS building was the second high-rise in the United States
to be fully air conditioned.[15]

Yet practicality is hardly such a simple issue in architecture, especially when the aim of a project is *ultra*practicality. Was
this "ultra" a matter of increase, meaning *extremely* practical, or
did it indicate architectural conditions that were somehow *beyond*
the practical? If so, what might they be? Would aesthetic content
be what one finds beyond the practical? Expediency, efficiency,
and need-based functionality of the sort promoted by doctrinaire
functionalists were surely not intended here. Consider the famous
banking room. Not too long after the building was finished, a new
lighting system was installed. One can assume that the illumina-
tion from recessed and indirect lighting, together with the broad
sweep of perimeter glazing facing the north and east, was discovered to be inadequate from a strictly functional point of view,
although one suspects the room seemed bright when first built.
William Jordy, not intending dispraise, described the interior
before the upgrade as "subdued" and "shadowy."[16] More encour-
agingly, he introduced the term "muted splendor" to define the
quality of the interior finishes. This is not quite the splendor of Le
Corbusier's Cartesian skyscraper. Frederick Gutheim, as I have
pointed out before, observed "a curious, haunting, and distinctive kind of beauty." These terms suggest, and early photographs
confirm, that the original condition of the room, while not practical by our standards because a little dim, was not without quality.
Of those who reported on it, all were impressed by its *dignity*.
It seems to me that this term, difficult as it may be to define,
requires thought.

Jordy pointed to matters of construction and finishing when explaining the building's ultrafunctional qualities. Surely nothing is so effective in giving the building its shadowy kind of beauty than the surface treatment (finishing) of its palpable body. Seemingly, this is also what makes its "laconic" space "haunting," what gives it such a strong sense of emptiness or loss, or, more positively, of readiness to receive. The conclusion to this line of thinking would seem to be that the building's dignity results from its unaffected simplicity, a confident forthrightness produced by scraping away peculiarities of circumstance and conventional motif. But the opposite is also true. Simple surfaces and settings give one the sense of anticipation, of potential, that something is about to occur, as if the architects were content to let the settings wait for or anticipate possible forms of occupation. The purpose of the settings, then, would not be to designate but to anticipate, to be empty of indication but full of potential, a potential not known to be their own.

What, then, is the relationship between this sense of potentiality and the tightfisted rationality we tend to associate with functionalism? Although both are oriented toward the future and concerned with the unfolding of events, the prediction of practices is rather different from openness toward their possible occurrence. In contemporary architecture this is hard to understand, because we tend to see design as an artistic sort of planning, which is in the end really a form of management or administration. George Howe described the building's rationale as follows: "[T]he design is 'modern' in the sense that it is based on economic and structural logic. It is, however, subdued and dignified in ornament and coloring." Considering modern architecture more broadly, he stressed the "social" meaning of architectural settings. Along the same lines, he stated his "conviction that architecture is social, not individual, that its ideal must conform for better or worse to the social ideal of its time."[17] He developed this thesis in 1932, the year PSFS was finished. Seven years later he made similar points in a paper on movement in architecture, but shifted from consideration of the ways people coexist to the ways buildings do. Speaking of the spatial structure of urban housing, he argued that "we no longer conceive of housing as a row of isolated dwellings on a street, but as an integrated community."[18] The house, he said, is part of a "spatial complex." Likewise, an office building, or a bank, must be enmeshed in its urban framework. While this interweaving of part and whole was decisive in the new architecture, Howe also maintained it was not new. It could be found in what he called "the primitive community." With this statement we have arrived, I think, at a topic of design that contributed as much to the dignity of the PSFS building as did its construction: the building's engagement with the city, its primitive situations and institutions—in this case *saving*, by which wealth, whatever the amount, is withheld in the present so that it can be donated in the future.

Of all the expressions of the "social ideal," the city was for Howe the most durable, eloquent, and apparent. In a letter to the philosopher Paul Weiss, he defined architecture as "the physiognomy of culture."[19] This wonderful definition, together with the preceding passages suggest that what is primitive in architecture, particularly in its physiognomy, is neither brutal form nor raw materials, but the social fabric in which its settings and situations are interlaced.

A new, or newly integrative, social program was accommodated by the PSFS building's elaborate stratification: from the lower landscape of the subway, up to the several levels of the street, the massive body of the setback block, and then higher still to the upper horizons of the penthouse, solarium, observatory, and sign. Obviously, before this time buildings had basements and first floors; but never had they been synthetically elaborated in this way, never so carefully interwoven with an underground

PSFS Building; distant view

PSFS Building; shops along Market Street

network and as the upper horizon of streetscape. Nor had the remote horizon of the city been so clearly seen as an aspect of office interiors, which was the result of the cantilevers and horizontality the architects were so insistent about. The same was true for the connections to the far distance established by the top of the building. The genius of the building is to integrate these strata into one section, giving each its dimension, settings, material, and luminous qualities and distance. The building is ultrapractical because it transcends itself as an accommodation of particular functions into an urban receptacle not only of these events but of many, many others besides.

Manifest latency

I do not want to suggest that there is a primitive sort of practicality *beyond* the actual events of the building, or that such a thing could be realized apart from them, as if something essential could be freed from all things accidental. "Primitive" does not necessarily mean distant or remote. What the poet Rainer Maria Rilke said of death is also true of the primitive; it is "a side of life that is turned away from us."[20] When speaking of practical matters, I propose that we replace the metaphor of "beyond" with "through," which is to say that in the case of the PSFS building, this new urban horizon was realized *through* the particularities of an institution of saving. This means the building's first task was (and is) to mediate the potentialities of its milieu, crystallizing its capacities, and drawing figures out of its background. Put simply, the urban framework is the building's source and soil of expression. But while it gives birth to architectural articulation, the urban horizon is never fully absorbed into those accomplishments, for it still exceeds every presentation—it is a side of life that is turned away from us. Architecture's primitive condition is neither immediate nor inaccessible, neither an extension of our individual sensibilities nor a distant *arche* or lost paradise; it is, instead, an aspect, or *dimension*, of prosaic existence, part of everyday affairs, just not obviously so—manifestly latent.

Settings in urban circumstances open themselves to shared experiences. Describing what is specific to human praxis, as opposed to animal instinct, Hans-Georg Gadamer suggested that the key is "acting in solidarity."[21] He also suggested that this occurs most visibly and vitally in the city. With these statements in mind, I would like to propose a three-part connection: the primitive to the practical, and both to the city as the embodiment of "acting in solidarity." Gadamer's term "solidarity" is at once familiar and difficult. So much of our thought and experience speaks against this, protective as we are of our individuality—its freedoms and expressions. We tend to posit solitude against solidarity, holding fast to the first when all else fails. Following Gadamer, I want to maintain that cities and societies are *not* collections of individuals. Although our dedication to individuality is entirely congenial to professional interests, it is reductive with respect to human experience, for it neglects the dependence of figures on their constitutive ground, in all its dimensions. Merleau-Ponty noted that just because we die alone does not imply that we live alone.[22] The town is a connective fabric that holds itself together through the cooperative labor of its constituents—building to building, person to person. This cooperation is hard to catch sight of, because we tend to concentrate on its manifestations, each of us and the things nearby. Their dependence on a framework that exceeds them is easier to grasp if they are viewed in action, behavior, or operation, for there never was an act that did not summon its energy and measure its outcome against some other thing or person, which is the outer face of some power or force of resistance. The city is the horizon of human interactivity or cooperation. Architecture's first or primitive dimension is not pure materiality—the so-called nature of materials—but the milieu or topography in which the materials make themselves manifest through suffering and resistance, which is to say work. Buildings perform, as do people. Speaking not of things but of people, Gadamer said that the first requirement of praxis is effort or labor. It involves living, and this means, he said, actuation of life: not only labor but making choices or indicating preferences; and that presupposes having an orientation that is historically and ethically constituted. Because it allows freedom and necessitates deliberation, practicality is not technical activity (a distinction neglected in functionalist thinking). But the key point is that none of this—labor, actuation, choice, or orientation—is possible without a frame of reference.

Again, the most difficult task is to see this framework as something other than the sum total of what analytical thinking discovers as its components, something different from a collection of buildings, streets, and gardens, or friends, neighbors, and strangers. Another city, architecture's primitive ground, will only become apparent if we imagine the conditions that exist before its elements are congealed or hardened into distinct entities. Within this horizon, which I have tried elsewhere to characterize as "topography," buildings are less objects than configurations, each a hinge or pivot in a matrix of engagements.[23] The key is not the so-called space between things but their prolongations into and through one another, according to different degrees of porosity and permeability, and configured after patterns of more or less typical events: reading a newspaper on a subway platform, buying a shirt in a clothing store, depositing a check in a bank, or having a meal above the town in a penthouse. The PSFS building did not so much internalize the city in its accommodation of these and other events as it opened itself to the town's structures and situations, some of which were quite stable within the cultural context, while others were emerging with the building itself. The building plays its part within this primitive condition by not closing itself up into itself, but by yielding to some of its pressures, resisting others, and catching its opportunities, of which—paradoxically—the building is one. Thus the building is at once enmeshed within a primordial framework that exceeds it and at the same time stands apart from that framework as its most visible manifestation and palpable embodiment.

Endnotes

1   Le Corbusier, *When the Cathedrals Were White* (New York: Reynal and Hitchcock, 1947), 54; first pub. as *Quand les cathédrales étaient blanches* (Paris: Librairie Plon, 1937).

2   Le Corbusier, *La Ville radieuse* (Boulogne-sur-Seine: L'Architecture d'Aujourd'hui, 1935). See particularly pt. 4, chap. 8: "A New City to Replace the Old."

3   Le Corbusier, *Cathedrals*, 63.

4   Ibid., 34.

5   Ibid., 137.

6   See Mardges Bacon, *Le Corbusier in America* (Cambridge, Mass.: MIT Press, 2001), 162.

7   This is discussed in Lorraine Welling Lanmon, *William Lescaze, Architect* (Philadelphia: The Art Alliance Press, 1987).

8   See the review in *Arts and Decoration* 28 (November 1927): 50–51.

9   Frederick Gutheim, "The Philadelphia Saving Fund Society Building: A Reappraisal," *Architectural Record* 166 (October 1949): 88–95.

10   Mircea Eliade, *Patterns in Comparative Religion* (New York: Sheed & Ward, 1958), 216.

11   Ibid., 216.

12   According to *Fortune* (December 1932): 68. Cited by William Jordy, *American Buildings and Their Architects*, vol. 4 (Garden City, N.Y.: Doubleday, 1972), 90.

13   As Jordy points out, "there were some precedents in Philadelphia" for placing the banking room on the second floor "so as to leave the ground level for revenue-producing shops." *American Buildings*, 91. One example is the building known as "One East Penn Square," completed in 1930. Nevertheless, the PSFS building makes remarkable use of this unusual feature.

14   See Jordy, *American Buildings*, 92.

15   The first was the Milam Building in San Antonio, Texas, completed in 1928. See Jordy, 97.

16   Jordy, *American Buildings*, 112. This aspect of the buildings has also been discussed in David Leatherbarrow and Mohsen Mostafavi, *Surface Architecture* (Cambridge, Mass.: MIT Press, 2002), 135–43.

17   George Howe, "Functional Aesthetics and the Social Ideal," *Pencil Points* 14, no. 4 (April 1932): 215–18.

18   Howe, "Going In and Coming Out—The Fundamental Architectural Experience," (unpub. ms., George Howe Collection, Avery Library, Columbia University), 10.

19   Howe, "The Architect and The Philosopher, A Dialogue by Correspondence." (unpub. ms., George Howe Collection, Avery Library, Columbia University); letter dated 25 June 1953.

20   Rainer Maria Rilke to Witold von Hulewicz (Nov. 13, 1925), in *Letters of Rainer Maria Rilke*, vol. 2, trans. J. B. Greene and M. D. Herter Norton (New York: W.W. Norton, 1947), 373.

21   Hans-Georg Gadamer, "Isolation as a Symptom of Self-Alienation," in *In Praise of Theory* (New Haven: Yale University Press, 1998), 113.

22   Maurice Merleau-Ponty, "The Philosopher and His Shadow," in *Signs* (Evanston, Ill.: Northwestern University Press, 1964), 175.

23   David Leatherbarrow, *Uncommon Ground: Architecture, Technology, and Topography* (Cambridge, Mass.: MIT Press, 2000).

Part 3

Topographies

CHAPTER 8

Skylines

It is true that much of the impact of modern Manhattan, much of its "aura," in [Walter] Benjamin's sense, whether viewed frontally or from the air, derives from its monumental outline, the invention of its skyline paralleling that of its site.

—Hubert Damisch, *Skyline: The Narcissistic City*

Perhaps only through a kind of inattention, the most benevolent form of betrayal, is one faithful to a place, to what ultimately changes very slowly.

—Aldo Rossi, *A Scientific Autobiography*

Maps help us find our way through cities; skylines give us memorable images of them. The geometries of both flatten architecture's three-dimensionality, but while the first presents a configuration no one can ever see, the second offers an image that invites appreciation. Plans may comprise the whole of a town, but we look to them mainly for information about a specific place in the city, a particular street, garden, or train station.

Sydney skyline

Philadelphia skyline

Renzo Piano Workshop, Aurora Place, Sydney

The skyline, by contrast, continually reasserts the town's unity, because its stepped line vaults over all the discrete properties that plans individuate. Unity such as this does not suppress difference, however, for every city's "monumental outline" includes some figures that are noticeable because unique—the World Trade Center in New York before the 9/11 attack, the Chrysler and Empire State buildings after.[1]

The case of Manhattan suggests that size is chiefly important in skyline definition. That this is not always the case is clear when cities on the edge of the Pacific are considered—a city such a Sydney, for example. No silhouette of Sydney would be complete without the famous Opera House. Yet, with all that has been said about that building, it has never been described as *big*. This first example suggests that shape and profile matter no less than size in skyline definition. Renzo Piano, when explaining the thinking behind his design of Aurora Place in Sydney (one kilometer away from the Opera House, in the heart of the city's business center and not on the harbor), referred to Jørn Utzon's distinctive profile as the "trademark" of the city.[2] Its importance was so great that insignificant other profiles were omitted from his preliminary sketches. Given its relatively low stature, the Opera House can only be seen as part of the city's skyline if one views the town from a distance—across the harbor if it is to be central, from the Botanical Gardens if a marginal position is adequate. The argument would seem to be that one gets to know a city by removing oneself from it, that while proximity constrains understanding, distance is discerning. This is just as true in other cities as it is in New York and Sydney. The one I know best is Philadelphia.

Distance and urban images

A distant view of ancient architecture's most famous monument, the Acropolis in Athens, inspired the design of one of modern

Athens skyline

New York skyline

architecture's most fascinating, the Philadelphia Saving Fund
Society (PSFS) building. Initially the comparison may seem
odd, for the most prominent aspect of the modern building's
appearance from a distance is its sign, the thirty-foot-high letters of which bear no similarity to any aspects of the buildings
on the hill in Athens. Much hinges on the meaning one gives to
the word "sign." But when George Howe, one of the designers of
the PSFS, proposed this likeness in 1930, writing in the sky was
not foremost in his thinking; instead, it was the building's massing and urban siting. The building was composed, he explained,
asymmetrically, as had been the Acropolis.

> By placing the entrances at the sides and setting the
> tower back more on the west against the adjoining
> property than on the east along the street front, in order
> to secure for all time an ample light well at a vulnerable
> point, an organic asymmetry has been produced far more
> interesting than the usual scholastic and unthinking axial
> symmetry. The soundest precedent for such asymmetries
> is to be found in the grouping of numerous buildings in
> Greek architecture, as on the Acropolis, for a modern
> building is really a group of many smaller buildings.[3]

Several fascinating ideas have been joined together in this summary: that the temporal distance between constructions that are
modern and those that are ancient is of no real consequence;
that architectural configurations are aggregate in character; that
ensembles of this kind are interesting because they are asymmetrical; that such an arrangement is organic; and that its operations can have unending duration, as in this building's light
"secured for all time."

In every guide to the city of Philadelphia, the PSFS
building is listed as one of the city's most significant monu-

ments, alongside Independence Hall and the Museum of Art, for example. Among these, PSFS is perhaps the most important to architects, which is to say it is the one that is most impressive and instructive. This estimation is more a matter of reception than intention, however, for prominent significance was not one of the explicit aims of the architects, as it might be for designers intent on "branding" such a structure these days. To the contrary, the aim of the PSFS architects was for a practical solution. But as I will show, this is true for some though not all of the elements of the building. It does not explain, for example, its distinctive contribution to the city's skyline.

Aldo Rossi wrote in his *Scientific Autobiography* that "[i]n order to be significant architecture must be forgotten."[4] Absence and inattention were so important to him when writing the book that he thought of calling it *Forgetting Architecture*. Rossi's built work may be taken to exemplify an architecture possessed of this tacit manner of significance, particularly his Gallaratese housing complex in Milan. He described the building as a big house that would be "at home anywhere along the Milanese waterway or any other Lombardian canal."[5] This is to say, I think, that the building is so typical as to be unremarkable, that its effectiveness does not involve insistence on one's attention, that it is content to play the part of the background for everyday life. Such *insignificant significance* was made particularly clear in Rossi's account of the Palazzo Ragione in Padua, not a building he designed but one he admired. He used the building's history to explain two kinds of permanence in architecture (pathological and propelling) and to develop a critique of naive functionalism. This critique allowed him to advance the argument that "form persists and comes to preside over a built work in a world where functions continually become modified."[6] Persistence is not prominence, however, for the primary condition Rossi described is urban, and that condition always presents an ensemble, a unity that joins and tran-

Aldo Rossi, Gallaratese, Milan, 1967–73; view of facade arcade

scends its component parts. Some parts can, indeed, concentrate the ensemble, but this does not mean they make steady demands on our awareness. The elements that constitute a building's form do, indeed, give it a degree of autonomy; but assumed in the *actuality* of the form, in the artifact as fact, is particularity of place, or *locus*, as Rossi said. Place, on this account, is not only geographical but historical, for each always presents itself as an inheritance. The history of a place makes it recognizable, even memorable, but also taken for granted, recessive, or withdrawing. Thus the paradox to which I have referred. Let me paraphrase Rossi again: in order to be significant, architecture must be forgotten.

While puzzling, it is nevertheless true that the buildings that merit continued study and interest, decade after decade, are those that do not continually obtrude themselves on everyday experience. Put more strongly, significant works are often those that are ordinarily unnoticed, despite the ambitions of some designers and patrons. These works sustain wonder but do not demand it, or do not do so incessantly. When one of my students expressed embarrassment in admitting that he had frequently walked by such a building in Philadelphia—the PSFS building—failing to notice it (despite the fact that he had been shown it in class), I explained that his neglect might not have displeased its architects. Their sense of a building was like Rossi's; they thought that as "an outward expression of the contemporary life process" the building's first task was to play its part in the workings of a street, block, and city, giving the patterns of contemporary life durable dimension, suitable enclosure, and expression. As I observed in Chapter 5, Le Corbusier, whose ideas George Howe often invoked, stressed unobtrusiveness when characterizing architectural furnishings: a chair, like "a good servant is discreet and self-effacing, in order to leave his master free." Entire buildings, too, I want to suggest, are alternately expressive and recessive, remarkably beautiful and laconic. In this way also they both transcend common sense and assume it. Gianni Vattimo, a contemporary philosopher who occasionally addresses architecture, seems to have had a similar conclusion in mind when he described the *background* character of good buildings and even of works of art.[7] This sense of the urban artifact as a backdrop for everyday life was stated even more forcefully by the early-twentieth-century Viennese writer Robert Musil in his account of monumental architecture. "Monuments," he observed, "are conspicuously inconspicuous. There is nothing in this world as invisible as a monument. They are no doubt erected to be seen—indeed, to attract attention. But at the same time they are impregnated with something that repels attention, causing the glance to roll right off, like water droplets off an oilcloth."[8] What is it about the monument that causes the glance "to roll right off?" Does the building's sky-plane possess the same "significant insignificance" as its ground-plane? Or does the background below become a foreground above?

Let me return to the ensemble George Howe identified as the model for the PSFS building. His account of the Acropolis as an asymmetrical grouping of buildings seems indebted to Le Corbusier. Yet Le Corbusier's description itself is not without precedent. He seems to have based his account on the writings of Auguste Choisy, at least in part. Howe himself would have come across Choisy's ideas while a student at the École des Beaux-Arts between 1908 (the year Choisy died) and 1913. Two passages from Choisy's account of irregularity in the "*pittoresque*" arrangement of buildings on the Athenian acropolis set out the conceptual foundation for Howe's position. Considering the entire site, Choisy wrote that "in this new Acropolis the apparent asymmetries are only a means of giving a picturesque aspect to the most cunningly balanced group of architecture there ever was." Considering the differences between part and whole, he observed: "[E]ach architectural motif, on its own, is symmetrical, but every group is treated like a landscape where the masses

Howe and Lescaze, PSFS Building, Philadelphia, 1931; view from sidewalk level

alone balance out."[9] As for Le Corbusier's view of the site as *pittoresque*, his sketches and photographs taken from a distance are most helpful, for in them the "irregularity" of the massing is vividly apparent. Le Corbusier also emphasized the coincidence of the site's near and far horizons—that is, the alignment of the top edge of the hill's stylobates with the shoreline at the foot of the mountains in the distance.

Now such an alignment, and the encompassed distance it assumes (conceals), is impossible to achieve in an urban context, say that of Philadelphia. The PSFS building is surrounded by a number of other structures that are just about as tall as it is, and most of them were built without any setback. Yet density is not the only cause of the modern building's occlusion; the parity of footing that results from the city's level terrain also contributes to this condition. Unlike the Parthenon, Erechtheum, Propylaea, and the other buildings that overlook Athens, PSFS stands on the same "platform" as everything in its vicinity. From within the city, then, sight lines toward it must be either oblique or ascending. A consequence of this is that views are always interrupted by aspects of intermediate figures that fragment its asymmetrical unity, defeating it.

From the other side of the Delaware River, Philadelphia is reached via the Benjamin Franklin Bridge, designed by Paul Cret and finished in 1922, four years before Howe (who was then still in the firm of Mellor, Meigs, and Howe) produced his first design for the PSFS building (1926). Although distant, PSFS is not lost to the view from the bridge, nor are its asymmetries fragmented, for the foothills of buildings in the foreground right up to its base are too low to obstruct sight of its upper mass and elevated peak. What's more, its sign, or the side of its sign that faces the bridge, seems perfectly perpendicular to one's view from that vantage point. This perpendicularity results from the eastward side of the sign being misaligned with the body of the building, rotated about 20°, as if it were a hinge.

Within the space of this "hinge," machinery for the air-conditioning system is hidden. The angle in plan also gives the sign's structure greater resistance against wind loads. But the requirements of distant viewing seem to have been equally decisive in the design. Although PSFS is not the tallest building on the city's skyline it is certainly one of its dominant or most insistent figures, partly because of its relative height but also because of its atypical "asymmetry" and because of its sign, by which the building turns its face to the bridge and makes itself legible from that distant approach.

If the building's top imitates the asymmetry of its base, it does so by compressing the spatiality of that arrangement into a figure that can be read as an outline or *profile*. That buildings should present themselves as lines in the sky has come to be a familiar notion. On reflection, this is also rather odd, for it assumes that the building, together with its urban context, is not what is seen or felt around us when we are involved in this or that situation—is not spatial—but is what stands apart from and before us in two dimensions, like a picture. *Malerisch* (pictorial) is the term Camillo Sitte used to describe this aspect of urban architecture, this look of the city, this *Stadtbild*.[10] A century ago he and others elaborated this way of seeing as a technique for designing cities. The most instrumental account of this way of seeing towns was provided by Hermann Maertens in *Optisches Maas für den Städtebau*, 1890.[11] In this text, as in Sitte's writings, distance is understood as perspective, securing one's "point of view" as a source of urban order. Such a view could also be called a landscape, if one stresses not the land- but the -scape, or scenic, part of the term.[12] Sitte concentrated on the framed or enclosed prospect (the *geschlossenes Architekturbild*), which resulted not only from density but from station points, whether planned or not. His ideas had practical consequence in Vienna. A good example is the Platz in front of the Votifkirche at one end of the famous Ringstrasse. Musil's account (cited previously in this chapter) of the remoteness of monuments (conspicuous inconspicuousness) was written just after this Platz was finished. For Sitte, such a forecourt clearing gave the monument appropriate standing. Five centuries earlier, in the Renaissance, Alberti suggested something similar, as a matter of civic decorum. An urban skyline is essentially different, however, because it is the view that encompasses the city's many internal openings, serving as the inclusive horizon of all local prospects. I would like to consider the topic of *profile* a little more fully, because I think it is a key to the question concerning the urban skyline.

Although it is now common in architectural usage, and has been since it served as the title of Lewis Mumford's popular column in the *New Yorker*, the term "skyline" is a relative newcomer to architectural discourse, scarcely used before the last decades of the nineteenth century.[13] Its early currency seems to have resulted from usage by the widely read architectural historian Montgomery Schuyler, whose writings for *Harper's Weekly* in 1897 were published under this title. Earlier still, and outside architectural criticism, the word seems to have named the line where earth and sky meet, in other words, the horizon. But in some instances of earlier architectural criticism, "skyline" was also used to indicate the profile of urban buildings. An article titled "Skyline," published in *American Architect and Building News*, cited an English critic's assessment of the importance of profile in metropolitan situations: "[I]n an important city like London, it is particularly essential that any building which has pretensions, and rears itself above its neighbors, should possess a decent profile."[14] In other texts, a number of terms were used synonymously: "outline," "trace," or "silhouette"—in all cases referring to the upper extreme of the city's several central buildings, as far removed from the plane of the horizon, the ground-plane, as possible.

Despite distance or perhaps because of it, this line was, in the first years of the twentieth century, thought to disclose something essential about the city. Earle Shultz, a New York office building manager in the 1920s, wrote: "The character and quality of any city can be told from a great distance by its skyline, but these buildings do more than merely advertise a city. They show the faith of many men in its destiny, and they create a like faith in others."[15] A rather more prominent figure, Cass Gilbert, the architect of the Woolworth Building (among many others), expressed himself as follows: "The changing skyline of New York is one of the marvels of a marvelous age...the skyscraper is a creation unique to this epoch. In its aspiring lines we behold the very symbol of a bold, adventurous people; restless, eager, and confident in their strength and power."[16] To ascertain what is characteristic of a city, then, to get close to its particular quality, it is necessary to remove oneself from it, distance it, make it remote—which is also to defamiliarize oneself with it.

Is the reverse likewise true, is the designer's task to defamiliarize the city, to make it, or its parts, "irregular," as Howe said of the PSFS building? If so, the concept of profile would be key in the understanding of urban architecture, as would be the unity of the ensemble, and distance.

Let me return to the water's edge—not of Renzo Piano's Sydney, Aldo Rossi's Milan, George Howe's Philadelphia, or Camillo Sitte's Vienna, but of Le Corbusier's New York.

> Monday morning when my ship stopped at Quarantine, I saw a fantastic, almost mystic city rising up in the mist. But the ship moves forward and the apparition is transformed into an image of incredible brutality and savagery. Here is certainly the most prominent manifestation of the power of modern times. This brutality and this savagery do not displease me. It is thus that great enterprises begin: by strength.[17]

Defining the city prior to entering it, Le Corbusier described the
view before him in terms that were remarkably similar to those
he had used to describe the Acropolis in both *Journey to the East*
and *Towards a New Architecture*. As before, the view from the
distance revealed something essential, not only about the city
but the modern world as well—power. While true, there is nothing familiar or comforting in this prospect. Still, it is amazing;
thus the language of the romantic sublime, as if a "delightful
terror" had come to reign over the senses.[18] The night of the
voyage was dispelled by the morning's disclosure, for out of the
mist Le Corbusier saw the ascent of the modern city. One could
assume that from the promenade deck, the shore would be a
line, a horizon, but nothing so definite was there. Elsewhere in
this same book, Le Corbusier used the term "vapor" to describe
this formless foundation. As the picture was sketched out more
fully, he said nothing about the city's intermediate levels, focus-
ing instead on what appeared above everything else. In the sky
he saw articulate and distinct profiles. Challenging the outward
and encompassing spread of the azure were the articulate and
distinct profiles of the skyscrapers, all together a "banner in the
sky," he said, a "fireworks rocket." Despite the striving of each
building, architect, and patron for uniqueness, all of them had
submitted to a "subjugating force," for unity, grouping, or con-
solidation is seen in this skyline, as in every other. New York,
Le Corbusier asserted, stands "above Manhattan like a rose-
colored stone in the blue of a maritime sky, New York at night is
like a limitless cluster of jewels. America is not small potatoes!
In the last twenty years, facing the old continent, it has set the
Jacob's ladder of the new times. It is a blow in the stomach that
strikes you like a hurricane."[19]

All of this is to say that size matters in skylines, even if
it isn't all that matters. Ascending the ladder meant increasing
height; the "subjugating force" to which Le Corbusier referred
was "magnitude." Many before and after him have commented

on this theme in American architecture and society, this desire for bigness.[20] The individual and individualistic efforts of the skyscraper builders vividly exemplified such longing for the taller, the tallest, building around. But if the desire for individual elevation motivated New York's rise out of the mist, a summary line was the result.

In *Towards a New Architecture*, the matter of profile played a central role in the definition of architecture. If architecture is the skillful, accurate, and magnificent play of masses seen in light, contours are the instruments or movements of this play. The subject was introduced as part of the discussion of artistic intention, the "pure creation of the mind." Clarity, the consequence of sharp definition, is the foundation of both understanding (reading a composition) and pleasure (the sensation of harmony). This observation led Le Corbusier to a working definition of "profile(s)" (*modénature*). It is or they are "the lineaments of the outward aspect" (*les traits du visage*).[21] The discussion that immediately follows this definition does not dwell on lines and angles, even less on practical matters such as construction, too long mistaken as the whole of architecture rather than a concern of building, which it really is. The discussion focuses instead on light and shade, which are properties of objects or materials, and therefore of surfaces. The shift from line to edge was important, for it allowed him to see the matter of profile definition as decisive for painters, sculptors, and architects, each of whom works with physical surfaces. Urban planners, not mentioned here in the text, can also be included in the group preoccupied with profile, insofar as they, too, are artists. Le Corbusier's beautiful and well-known drawing of Buenos Aires, with the waters of the Río de la Plata in the foreground and five illuminated building blocks against the dark and distant sky, clearly shows the potential of urban profiles to rise out of the mist. In Le Corbusier's vocabulary, a common synonym for profile clarity is "precision," but his caption under a cropped photo of a triglyph from the Parthenon suggests that it reveals "Austere Profiles. Doric morality."[22] This usage indicates what he believed was really at stake in the matter of outline definition; geometry was a sign of "life" in its broadest or fullest sense, life ruled sternly by a sense of severity and simplicity. That the Greeks had been concerned with profile was made clear to him by Auguste Choisy: *"[L]a modénature proprement dite est essentiellement grecque."*[23]

Distance not only depends on the building's relationship to its site but determines it. Buildings must make themselves available to experience from not one but at least three distances: the local (even intimate) horizons of enclosure, the ambient surround of the building's immediate vicinity, and the distant reaches of its extended topography. Modes of disclosure appropriate to each of these distances are variously proportioned in different building types. Monuments, for example, have the peculiarity of keeping themselves distant from nearly all points of view; houses by contrast offer very little to remote sightings.

The lines and outlines of the Acropolis occupied Le Corbusier's attention throughout his career. Yet whenever seen from afar, the site's several buildings appeared to him as a unified group: "one solid block." The massiness of this amalgam is the corporeal wholeness to which I referred at the very beginning of this chapter where I introduced the distinction between what is shown on maps and what is perceived in three dimensions. In his writings and drawings, Le Corbusier proposed a striking set of characterizations of the hill in Athens. Of the expectedly topographical terms, he repeated "flat summit" most often.[24] Also expected is a geometric rendering; the Parthenon is a "yellow cube." To this geometry was ascribed governing rank with the term "sovereign cube," conflating topographical with political elevation. But the hill and its figure were also personified. It was a "gigantic apparition," an "unconquerable titan"; and with reference to the bloody battles of Homeric myth, Le Corbusier called the big chunk of rock a "tragic carcass." But even more striking are the maritime images, suggesting that this building/block/boat was anchored in the midst of some uncharted sea. He called the Acropolis a "hull of rock" and the Parthenon at night "a black marble pilot." This argues for governance once again and renders the status of the governed as formless. He said the same thing about the streets of premodern Paris. Elsewhere in his account, a shift to textile imagery returned him to the problem of the horizon: The temple on the summit is a "dark knot" that binds together sea and sky. I like this image of the building concentrating the landscape. Giving the "marble pilot" an outlook, he ascribed to its place the role of a "contemplator of the sea"; it is a "block from another world," which places "man [whoever takes up its vantage] above the world." Here, again, is the idea of distance, as if the building's chief task were to keep itself remote, to stage a voluntary retreat from the practices of everyday life—at least from the obvious signs of those practices. But the summit's superior standing was destabilized by the last and most fascinating set of terms Le Corbusier introduced. Lying down flat on your stomach on the base platform of the Propylaea, he said, you can marvel at the alabaster mass below. He called this platform an "artificial ground," which is to say, one that is removed from the other ground (earlier associated with the sea below the rock hull). Because the platform is raised up, he also referred to it as a "hoist." And considering the column shaft, he praised its "halo base," which assumed an exchange of a luminous crown for dusty feet. My suggestion that the irregular roof profile of the PSFS building represents the asymmetry of its base proposes an equivalent substitution.

Can the same be said for other good urban buildings and the skylines they define: that the geometries below are mirrored by those above, that ground-plane prefigures sky-plane, that the elements that variously resist and accommodate ambient forces below are paralleled by analogous elements above?

Returning for a moment to Renzo Piano's Aurora Place, this argument would mean that the configuration of the skyline embodies the characteristics of the building's base. Indeed, this seems to be the case. In the absence of a "podium," which is the ground level equivalent to an undifferentiated rooftop "penthouse," there are four aspects of the Aurora Place ground-plane that particularize the project: (1) mediation between the different levels of the surrounding streets; (2) continuities with the patterns of movement along these streets; (3) interconnections between these patterns in the building's central public space; and (4) the reconfiguration of orientation by virtue of this mediation, continuity, and interconnection. If the argument for displacement is valid, these would need equivalents in the building's sky-plane. Levels of surrounding streets would not be mediated, but the upper levels of the tall buildings at the city center and of the lower roofs of the buildings that front the Botanical Gardens would be. Likewise, continuities would not be established with patterns of pedestrian movement but with the flows and forces of the environment, particularly wind and sunshine. Thirdly, the rooftop would centralize not the configuration of the nearby blocks but the distinctive figures in the wider horizon—particularly the Opera House, but also the bridge and the boats in the harbor, hence the sail imagery. If the building's upper profile acted in these ways, it would, like the ground-plane, restructure orientation within the city. Both Andrew Metcalf and Peter Buchanan, in their accounts of the Aurora Place building, attest to the ways it remade the city by weaving the "influence of Sydney's world renowned building [the Opera House] into the city's hinterland."[25] The primary task of the building's upper levels is to make its ground level order apparent for a distant view.

The same sort of thing happened in both the PSFS building and Le Corbusier's view of the Parthenon (Howe's model). Returning to Le Corbusier's images of the Acropolis and listing them as a summary of what can be expected from a skyline, we have the following: the summit distances itself from the surrounding city in two ways; the "eternal dialogue between architectural marbles and the horizon of the sea" aligns their lateral extension, just as it knots together and compresses their vertical separation.

In each of these examples, what Howe called "irregularity" presented itself in profile. This is not to say that this architecture lacked depth or three-dimensionality, but that from afar spatiality was compacted into contour or outline. Local articulation of elements was reduced to achieve this, their depth was also decreased, and their edges were left unbroken. Sitte's term *malerisch* is perfectly apt for this mode of appearance. Despite Le Corbusier's dismissal of what he took to be Sitte's arguments for "picturesque" town planning, the former's distance viewing can also be called "pictorial." Writing about himself, Le Corbusier identified the Greek landscape as the source of his first painting. Serving as his own biographer, he wrote: "His first picture [*La Cheminée*] dates from November 1918. It was an efflorescence of the landscapes [*émanation des paysages*] of Greece: space and light."[26] The block at its center rises from its platform the way the "yellow cube" rose up from the landscape stretching between Piraeus and the elevated rock of Mount Pentelicus. Contour definition (*modénature*) is as decisive on the canvas as it was under the light of the Greek sun. This early painting does not have the thickened depth of the canvases that were to follow in the next few years, but its unsaturated hues, reduced modeling, and indefinite field require of contour the accomplishment of *definition*. Because of the picture's three-fold lack (topographical depth, surface articulation, and modeling) and the lowered vantage point of the spectator, the figures are decidedly remote—clearly defined but distant.

This view of a painted cube from below parallels those one can take of a building from above—above city streets, that is. The profile of the PSFS building, I suggested, discloses itself most fully from the Benjamin Franklin Bridge about twenty blocks away, above the river and the urban network. Aurora Place in Sydney also presents a profile to a distant view, from across the harbor or the far side of the Botanical Gardens. Although legible in two dimensions only, what appears from afar is also what exists and is known in its full spatiality, at the building's base, where it plays its part in the everyday life of the city and can be easily forgotten.

Endnotes

Epigraph 1 Hubert Damish, *Skyline: The Narcissistic City* (Stanford: Stanford University Press, 2001), 93.
Epigraph 2 Aldo Rossi, *A Scientific Autobiography* (Cambridge, Mass.: MIT Press, 1981), 72.

1   Hubert Damisch, *Skyline: The Narcissistic City* (Stanford: Stanford University Press, 2001), see page 93 for his summary comments on the city profile.
2   "I believe the tower in Sydney...will be my most high-tech design. It has to be when you have the Opera House as the city's trademark." Cited in Bonnie Churchill, "Diverse Projects Cover Italian Architect's Drawing Board," *Christian Science Monitor* (24 April 1998).
3   George Howe, Howe to James Willcox, 25 July 1930, cited in William Jordy, "PSFS: Its Development and Its Significance," *JSAH* 21 (May 1962): 52.
4   Also Rossi, *A Scientific Autobiography* (Cambridge, Mass.: MIT Press, 1981), 45. On forgetting, see pages 34 and 78. See also page 72 for a wonderful definition of inattention as "the most benevolent form of betrayal."
5   Cited in *Aldo Rossi Buildings and Projects*, ed. Peter Arnell and Ted Bickford (New York: Rizzoli, 1985), 75.
6   Rossi, *The Architecture of the City* (Cambridge, Mass.: MIT Press, 1982), 29–32, 46–48, 114–18.
7   Gianni Vattimo, *The End of Modernity* (Baltimore: Johns Hopkins University Press, 1988), 87.
8   Robert Musil, "Monuments," in *Posthumous Papers of a Living Author* (Hygiene, Col.: Eridanos Library, 1987), 61.
9   Auguste Choisy, *Histoire de l'architecture*, 1899 (Paris: Bibliothèque de L'Image, 1996), 409–22.

10   Camillo Sitte, "City Planning According to Artistic Principles," in *Camillo Sitte: The Birth of Modern City Planning*, ed. George Collins and Christiane Craseman Collins (New York: Rizzoli, 1986).

11   Hermann Maertens, *Optisches Maas für den Städtebau* (Bonn: Cohen, 1890).

12   On this term, see John Dixon Hunt, *Greater Perfections* (Philadelphia: University of Pennsylvania Press, 2000), 1, 217, 239, 258.

13   A thorough and fascinating study of this term and the whole problem of skyscrapers is set out in Thomas A. P. Leeuwen, *The Skyward Trend of Thought* (Cambridge, Mass.: MIT Press, 1986). A shorter, more recent study can be found in William R. Taylor, *In Pursuit of Gotham* (Oxford: Oxford University Press, 1992), esp. chap. 2.

14   Cited in Leeuwen, *Skyward Trend*, 5.

15   Cited in Earle Shultz and Walter Simmons, *Offices in the Sky* (Indianapolis: Bobbs-Merrill, 1959), 12; also quoted and discussed in Leeuwen, *Skyward Trend*, 84.

16   Cited in Leeuwen, *Skyward Trend*, 84. For more on Gilbert's view of the skyscraper's role in redefining the city skyline, see *Inventing the Skyline: The Architecture of Cass Gilbert*, ed. Margaret Heilbrun, (New York: Columbia University Press, 2000), esp. chap. 5.

17   Le Corbusier, *When the Cathedrals Were White* (New York: Reynal & Hitchcock, 1947), 34; originally, *Quand les cathédrales étaient blanches* (Paris: Librairie Plon, 1937), 49.

18   That terrifying scenes can be delightful is explained in Edmund Burke, *A Philosophical Enquiry into the Origin of Our Ideas of the Sublime and Beautiful* (1757), (London: Routledge and Kegan Paul, 1958), 134–135.

19   Le Corbusier, *Cathedrals*, 42; *Cathédrales*, 59.

20   It is well known that Rem Koolhaas has made much of "bigness." For present purposes, his early study of New York, *Delirious New York* (Oxford: Oxford University Press, 1978) is more useful than later manifestos.

21   Le Corbusier, *Towards a New Architecture* (London: Architectural Press, 1927), 202; *Vers une architecture* (Paris: Les Éditions G. Crès, 1923), 178.

22   Le Corbusier, *Towards*, 203; *Vers*, 179.

23   Choisy, *Histoire de l'architecture*, 290.

24   Le Corbusier, *Journey to the East* (Cambridge, Mass.,: MIT Press, 1987), 209. The other terms, listed in the following lines, are given between pages 209 and 238 of the English edition. The text was originally pub. as *Le Voyage d'Orient* (Paris: Forces Vives, 1966).

25   Andrew Metcalf, *Aurora Place: Renzo Piano Sydney* (Sydney: Watermark Press, 2001), 28–29; Peter Buchanan, *Renzo Piano Building Workshop: Complete Works*, vol. 4 (London: Phaidon, 2000), 220.

26   Le Corbusier, *Creation Is a Patient Search* (New York: Praeger, 1960), 49.

CHAPTER 9

Landings and Crossings

The open they came into by these moves
Stood opener, hoops came off the world,
They could feel the February air...

—Seamus Heaney, "Crossings"

Crossing the center of the Lewis Glucksman Gallery at University College Cork is a wide landing that both ends a flight of steps climbing from a river walk and begins a ramp that slopes gently upward to meet a path heading to the heart of the university. The prominence of this central platform is striking, because landings are normally thought of as marginal and discrete elements within buildings. Crossed in the course of vertical circulation, they typically serve as turning or resting points in a stairway. With continuity of movement principally in mind, most landings would seem to differ from a stairway's many treads only in dimension—they are simply a bit deeper than all the other steps. That they can stand for more than this, that they can possess spatial, social, and seasonal meanings, like the "crossings" described by Heaney in the epigraph above, is apparent when one considers landings outside buildings, along routes built at the scale of topography, through gardens, parks, or towns. Here landings serve as *clearings* by conferring orientation and giving the sense that something new is about to begin. Heaney's

O'Donnell + Tuomey, Lewis Glucksman Gallery, Cork, 2005; view from campus entrance

image of "February air" can be understood in a similar way, expressing the combined sense of unwrapping and awakening one feels after the "hoops have come off" the world, a feeling of release and possibility that ends the warmed seclusion of late winter. The same quality is achieved in the central landing of the Glucksman Gallery and elsewhere in the building, as I will try to show.

Thinking more largely, not of topography but of territory, land in itself can be viewed as a landing, flanked not by treads and risers but by lakes, rivers, or oceans. A landing then is not only a thing but an event; to land is to take the arrival step. Heaney's view of crossings suggests that something more than connection occurs in settings such as these. Landings at any scale—territory, town, or building—are also the means by which "the open" is allowed to stand "opener," unveiling what was previously unseen, allowing potentialities to actualize themselves. The Glucksman Gallery shows this particularly clearly. Its landings allow the town's topography to be crossed in ways that not only open settings into one another but also let them withdraw into themselves. Put differently, the gallery's ways of arresting and initiating changes in level involve sideways reach and lateral differentiation. Landings in the Glucksman Gallery are the means by which the terrain is both crossed over and crossed out. Serving as instruments of spatial continuity, they are at the same time structural facts and social emblems that have achieved and express *stability*. That stasis can have this double sense needs a little explanation. When the philosopher Edmund Husserl called for a reversal of the Copernican revolution, he developed his argument on the basis of an undeniable commonplace of prosaic experience: the sidewalk or soil on which one stands is not a miniscule patch of the planet's crust revolving around the sun, but a substrate more secure and stable than any other.[1] One must, he observed, adopt the theoretical attitude to imagine the earth moving. "We Copernicans, we moderns," he said, tend to think of this earth as "one of the stars, moving like all the rest." But when we think of it this way, we invoke a second-order concept. In a pre-Copernican view, a view that is at once more radical than and faithful to our actual (pretheoretical) experience of the world, the earth does not rotate or spin. In fact, it takes a great effort of imagination to think that it does. Every time we get up to walk, we hold just the reverse. "The earth," Husserl argued, "is the ark which makes possible in the first place the sense of motion, and all rest as a mode of motion. But its rest [the earth's] is not a mode of motion." For us to move, the earth must not. Much of what I want to say about the Glucksman Gallery concerns the back and forth of movement and rest, or the role that its landings play in the crossings that integrate and differentiate the several parts of the building and town. Unmoving, they allow movement, the sort of movement that is both integrative and exploratory. Their stability is not only tectonic but temporal; like habits and institutions, it is lasting.

Movement by means of landings goes against the concept of *flow*, which gets so much prominence in contemporary theorizing. Elsewhere I have discussed the fact that this image of movement is not new to architecture; half a century ago, George Howe described "flowing space" as *"the concept of our time,"*[2] and the so-called fathers of the modern movement, Frank Lloyd Wright, Theo van Doesburg, Mies van der Rohe, and Sigfried Giedion, asserted more or less the same thing. For them, and for many others since, flowing space represented the fundamental discovery of modern architecture, providing the stage for new patterns of life that were to be healthy and free. Nowadays, flow can characterize virtually all aspects of a building: its spatial structure, iconography, "information," even its construction detailing (achieved by virtue of new software technologies). If the building is not to be a continuous ramp, however, it must have points from which movement begins and at which it ends: landings. The Glucksman Gallery acknowledges this principle not once or twice, but repeatedly, stopping and restarting passage for the sake of spatial definition and orientation.

In the early stages of project making, the single most important task is to understand the different characteristics of the site's wider milieu, for a basic function of the building is to serve as the means by which they cross over and into one another. The Glucksman Gallery stands at the edge of University College Cork. Its marginal position allows it to mediate many conditions, two of which are often seen in opposition: the campus and the town. The building's northward and westward prospects make its double orientation vividly clear. On its north side the building faces an urban landscape of great density. Just beyond the lawn that limits the gallery's ground-floor "river room" runs a garden path that rings the campus at its lowest level. The trees lining this walk rise above the gallery's upper decks and shade the river, a southern channel of the River Lee. On the opposite bank of the river's twenty-meter width stand the private yards and back facades of a row of houses, sheltered somewhat by fences and bushes. In front of them runs one of Cork's main east-west arteries, the Western Road. Although unseen, its traffic can be heard from the river walk. In the nineteenth century, this road also coincided with a rail line that had its terminus at the edge of the medieval settlement. An equally important topographical parallel lies still farther northward from the gallery, the Mardyke. As its name indicates, a raised mound once formed this line. Centuries ago, it acted as a "parade" heading outward from the town center, bisecting the marshland between the southern and northern channels of the Lee. Still farther north, on the other side of the northern channel, the suburbs of Cork rise on the hills that enclose the entire town. From those summits in the distance, to the valley in which the gallery stands,

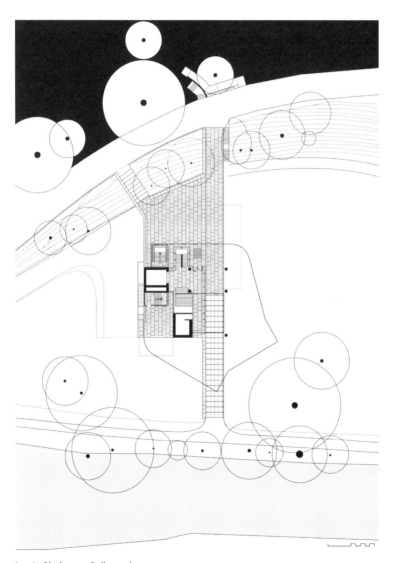

Lewis Glucksman Gallery; plan

the following elements cross in front of one another: a lawn, tree screen, river walk and river, backs and fronts of a housing terrace, a crosstown highway, remnants of an ancient dyke, another river, houses, and hills. These layers are not unapparent from the building, for its main axis or line of approach forms an exact perpendicular to all of them.

While the building's orientation toward the town is layered in depth, its prospect toward the center of the university opens onto a series of levels (platforms or terraces) stacked up to the height of the old university quadrangle. At right angles to the river room is the gallery's café, facing westward. Like a baroque *sala terrena*, it, too, opens onto the lawn that edges the building's base. When the café's glazed doors are slid sideways, the interior extends onto a wide deck, half shaded by the cantilevered galleries above. This "landing" leads to a green that is much wider than its northern counterpart, filling the entire space left by the ancient meander of the river. In the future, this lawn will display works of art, but now it is used as a park. Centuries of erosion have exposed the geological substrate of the mound on which the oldest parts of the university stand. Looking westward from the gallery, one sees a wall of limestone in the near distance, only partly screened by trees. A walkway up the slope leads to the university quadrangle, built in 1845 by Thomas Deane. Slightly farther from the gallery, but a little lower than the quadrangle and closer to the river, is a remnant of the county jail, built in 1818 as an extension to facilities constructed in the late eighteenth century. Well before then, before Queen Victoria's advisory committee proposed that an open site near the prison should be the location of Cork's new university, the summit had been the location of a monastery. Each of these levels has its counterpart in the gallery, as a look at the building's side elevation and section will show.

A small detail in the building's upper level is a remarkable example of this coupling of near and far. The line at the base of the old quadrangle coincides exactly with the split between the upper and lower sections of the two-part windows in Gallery 1. A "deep section" (showing the building's interiors together with their exterior backdrop) reveals this coincidence very clearly. That there are windows in an art gallery is itself an interesting fact. That the line of their division corresponds to a level in the distance is even more so. André Malraux's famous text *Museum Without Walls* was written in opposition to the enclosed sense of "art for its own sake" that had become common fifty years ago, the result of which might be called museums without openings. O'Donnell + Tuomey took a complementary opposite stance. By rejecting the introverted and isolated qualities of most modern galleries, and engaging their building with the town, they have opened the world of art into life.

The two-part windows bring to mind Kahn's Exeter Library, but unlike Kahn's example, this split operates on different planes. The lower part of the aperture is basically a window wall—glazed from top to bottom and side to side—that has been rotated outward to face some point in the distance (the quadrangle in one case, the houses opposite the river in the other). Above, the glazing remains coplanar with the white wall. The space created by these crossing planes is balconylike, part of the room and outside it. Placing a work of art—a piece of sculpture, for example—into this bay achieves a remarkable coordination of distances and contents. No longer are the landscape and town so far away and the work of art so close by; qualities of the environment have entered the room's depth (as ambient light and shadow), and the work of art stands before spectators both in and outside the building. To find equivalent crossings at a building's edge, one would have to turn to the better examples of baroque architecture.

Extending beyond the ramp that forms the main approach to the building, the large volume containing the galleries partly covers an open-air deck in front of the ground-level

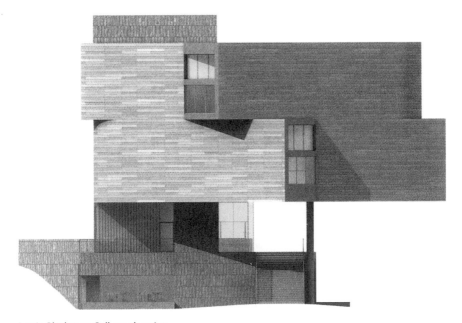

Lewis Glucksman Gallery; elevation

café. This deck, like the gallery "balcony," crosses distinct settings into one another. Similar eateries can be found in most galleries and museums these days. Yet this café is unlike most because of its marginal position and its interconnectedness with settings outside the building. Obviously, it can be reached from within the gallery; in plan it is positioned diagonally opposite the river room, to the east of the landing at the base of the central stair. But when its full-height sliding doors are open, the café is also accessible from the campus walkway above, by means of a small stairway that parallels the entry ramp, and from the great lawn onto which it reaches. If its deck is understood as a landing, the café can be seen to coordinate at least three crossings: the diagonal of public rooms at the building's base; a shortcut from the campus path to the river; or any wandering across the lawn outside the café, through the leafy green that surrounds the gallery. This role would seem to make it open, like the deck above. But as a room, the café possesses all the qualities the forecourt landing lacks: darkness, depth, and limited horizontal extent, in other words, enclosure. Its contrast with the terrace above is most apparent when seen from the lawn.

From a distance, the café appears as a black hollow in the white mass of the building's base. Inhabited platforms are something of a commonplace in modern architecture; a few of the best known are Mies's New National Gallery in Berlin, Utzon's Sydney Opera House, and (closer in subject matter) Kahn's British Art Center. This one seems to conceal its contents more than those others, however, as the very sharp contrast between its shadowed depth and the patterned flatness of the plinth suggests. The building's base is obtrusively white, as if it wanted to show its separateness from the land, or from the river nearby. But a closer look at the site's stone, as it stands out from the soil on the face of the escarpment, reveals the congeniality of the building's base with the land; the cliff wall, too, has shadowed slices in the depths of its surface, and these, like the dark cut in the plinth, contrast with the white of the limestone. What is more, the bonelike stone gives a sense of permanence to both the base and the cliff.

The contrasts that exist outside of the building are echoed in the café's interior. Bounded by walls on three sides and a frame on the fourth, the room's materials and colors amplify the "tectonic" opposition of the thick walls against the supports and screens of the fourth. Limestone panels like those on the exterior clad the two walls at each end. The dimensions of each panel are small, and their pattern is vertical, while the reverse happens on the frame side, where large-scale glazed horizontals dominate. The long wall that parallels the columns and glass surfaces is designed with recesses that provide space for equipment. Thus, the two long walls could not be more opposed in quality: thick and thin, earthy and shiny, recessive and expansive. While the likeness between the ceiling and floor surfaces gives unity to the room, these oppositions and lateral references also allow the café to escape its own boundaries. Seen in reverse, it is not a thing in itself but a modulation of or divergence from its milieu. Like any example of the baroque *sala terrena*, its crossovers into its vicinity are key to its character. Owned neither by the building nor by the garden, the room belongs to both.

Apart from housing the café and the delivery and service areas, the primary function of the building's broad base would seem to be support of the entry forecourt. Yet because it ends both the ramp that descends from the campus path and the steps that rise from the river walk, this space can also be seen as a landing that is proportioned not to the gallery but to its vicinity. When seen at this scale and understood as part of the campus and town, the forecourt stands between the two major lines of approach, the stair and ramp, as well as a number of minor ones: the shortcut from the campus path down to the café lawn; a second approach from lower down the campus path; and a small stair at the opposite corner of the plan that descends to the service yard to the west of the building.

Nothing in particular is made of the confluence of these routes; instead, the space seems happy to wait for events to occur, like a tray or table on which things are placed now and then, only to be removed at some later time. While nothing of the basilican monumentality of Kahn's courtyard at the Jonas Salk Institute characterizes this clearing, it exercises a similar restraint. Receptiveness is the result, which only serves to emphasize the forecourt's integrative function as the crossing of several routes and its role as a landing, the chief purpose of which is to *open toward* unforeseen conditions. As the architects have left it, the content of the space is "not yet" decided. Not only is movement paused but also meaning; while the forecourt reaches toward the various elements nearby, it stops short of each of them, resisting their claims. Allowed to stand *beyond* the forecourt, the surrounding situations still show what existed *before* the landing stepped onto the site, actualizing history by coupling a topographical inheritance with an architectural possibility. If anything is staged on the deck, it is a play of shadows across the dry grid, shadows cast by precisely those figures the landing keeps at a distance.

Deeply shaded by the galleries above, the entry hall's rich intensity contrasts sharply with the tacit spread of the forecourt. Despite its relative darkness (or maybe because of it, like a camera obscura), this setting is the most integrative of all the building's crossings, bringing within reach aspects of all that is around: the forecourt behind and the town ahead, the galleries above and the river below. Here also are a great staircase that leads upward, an elevator, and a showcase straight ahead, which is as yet waiting for (a) work to be installed. The reflections of leaves and clouds suffuse all of these places, as does the play of light they supply, quickening the qualities of the foyer's materials and transparencies. Through glazing on nearly all sides, aspects of the surroundings emerge frontally and obliquely, at varying distances and elevations. Hierarchy of significance doesn't seem to be chiefly important—although it would be hard to imagine anything other than a frontal position for the main stair—instead, orientation to the characters that make up the topography's various opportunities. The premise being argued is that topographical depth contains a constellation of sublunar stars, points within the urban horizon that are familiar enough to provide movement (and experience) with orientation. Unassembled but made apparent, they confer spatial knowledge. But the configuration also calls for a decision: What next? It is hard to imagine circumstances that would allow for a more well-informed choice about which way to move.

A decisive aspect of the gallery's landings and crossings, and of the one at the entry in particular, is their sense of freedom. Freedom in this context means more than just the modernist "flow," the goal of achieving an absence of "external" limitations to allow for movement that is independent, sovereign, or autarkic. The freedom I would like to evoke here is not of movement but of the object, not unrestricted passage through the interior's several settings, but independence from the constraints of the inherited context—the city being the most restrictive of contexts. Of course, there are both conceptual and practical problems with this conception of freedom. When it attempts a categorical separation from its vicinity, the building cuts itself off from the very conditions that grant it its reality and identity. Sovereignty in architecture cannot mean unconditional independence, for no building can stand apart from its context. Buildings are created out of materials that are available at or brought to a location; they are built with labor practices that are common or possible there; they depend on social patterns, natural and civic ecologies, cultural memories and aspirations, and so on. The freedom they express—the freedom of their stance—can only be understood *within* these conditions. The identity of a building does not result from absolute sameness with others in its vicinity, or from absolute difference, but from degrees of both. In the absence of a background, no figure could appear—the second presupposes the first, against which it shows itself. It is precisely this dependence of the figure on its ground that suggests another sense of the building's freedom, a freedom that arises out of the conditions that are given to design, not apart from them.

The freedom that characterizes the entry to the Glucksman Gallery lies in its function as a place for well-informed decision making. No decision is more difficult than the one made in absence of understanding, nor is any such choice really meaningful. Self-determination occurs through decisions that are made *in the midst* of circumstances, particularly conflictual circumstances. The paradoxical term "freestanding participation" aptly describes this allocentric situation, which applies to the gallery as a whole and its entry in particular. The task of the entry space is to draw together the several opportunities presented by the ambient circumstances and offer them to movement as a context of choice. The more the differences of the surroundings' various situations are made apparent, the more significant will be the choice of one or another. Herein lies the freedom that we experience in this space. Buildings do not sustain autonomy by divorcing themselves from "external constraints" but by using those very limitations as a framework for action.

While the gallery's engagement with its topography is apparent in its entry space, this interweaving is equally clear in its elevations. In the history of art, figures that are torn between several alternative, equally attractive, choices are often depicted as experiencing an internal conflict that has an impact on their physical composition. In mannerist and baroque painting and sculpture, this type of composition is known as *contrapposto* and

Michelangelo, *Battle of Cascina,* study, c. 1504–06; British Museum

has a number of typical characteristics. The first is that aspects of the figure's front and back are displayed simultaneously. A second and analogous characteristic of *contrapposto* is an opposition between the way the figure faces (or looks) and reaches. There is a wonderful drawing by Michelangelo of the Battle of Cascina that shows a single figure extending itself in four or five directions: one leg pointing to the left, another straight downward, the waist facing forward, the head twisted completely around to the rear, and an arm extending to the right—a figure truly *engaged* in battle, torn, one might say, in different directions. In this case, and in similar designs, contrary movements lead to a third characteristic of *contrapposto* composition: axial disequilibrium. The equivalent (structural) principle in architecture would be asymmetrical balance, kept in static equilibrium by means of cantilevers.

David Summers, in his account of *contrapposto* (cited in my introductory chapter), observed that the aim of "counterpositioning" was to use variety to give the sense of movement, for nothing brings a work to life as much as movement. But the key is that the movement of a body or any of its parts is always toward or away from some attractive or displeasing figure within its milieu; the figure comes to life, or defines itself, by taking a stand for or against conditions outside itself. Both axial disequilibrium, which allows the simultaneous appearance of front and back, and reaching in opposite directions are prompted by conditions outside the body. A figure's profile—an architectural elevation, for instance—indicates the choices it has made in the midst of the circumstances that surround it. Put differently, freedom, as described above, finds its foothold in a context of antithetical surroundings—the sort that can be found in just about any urban situation. There is no other way of understanding the Glucksman Gallery's *contrapposto* profile. It is irregular, distended, even convulsive, by virtue of being engaged in the contraries of its vicinity.

Given the "interest" this building shows in the many aspects of its surrounds, it may seem sensible to describe it as a kind of nexus or knot that binds together and concentrates the community of routes that cross its property. This image only applies, however, as long as it does not involve a sense of centrality, in the magnetic meaning of that word—for the building, at least the landing at the midpoint of its main axis, is more like a junction than a gathering point. What is more, it is not only planimetric but a spatial or volumetric intersection. A good way to think of it is to imagine a Loosian *Raumplan* made fully topographical. Many critics have characterized Loos's *Raumplan* designs as internal configurations, severed from their topographical frame of reference, although the buildings' apertures reveal linkage between inside and out. In the case of the Glucksman Gallery, however, the interconnections that Loos condensed onto a building's skin are prolonged into the reach of the gallery's volumes, toward the "external" situations they seek to engage. This is why its pattern of distribution can be called an allocentric order—centered outside itself.

Perhaps nothing clouds our understanding of a building's fundamental inherence in its milieu so much as our inflated and ill-conceived sense of architectural authorship. Because there are artists, there are works of art. The singularity of the second mirrors the individuality of the first. A long study would be required to explain the historical constitution of this conception. For present purposes it may be sufficient to point out that even if it makes sense in painting or music, the notion of a single author for a work of architecture is patently false. For many buildings, the owner or client is as important in the definition of the use program as the architect. While the materials and processes of construction are prescribed in the architect's drawings, models, and specifications, the control they exercise is never absolute. One doesn't have to accept Ruskin's argument about the craft origin of meaningful articulation to recognize the formative role of building labor, to

Le Corbusier, Pavillon Suisse, Cité Internationale Universitaire de Paris, 1933; entry hall

say nothing of the role that (undesigned) material properties play in the sense of the work. And once the construction is complete, internal and external influences continue to modify what was intended in the "initial design." With just these simple observations set out, it should be obvious that many agents have a hand in giving a building its definition: professional, nonprofessional, and environmental. Once this is realized, once the several powers at work in a building's genesis and continual modification are recognized, its inherence in the world will not be so hard to grasp. Failing this, one cannot do justice to the ways a building offers itself to experience.

The forecourt landing of the Glucksman Gallery is a place where aspects of the extended topography cross over and into one another. At no point on this level does any part show itself fully. Standing on the forecourt, the stair within the entry hall is obvious, but seen darkly, under the shadow cast by the galleries above. The same obscurity blankets the showcase, but it receives light from the sky above the river. No vantage point can be taken that would isolate any of these parts from the others. Inclusions, on the other hand, are many: leaves and clouds are included in the gallery's "balcony" window; the face of the town behind the campus entry looks over the wide rim of the forecourt; the column that partially limits the café below is among those that line the opposite side of the wide deck. Experience is not offered single objects but aspects of many, not items side by side but a field, a landscape, or topography whose depth is structured by the mutual envelopment of things. Within such a horizon, no room, court, or lawn appears whole and complete in itself, but always partially blocked by and blocking others. This is because each plunges its roots into the midst of its world as the site and soil of its unique divergence. Nor is the famous figure–background stable, as the two exchange roles depending on perceptual and practical interests, and the margins they share lead to reciprocal commingling and infiltration.

Lewis Glucksman Gallery; entry hall

Lewis Glucksman Gallery; entry platform

In every project there is the site, and there are the building's settings. The first is given and the second are designed. No truism in architecture is more obvious. But the configuration and posture of the Glucksman Gallery show that the reality of the building is not comprehended by this postulate. Each of the two—the site and the setting—crosses into the other in such a fashion that the limit between them is as indeterminate as it is incontestable. Each of the rooms in this building makes allusions to others nearby and far away—that much is clear. Less obvious but even more important is the realization that each constitutes itself as a room by virtue of these allusions. Thus, the gallery's most radical lesson is that project making is not limited to determination but requires a specifically architectural sort of indetermination, a disintegration of the object that promotes the leakage of settings into one another, resulting in a configuration of both kinships and differences, as in a family. In other words, the task taken up in the design of this building was not the definition of forms but the orchestration of relationships.

In architecture, depth is a phenomenon of "congeniality" in the etymological sense of that word: of like, common, or kindred origin. The congenial depth of the Glucksman Gallery is at once inviting and challenging. The architect, John Tuomey, once used the term "strangely familiar" to name its remote immediacy. If, indeed, the building crosses paths by crossing out their individuality, its chief aim is to serve as an emblem of what was otherwise unseen but integral about the world in which it stands.

Endnotes

Epigraph Seamus Heaney, "Crossings," in *Seeing Things* (New York: The Noonday Press, 1993), 84.

1   Edmund Husserl, "Foundational Investigations of the Phenomenological Origin of the Spatiality of Nature, in *Husserl Shorter Works*, ed. Peter McCormick and Frederick Elliston, (Notre Dame, Ind.: University of Notre Dame Press, 1981), 222–33.
2   See David Leatherbarrow, *Uncommon Ground: Architecture, Technology, and Topography* (Cambridge, Mass.: MIT Press, 2000), 176–80.

CHAPTER 10

Space in and out of Architecture

When architects describe architecture, the term they use most frequently is *space*. Two cognates are also common: *spaces* and *spatiality*. As is true with all well-worn vocabulary, these words fit their objects rather loosely.[1] Yet when considered in the sequence I have just set out, an argument suggests itself about the varying concreteness or abstraction of what these terms signify. Space, as something more or less conceptual and universal can be distinguished from spaces because the latter are at once particular and factual, known directly or immediately as the fabric and framework of our lives. Spatiality, by contrast, points not to the phenomena themselves but to one's experience and sense of them. The three terms can also be distinguished with respect to their role in the development of an architectural work. Space is congenial to an instrumental sort of production, because technique is know-how that is free from circumstantial particulars. Discrete spaces, by contrast, do not point directly to productivity but can sustain it, when design is understood as ingenuity. Here, too, spatiality offers itself as a term of comparison, by means of which the universal "there is" of space is grasped in the concrete experience of a specific location. Put differently, spatiality is the key to mediating the alternative between *conceiving* abstract space and *perceiving* actual spaces.

In what follows, I shall develop these distinctions. To do so, I have divided this chapter into two parts: a historiographic and a theoretical part. First, I will briefly review the emergence of the concept of space in architectural discourse. Although my focus will be on theories developed in late-nineteenth- and early-twentieth-century writing, I will begin with the later history of the story, a building and set of ideas developed in Philadelphia in the 1930s and 1940s, to which I have already referred in this book in Chapter 7 and 8. The building is the Philadelphia Saving Fund Society building, and the ideas were developed by one of its architects, George Howe, who wrote a paper in 1939 called "Going In and Coming Out—the Fundamental Architectural Experience," from which this present chapter title partly derives.[2] Howe's text and building introduce the problem of movement, which I see as a key to spatiality. Having considered the PSFS building earlier in this book, my attention to its particular qualities in this chapter will be brief.

I will start in Philadelphia, but not end there. Howe elaborated ideas set forth by an historian he thought very highly of, even though few read him today, Oswald Spengler. Spengler's ideas open the question of space into the main currents of mid- to late-nineteenth-century German thought. In developing his arguments, he made use of concepts of cultural experience, particularly symbolization, developed in late romanticism. For the purposes of this study, I will consider just one contributor to this broad tradition, Gottfried Semper, particularly his theory of formal beauty. Here, as with Spengler and Howe, there is attention to movement as a key to spatiality, but also to related concepts of direction and orientation. Semper's thought had great impact on Viennese theory and practice. In my brief account of his influence on early-twentieth-century architecture, I will consider the works of a theorist, August Schmarsow, and an architect, Adolf Loos. Loos's work will point me back toward the problem of going in and coming out—the matter of transitional or marginal space—and thus to Howe, completing the circle. A number of historians have clarified parts of this tradition: Werner Oechslin, Harry Mallgrave, Wolfgang Herrmann, Kurt Badt, and, more recently, Tonkao Panin.[3] With my interpretative comments, I will try to build upon the descriptions and arguments they have put forward.

After this historiographic introduction, I want to give a more theoretical account of the relationships between space, spaces, and spatiality. I will try to draw out the implications of the ideas of the historians and theorists I have reviewed and allude to some of the philosophical arguments developed within the same traditions, principally those of Edmund Husserl, Maurice Merleau-Ponty, and Jan Patočka:[4] Husserl's observations on the spatiality of nature, Merleau-Ponty's account of the perception of depth, and Patočka's account of the dependence of spatiality on movement. In brief, I will try to show that space is a second-order concept, the result of a process of abstraction, hardly wrong or misguided in itself—in fact, essential for architecture—but derivative just the same. While individual spaces and spatiality reciprocate one another, each place transcends itself into a wider frame of reference. Space is a symbolization of one or a few aspects of this wider horizon; its extensity, for example.

One last preliminary: there will be a methodological prejudice or antiprejudice in my account. In this chapter my aim is not to elucidate or develop concepts that are immediately congenial to design, at least to design as widely understood. Instead, I want to develop and elucidate concepts that help us understand more fully the nature and reality of spatial experience. I have set this as my task, because I believe questions of methodology should follow those of anthropology, that insights into the second should guide proposals for the first. The prejudice here in is favor of the world as it is lived in, not as it is made.

George Howe's paper "Going In and Coming Out" was presented at the Philadelphia Art Alliance in 1939, on the occasion of the opening of an exhibition of recent housing projects in the United States. His argument addresses housing, but also ranges across other territories: philosophy, art theory, and modern history. Linking many of his arguments is the concept of *continuity*. In view of the work shown, and of modern architecture generally, he observed: "We no longer conceive of housing as a row of isolated dwellings on a street, but as an integrated community. [And further] we no longer think of the house as a place to sleep, eat and rear a family in, but as part of a spatial complex, a place to go into and out of with human dignity to work, to play and to study."[5] The key point here is the sense of *interconnectedness* established by this complex or configuration of places. Despite the fact that they are often designed individually, buildings are never experienced that way; far from existing on their own, they always distinguish and define themselves with respect to settings and situations in their milieu, according to degrees of difference and similarity. Put simply, every part is also a counterpart. Howe historicized this point later in his talk: "It seems to me the great justification of the modern approach to the design of the house is that the house cannot be divorced from the complex of the community."[6]

The new spatiality was not limited to disciplinary concerns, however. Nor was it the result of design or architectural production alone. Howe felt he had identified a transformation that affected all departments of life and the whole of modern culture. "The world of tomorrow should not be a series of disconnected spaces, the one human in scale and drab in design [he means mass housing], the next superhuman in scale and glittering in pretentious finery. We must maintain the importance of the connecting points from which successive dimensions are measured, dimensions of direction, intensity and velocity, these

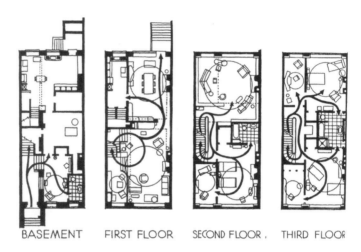

BASEMENT   FIRST FLOOR   SECOND FLOOR .   THIRD FLOOR

George Howe, Maurice J. Speiser House, Philadelphia, 1935; plan

are the points of going in and coming out."[7] These connecting points were thus integrative in a number of ways: different scales were joined together (the crosstown subway and the sidewalk), also different speeds (of the alley and avenue) and directions (toward and away from the town center, for example).

In point of fact, Howe's PSFS building accomplishes exactly these sorts of interconnection—although he did not mention that building in his talk. He referred instead to the masters of the modern movement. Speaking not of movement but of the dependency of settings (space) on situations (human praxis), he took the work of Loos and Le Corbusier as models: "The house, someone has said [here he means Loos], is not architecture at all, in the sense in which a cathedral or a temple is architecture, it is the product of a way of life, not an object to be looked at in the light [here he means Le Corbusier]."[8] I will return to this accent on the "way of life," because it will help me demonstrate the derivative character of space concepts.

Howe's criticism of Le Corbusier's definition of architecture as the play of forms in light should not be taken as a wholesale rejection of the latter's work. Slightly later in this same text, Howe identified Le Corbusier and Wright as the architects whose works most perfectly illustrate the new spatiality: "In the houses designed by the masters I have mentioned, we no longer approach the front door head-on, but indirectly, sometimes tortuously. The act of going in and coming out no longer seems to symbolize the passage from one compartment of space to another, but rather the observation of a point defining a change in direction, intensity or velocity."[9] To make Howe's point plain, I adduce two examples of indirect movement and spatial continuity, Wright's Unity Temple and Le Corbusier's Maisons La Roche and Jeanneret.

Passage into and through Wright's Unity Temple involves a striking number of turns and varieties of views.

Robert McCarter counted seven turns and a walk twice the length of the entire building just to get from sidewalk to sanctuary.[10] The entry foyer is a decisive point of orientation in the early stages of the sequence. Because of its low ceiling and the vertical compression it suggests, there is a heightened sense of opportunities at the edges of the room, or an expansion of lateral awareness. The key point of release leads into the so-called cloister, an ambulatory around the lower level, which skirts the main sanctuary. En route, the latter setting is glimpsed indirectly, increasing one's sense of anticipation. Through openings between the sanctuary floor and the cloister ceiling, one can see from the darkness of the hallway into the warm light of the space above. Wright explained this glimpsing or glancing awareness with comments on propriety: "[T]hose entering would be imperceptible to the audience. This would preserve the quiet and dignity of the room itself."[11] But the main point, I think, is the delay, the partial disclosure, or simultaneity of revealing and hiding. For Howe, this meander was a good thing, because modern spatiality involves continuities, sequences, and connections—not movement *in space* but *through spaces*.

As for Le Corbusier, a well-known indication of his development of the new spatiality is the *promenade architectural*. Although he explored the motif in several projects, its introduction in his *Oeuvre Complète* occurred in his description of Maisons La Roche and Jeanneret. His account began not with movement but vision; first you enter and the spectacle unfolds in succession before your eyes.[12] The sequence that follows is not of rooms but of their parts, because some elements of each obscure the full comprehension of those that follow. His statement of principle is this: "[Y]ou follow an itinerary and the perspectives develop with great variety."[13] As with many writers in the picturesque tradition, rambling movement prolongs the succession of partial prospects. But partiality indicates both lack

Frank Lloyd Wright, Unity Temple, Oak Park, Illinois, 1906; entry walk

Unity Temple; entry hall

Unity Temple; cloister view

and surplus. Although occlusion requires concealment, it also prompts discovery.

Presupposed in both of these cases—Unity Temple and Maisons La Roche and Jeanneret—is a sense of the perceiving body as the zero-point of spatial structure. Space for Howe is not given to experience except from the vantage of an individual's point of view—feet on the ground, in some concrete situation. I will try to show further on that the original dimension is the one we tend to see as the third, depth, which in fact is nothing like height and breadth. But for the moment, let me observe that for Howe, like Le Corbusier and Wright, the key to the order of space is the body moving through settings—going in and coming out, as he said—without which settings lack order, even if they have clear geometry. My last quotation from Howe can serve as a summary statement of this principle:

> Architecture cannot be limited to four walls and a roof,
> however complex the system of subdivisions they enclose,
> or as a system of posts and planes, transparent or opaque.
> To experience the meaning of . . . space in an architec-
> tural, or purely human, sense it is not enough to look at
> its visible form . . . To feel space the observer must flow
> through it, he must go in and come out, become con-
> scious of the indoors and the outdoors as related parts of
> a continuous whole.[14]

Continuity, interconnectivity, and complexity all presuppose the perceiving body's movement through settings as they unfold in sequence and open themselves through frontal and oblique views.

I have suggested that Howe's sense of space was influenced by Oswald Spengler's. He received a copy of *Decline of the West* in 1926.[15] It had been published that year in English, eight years after it first appeared in German.[16] Its impact on Howe's thinking cannot easily be overstated; he described it as "a major event" in his life. Like many American readers in the late 1920s, Howe was especially fond of Spengler's comparison between the Temple of Poseidon at Paestum (really the Hera Temple) and the cathedral at Ulm. The contrast appears in a chapter called "Symbolism and Space." Comparing Greek and Gothic buildings as symbolisms of the peoples, cultures, or spirits that built them, Spengler wrote: "While the Gothic style soars, the Ionic hovers. The interior of the cathedral pulls up with primeval force, but the temple is laid down in majestic rest."[17] Later, in a chapter on the "Arts of Form," he continued the comparison: "[T]he Temple of Poseidon at Paestum and the Minster at Ulm, works of the ripest Doric and ripest Gothic, differ as precisely as the Euclidean geometry of bodily-bounding surfaces differs from the analytical geometry of the position of points in space referred to spatial axes. All Classical building begins from the outside, all Western from the inside."[18] Spengler continued like this at some length, linking architecture with culturally specific conceptions of space. For Howe, the argument was not only persuasive historically but inspiring professionally. In 1954, he recalled that the passage had

> produced an immediate and violent impact... Having
> discovered through the interpretation of the past, an
> intimate relationship between mathematics and science
> on the one hand and architecture on the other, a relation-
> ship of form and spiritual content, not of dry technology,
> I decided... to seek out the same sort of relationship in
> the architecture of the present, representing the con-
> tinuation, or revival of the gothic craving "for a style
> which drives through walls into the limitless universe of
> space" and makes both the exterior and the interior of
> the building complementary images of one and the same
> world-feeling.[19]

If, as Spengler argued, each of the great cultures had arrived at its own language of world-feeling, its own symbolism of space, the same should be true for the present, or so Howe imagined. In a 1947 paper called "Flowing Space: The Concept of Our Time," he distinguished the modern concept from the static Greek and ascending Gothic as a kind of space in which "all is in flux... the flow of traffic, of production, and of people."[20] This is why modern buildings have replaced boxed-in enclosures with aggregates of planes of reference; instead of walls or facades, the architecture of the new age is composed of elements that guide and direct continual movement: partitions, screens, changes in level, and so on.

Despite the fact that Spengler's historiography has been sharply criticized by many scholars and his method rejected by many philosophers, his arguments merit some attention, because they introduce themes that more than a few twentieth-century architects also proposed. One of Spengler's most important points is implicit in Howe's sense of the succession of space concepts: that there is not one concept of space but many, that there is nothing like a nature of space, for each is a historically conditioned symbolism of spatial experience. Spengler observed that "a few years after the completion of Kant's main work Gauss discovered the first of the non-Euclidean geometries. These, irreproachably demonstrated... that there are several strictly mathematical kinds of three-dimensional extension, all of which are *a priori* certain, and none of which can be singled out to rank as the genuine form of perception."[21] Concerning the impact of these geometries, Morris Kline, the great historian of mathematics, observed that in the mid-nineteenth century, after the publication of the works of Gauss, Lobatchevsky, and Riemann, many mathematicians were convinced that a non-Euclidean geometry could be the geometry of physical space and that we could no longer be sure which geometry was true.

Kline also wrote: "[T]he mere fact that there could be alternative geometries was itself a shock. But the greater shock was that one could no longer be sure which geometry was true or whether any one of them was true."[22] I will return to this point, for it shows the need to pass from discussion of geometry and space to spatiality, if we are to deal with the problem rigorously and remain faithful to concrete experience.

The second point I want to take from Spengler also relates to the matter of spatial experience. Having demonstrated the transience of peoples and their symbols, and shown the continual and widespread preoccupation of cultures with emblems of death—as that which ends transience—he claimed to have discovered a new approach to the problem of space. I quote two key passages. The first is: "From the moment of our awakening, the fateful and directed life appears in the phenomenal life as an experienced *depth*. Everything extends itself, but it is not yet 'space,' not something established in itself but a self-extension continued from the moving here to the moving there."[23] The second passage reads: "From now on, we shall consider the *kind of extension as the prime symbol of a Culture*."[24] I believe these passages provided Howe with the key to his sense of the fundamental architectural experience—going in and coming out.

Spengler continued by acknowledging that depth, length, and breadth are, indeed, seen as equivalent in mathematics, depth being seen as the third dimension. He suggested, however, that this is misleading, "for in our impression of the spatial world these elements are unquestionably not equivalent, let alone homogeneous. Depth is a representation of expression, with which the world as such begins."[25] Obviously, this is a big statement. He explained himself by saying that extension into depth converts contemplation into sensation; it initiates, but is also the consequence of, activity; further, it is voluntary and creative, an emblem and experience of life that is outward and expressive. He made an analogous point with respect to the concept of dimension. Depth is so unlike width and breadth that the term "dimension" should only be used for the former: it means extension not extensions. "The idea of the three directions is an out-and-out abstraction and is not contained in the immediate extension feeling of the body. Direction as such... gives rise to the mysterious *animal* [he means horizontal] sense of right and left and vegetal [he means vertical] characteristic of below-to-above, earth to heaven."[26] While odd, this last observation is fascinating because it parallels arguments published not long before, made by two architectural theorists, Gottfried Semper and August Schmarsow.

Gottfried Semper addressed the problem of space in a number of his writings, but nowhere more directly than in the Prolegomena to his massive book *Style*.[27] That introductory text, however, is largely a republication of his paper on the "Attributes of Formal Beauty," intended to introduce a study called *Theory of Formal Beauty*.[28] Semper's argument is difficult to grasp for two reasons; despite his many revisions, it remains unfinished, and the illustration of its concepts is fuller than its explanation of them. Set out in summary form, Semper's argument is as follows. Beauty is not so much an attribute of a work, but its effect. While there are a number of diverse elements active within a beautiful object, three that generate form correspond to the three spatial dimensions of height, width, and depth. As for the conditions necessary for formal beauty to emerge, there are again three: symmetry, proportionality, and direction. Semper illustrated these with a discussion of snowflakes and crystals. This discussion introduced the concept of the radial line, which led him to the related notion of the axis. An axis, for Semper, is at once a line of force and, for living organisms, a line of both movement and orientation. In his account, there are axes of symmetry, proportionality, and direction. In different living organisms, these axes variously align and diverge from one another. In one animal an axis of proportionality may be vertical, while the axis of movement may be horizontal. In fish, however, axes of symmetry and direction coincide. Semper's discussion of direction is particularly difficult, because he couples directionality with a notion of vital forces. We have seen this in Spengler too; he characterized vegetal movement as vertical, animal as horizontal. Semper is more specific and elaborate:

> [T]he vital force, though it works in all directions, tends
> to follow one main direction, which in plants is generally
> directed vertically against the force of gravity. In most
> animals it is defined by the dorsal vertebrae, which are in
> most animals arranged horizontally, and thus it coincides
> with the direction of the will. With humans it is again
> vertical; it does not coincide with the direction of the will
> but forms a right angle to it.[29]

This concept of the will corresponds to what Spengler wrote about the outwardness of expression.

This complicated and somewhat esoteric anthropology has bearing on architecture, because works of art follow the laws of nature. In other words, the attributes of beauty in works of nature are the same as those in works of art: "[T]he principles of formal configuration [in art] must be in strict accordance with the laws of nature."[30] "Thus it happens," Semper observed, "that in art, as in nature—now through crystalline regularity, now through the dominance of symmetry, now through exceptional proportional development, and finally through special emphasis given to direction—the idea becomes manifested in a clear and distinct way."[31] This observation of differing emphases opens the possibility of classifying architectural works and writing their history. Symmetry prevails in works that belong to the class of memorials. Proportionality, by contrast, dominates in works with high domes or, still more emphatically, in those with towers, whose symmetries are overmatched by the proportionality of the ascending forms. Here again is an anticipation of what we see in Spengler and Howe, particularly the comparison between the Poseidon temple and the Ulm cathedral, works that are earthbound or heavenly striving. Directional organization, Semper suggested, is the leading principle in many works of the technical arts and of architecture: the ship and chariot in the first case, countless buildings in the second.

Semper was not alone in relating the configuration of architecture to works of nature, particularly the human body. Because he defined architecture as "the creatress of space," August Schmarsow is the most significant of these thinkers. Like Semper, he argued that works of art and nature have the same structure. The most important of natural works is the human body. For Schmarsow, like Semper, the configuration of the human body is axial. "We carry the dominant coordinate of the axial system within ourselves in the vertical line that runs from head to toe."[32] The obelisk, Schmarsow argued, is an equivalent or comparable configuration. But because the principal concern for architecture is enclosure, the most important axis or dimension for space creation is depth. The decisive point is this: the organization of the body—upright but forward looking—confers upon the body's surroundings similar structure and orientation: "[T]he spatial construct is, so to speak, an emanation of the human being present, a projection from within the subject, irrespective of whether we physically place ourselves inside the space or mentally project ourselves into it."[33] Also like Semper, Schmarsow coupled axial dimensions with conditions of formal beauty: verticality to proportion, horizontality to symmetry, and depth to both directionality and the measure of movement, rhythm—the aesthetic consequence of not just bodily motility but also of breathing and heartbeat. The point I want to stress, however, is Schmarsow's understanding of movement as the key factor in forming space. Like Carl Stumpf before him and Edmund Husserl after, Schmarsow based his concept of abstract space on a more fundamental and originating sense of space that is both localized and centered. Kinesthesis is the constitutive factor in the formation of space. "[O]ut of many spaces," argued Stumpf, "arises one space; this is explained by the continuity of space."[34] Husserl argued that "all spatiality is constituted through movement, the movement of the object itself and the movement of the I."[35]

This passage from Husserl appears in a text called *Thing and Space*. I will return to his argument shortly, but first I would like to point to an architect whose work demonstrates an equivalent understanding of spatiality. Husserl's text was written in 1907. One year later, Adolf Loos started work on his well-known clothing store and apartment building on Michaelerplatz in Vienna, a building he identified as one in which he first established the *Raumplan* configuration of spaces. He had in mind the relationship between the settings on the mezzanine level and the main display space.

The key point, as many commentators have indicated, is differentiation. This is achieved through several architectural means: the setting's size, shape, and position; the choice of construction materials and their finishing; the source and quality of lighting; and the specification of furnishings and fittings. All of this assumes the differentiation of purposes within the institution: display, orientation, sales, fittings, and so on. Beginning in the Michaelerplatz, a modern and metropolitan public space, a sequence of variously qualified settings ends in an approximately domestic mezzanine interior, the department for custom tailoring. Together with these two opposite endpoints, the several "characters" one confronts along this sequence are those

Adolf Loos, Michaelerhaus, Vienna, 1909; mezzanine levels

that were required by the institution. A particularly economical integration of this range is achieved by the midlevel landing of the stair that leads from the main shopping hall to the mezzanine display tables and windows, for there one can see aspects of the institution's key situations: display of goods, choice among alternatives, tailoring, and buying. The integration of these situations is spatial and practical, but also physical. Polished surfaces, mirrors, and glass panels amplify the play of aspects of several settings.

For his part, Loos stressed the differentiation of settings according to room level and height. All of the settings just named have different ceiling heights. Perhaps the best way to summarize this spatial structure is to cite Loos himself:

> I design no plans, facades, sections, I design space. In fact, there is neither a ground floor, nor a first floor, nor a basement in my designs, there are only integrated rooms, anterooms, and terraces. Every room requires a specific height—the dining room needs a different one from that of the larder—therefore the ceilings are arranged at different levels. Then one has to integrate all these rooms in such a manner that the transition [Übergang] is not only imperceptible and natural, but also functional.[36]

The "space" to which he refers is not the abstract and homogeneous continuum posited in Cartesian geometry, but a richly qualified ensemble of settings differentiated from one another but also integrated by means of movements, transitions, and continuities that are simultaneously visual, ambulatory, and practical. It was transitions of this sort that Howe had in mind when he described the fundamental architectural experience as "going in and coming out," cited at the beginning of this chapter (see pages 240–44).

Modern architecture has been assailed by many post-modern critics as a style of building that imposed on the modern city and on our lives a set of objects that did not belong to the context in which they were inserted. This criticism was also made of building projects in the nineteenth century, not houses and theaters, but railway stations. If engineering works could be tolerated as practical and economic necessities, works of architecture could not. The chief differences these buildings were said to possess resulted from a number of factors, among them lack of ornament, the use of new materials or of old materials used in new ways, large sizes. When these formal and physical characteristics were coupled with an assumed rejection of the past, sanctioned by political and aesthetic arguments for renewal, the new architecture was widely viewed as either indifferent or hostile to its inherited context. The framework of modern design, we have been told, was abstract space, not the given city. Dissatisfaction with modern architecture has led some critics to reject what has been taken to be its theoretical foundation—space. This explains in part the strong interest in place theory among some of these writers. We seem to be presented with an alternative between space and spaces, between a relativity of direction or orientation and particular content. I said at the outset of this chapter, I would rather not accept this alternative, hence my concern for spatiality.

The arguments and projects of Howe, Wright, Le Corbusier, and Loos suggest that the common conception of modern architecture's autonomy is false. I believe I have shown that modern buildings were not designed as objects in space, but as ensembles of settings that were part of their milieu, because they were always understood to be coextensive with it. Now it is certainly true that traditional ornamentation, together with its privileged site, the facade, was largely abandoned in early-twentieth-century architecture, but substituting for it (as a means of ordering the building) was a new understanding of spatial depth. Pictorial *signs* of architectural order were replaced by a more radical understanding of spatial and practical *configuration*: two-dimensional patterns were substituted by three-dimensional ensembles. Obviously, art and architectural theorists had considered three-dimensionality and depth before; it had been a topic of study and representation at least since the Renaissance. Still, I believe it is entirely correct to say that four centuries after the Renaissance "rediscovery of linear perspective," spatial depth still needed reconsideration. Writing at the time of Schmarsow and Loos, the art historian Fritz Novotny argued that in paintings by artists as different as Paul Cézanne, Henri Matisse, and Gustav Klimt, we witness the end of scientific perspective.[37] Merleau-Ponty's studies of Cézanne and Paul Klee make the same point.[38] Certainly the well-known flatness of early modern paintings suggests that the early twentieth century inaugurated a new spatiality. While improbable or surprising as an assertion, I think it is fair to say that the end of perspectival space, signaled by the flattening of constructed three-dimensionality, heralds the beginning of a new and fuller sense of depth—not constructed (after having been conceived) but lived. The end of the perspectival tradition also led to the discovery of depth as the first, not the third, dimension.[39]

The chief difficulty in discussing depth is that it cannot be perceived as such. Unlike height and breadth, the intervals or lengths of which conceal nothing in their wide or narrow spread, depth never appears as complete in itself or all of a piece; the distance it opens is always discontinuous, because some of its parts are hidden behind the figures that populate its spread, no matter whether it is the depth of a bookcase in the study, the balcony outside its window, or the urban block into which it extends. Perhaps it was for this reason—depth's nontransparency—that the Irish philosopher George Berkeley said that it cannot be perceived.[40]

It we suspend our assumptions about the unity of isotropic space, however, and likewise doubt the equivalence assumed
to exist among the three dimensions; if we try instead to remain
faithful to our concrete experience, we can begin to see that
depth is not an interval between things, between buildings, gardens, or streets (seen from an airplane), but the medium of their
interconnection as they provide the framework for the practices
of everyday life—taking a book off the shelf, calling to one's children from the balcony, or picking up the newspaper from the
sidewalk.[41] The settings for these events are not things in space
(even if that is how I have listed them) but instruments of their
connection and continuity. I believe this is what Howe stated
with such insistence in his comments on the interconnectedness
of spatial ensembles, the internal coherence of the "spatial com-
plexes" or "integrated communities" that characterize the modern world. Buildings have their place (exist unto themselves),
because they conceal aspects of one another. Merleau-Ponty
described the relationships between things in depth as follows:
"[T]hey are rivals before my sight precisely because each one is
in its own place. Their exteriority is known in their envelopment
and their mutual dependence in their autonomy."[42]

Depth as mutuality or reciprocal envelopment helps us
understand Howe's sense of the building or the architectural
setting as something defined by degrees of difference from and
similarity to configurations within its milieu. Each situation
within a building is enmeshed in a wider context or stuck in its
vicinity. The famous escalator in the PSFS building cannot be
understood apart from the speed of the subway below and the
scale of the banking room above. The shops at the building's
base belong as much to the commercial character of this part of
the city and the intercity rail line across the street as they do to
the building itself. These relationships and interconnections are
both practical and perceptual. Viewing the PSFS entry sequence

in reverse—in other words, grasping the depth of the public domain from within (toward the street)—one sees not things in space but their encroachment on one another, their porosity or promiscuity, suggesting that the identity and dimensionality of things emerges out of their copresence among one another. In this case, as in many others, light exposes the porosity and interconnection of settings; light levels in one setting depend on the higher or lower reflectivity of another. On this account, the identity or selfsameness of a setting or building results from its divergence from other settings in the depth of its milieu. For this to be the case, the ambient terrain must be allowed to act as the building's first premise; the city—its typical configurations and its particular characters—must act as the medium of architectural definition. This allows the building's spaces to originate in the spatial order of the "pre-given" situation.

For this reason, talk of space will always be distracting if it is seen as a neutral or homogeneous field in which independently conceived objects are placed. Space must, instead, be seen or understood to represent a *field of variations*.[43] Both characteristics are key: the unity or selfsameness of the field and the variations within it. The vicinity of the PSFS building, like every other neighborhood in the town, has its own character, ambience, or determinant quality—its *Stimmung*. This character results less from the sameness of buildings, gardens, and rooms than from their alterations of the regional norm. Sameness is not the issue but similarity.

The experience of depth, or in the case just mentioned, the thickness of the public realm, is not always, perhaps not even normally, frontal. The modern architects mentioned in this text often referred to oblique views. This is also the way they drew and photographed their buildings. I think it is fair to say that these works were also conceived obliquely. It is well known that Wright often implied diagonal movement in his plan com-

Le Corbusier, Maison la Roche, Paris, 1923–24; interior

positions. I believe it is a key to the structure and experience of architectural spatiality. If paintings or pictorial figures offer their contents in face-to-face encounters, architectural settings present themselves this way and at the margins of the frontal view. When one recognizes the lateral or oblique givenness of the milieu, one also catches sight of its invitation to further inspection, for marginal views are always partial. Wright, Le Corbusier, and Loos all proposed a decompartmentalized spatiality (the open plan, the free plan, and the *Raumplan*). Each of these configurations is a means by which the room or building transcends itself into its vicinity; or, in reverse, the means by which the potentials of the vicinity enter into and qualify the building's several settings. Howe described modern spatiality as passage through elements, not movement from room to room. This was to be accomplished not through doors and windows in walls but by breaks and open corners between partitions, screens, and changes of level. The developments in modern building technology—particularly the structural frame—did not give rise to the new spatiality but were required by it, by its desire for lateral connectedness, for continuity between the building and its milieu. Frontality is a special condition in architecture. Obliquity, by contrast, is the norm. The settings we inhabit are always excessive and deficient, they infiltrate (and prejudice) our sense of the locations they lead into, just as they depend on those same locations for qualities they require but do not possess. The essential laterality of architecture opens experience into the wider horizon's inexhaustible excess. This is also where architectural space transcends itself into the natural world.

The arguments about axiality offered by Spengler, Semper, and Schmarsow indicated the mosaic and differential character of modern spatiality. Directionality was also a key theme in their arguments about axes, as they exist in people, nature, and artifacts. These three authors suggested that directionality assumes or is the outcome of some kind of vital force that concentrates its energy along some line of influence or effect. I do not want to inquire here into what that force or energy might be (in Spengler it seems akin to Henri Bergson's vitalism, for example), but instead, simply to recall that Semper argued that plants are proportioned or articulated along a vertical axis of direction, which manifests an upward striving. The key point with respect to spatiality is that movement of this sort, and perhaps any other, occurs over and against a counterforce: upward striving measures its success against the downward pull of gravity. The philosopher Erwin Strauss once said that one reason we walk forward is to keep ourselves from falling downward.[44] More interesting for art is his related observation about dance, that its movements celebrate the body's capacity to resist the downward pull of gravity, or the body's heaviness and weight. The force–counterforce relationship posits once again the contextuality of definition; the plant's verticality is a sign of its standing against ambient forces that would reduce it to horizontality. Can we not say that buildings also define themselves through resistance to ambient forces—forces of all sorts (gravity, climate, flows of people, and so on)? If this can be said, we should conclude, I think, that the configuration of the part—the dimensions, distances, and arrangement of the building—presupposes a wider frame of reference as the context of its differentiation. The movement from space, through spatiality to spaces, points toward the play of forces in the natural world as space's most radical foundation. This has been stated, persuasively I believe, by Merleau-Ponty: "I never wholly live in varieties of human space, but am always ultimately rooted in a natural and non-human space...which foreshadows the horizons of possible objectivity, and frees me from every particular setting only because it ties me to the nature or primordial world which includes all of them."[45]

Endnotes

1   The most recent thorough study of the term "space" is contained in Adrian Forty, *Words and Buildings: A Vocabulary of Modern Architecture* (London: Thames & Hudson, 2000), 256–75.

2   George Howe, "Going In and Coming Out—the Fundamental Architectural Experience" (unpublished) George Howe Papers, Avery Library, Columbia University.

3   Werner Oechslin, *Otto Wagner, Adolf Loos, and the Road to Modern Architecture* (Cambridge: Cambridge University Press, 2002). Also useful for what I will argue are Werner Oechslin and Winfried Nerdinger, *Gottfried Semper (1803–1879): Architektur und Wissenschaft* (München: Prestel, 2003); Harry Mallgrave, *Modern Architectural Theory* (Cambridge: Cambridge University Press, 2005); Wolfgang Herrmann, *Gottfried Semper: In Search of Architecture* (Cambridge, Mass.: MIT Press, 1984); Kurt Badt, *Raumphantasie und Raumillusionen* (Köln: M. Dumont Schauberg, 1963); and Tonkao Panin, Ph.D. Dissertation, School of Design, University of Pennsylvania, 2003.

4   Edmund Husserl, *Ding und Raum* (1907) (Den Haag: Nijhoff, 1973); an English translation has appeared under the title *Thing and Space: Lectures of 1907*, trans. Richard Rojcewicz (Dordrecht: Kluwer, 1997). Also see Maurice Merleau-Ponty, "Space," in *Phenomenology of Perception*, trans. Colin Smith (New York: Humanities Press, 1962); and Jan Patočka, *Body, Community, Language, World* (Chicago: Open Court, 1998), fifth, seventeenth, and twentieth lectures.

5   Howe, "Going In and Coming Out," 10.

6   Ibid., 11.

7   Ibid., 7.

8   Ibid., 3.

9   Ibid., 8.

10 Robert McCarter, an authoritative Wright scholar, makes this point in *Frank Lloyd Wright* (London: Phaidon Press, 1997).

11 Frank Lloyd Wright, *An Autobiography* (New York: Duell, Sloan and Pearce, 1943), 155.

12 Le Corbusier, *Oeuvre Complète*, vol. 1 (London: Thames and Hudson, 1964), 60.

13 Cited in Stanislaus von Moos and Arthur Rüegg, eds., *Le Corbusier before Le Corbusier* (New Haven: Yale University Press, 2002), 41.

14 Howe, "Going In and Coming Out," 2.

15 Robert A. M. Stern, *George Howe* (New Haven: Yale University Press, 1975), 66.

16 Oswald Spengler, *Decline of the West* (London: George Allen & Unwin, 1926). (Originally pub. as *Der Untergang des Abendlandes, Gestalt und Wirklichkeit* [München: C. H. Beck, 1918]).

17 Spengler, *Decline*, 177.

18 Ibid., 224.

19 Cited in Stern, *George Howe*, 66.

20 Howe, "Flowing Space: The Concept of Our Time," in Thomas Creighton, ed., *Building for Modern Man: A Symposium* (Princeton: Princeton University Press), 164–69. I have discussed this paper at some length in *Uncommon Ground: Architecure, Technology and Topography* (Cambridge, Mass.: MIT Press, 2000), 177–80.

21 Spengler, *Decline*, 171.

22 Morris Kline, *Mathematics, the Loss of Certainty* (Oxford: Oxford University Press, 1980), 88.

23 Spengler, *Decline*, 168.

24 Ibid., 174.

25 Ibid., 168.

26 Ibid., 169.

27   Gottfried Semper, *Style in the Technical and Tectonic Arts; or, Practical Aesthetics*, Harry
      Francis Mallgrave, trans. and intro. (Los Angeles: Getty Research Institute, 2004).
28   Gottfried Semper, "Attributes of Formal Beauty," in Wolfgang Herrmann, *Gottfried
      Semper*, 219–44.
29   Semper, *Style*, 90.
30   Ibid., 92.
31   Ibid., 96.
32   August Schmarsow, "Essence of Architectural Creation," in *Empathy, Form, and Space*, ed.
      Harry Francis Mallgrave and Eleftherios Ikonomou (Los Angeles: Getty Research Institute,
      1994), 288.
33   Ibid., 289.
34   Carl Stumpf, "Ursprung der Raumvorstellung," cited in Mallgrave and Ikonomou, *Empathy,
      Form, and Space*, 60.
35   Husserl, *Ding und Raum*, section 154; *Thing and Space*, 131.
36   Adolf Loos, cited in Karel Lhota, "Architekt A. Loos: Adolf Loos spricht," *Ausschnitte aus
      Aufzeichnungen*, in *Architekt SIA*, 8 (1933): 137–43.
37   Fritz Novotny, *Cézanne und das Ende der Wissenschaftlichen Perspektive* (Vienna: Anton
      Schroll, 1938).
38   Maurice Merleau-Ponty, "Eye and Mind," in *The Primacy of Perception*, ed. James Edie
      (Evanston, Ill.: Northwestern University Press, 1964); and "Cézanne's Doubt," in *Sense and
      Non-sense* (Evanston, Ill.: Northwestern University Press, 1964).
39   Merleau-Ponty, "Space." This discussion is elaborated in Joseph Kockelmans, "Merleau-
      Ponty on Space Perception and Space," in Joseph Kockelmans and Theodore Kisiel,
      Phenomenology and the Natural Sciences (Evanston, Ill.: Northwestern University Press,
      1970); by Edward Casey, "The Element of Voluminousness" in *Merleau-Ponty Vivant*,
      ed. M. C. Dillon (Albany: State University of New York, 1991); and most suggestively by
      Renaud Barbaras, *The Being of the Phenomenon* (Bloomington: Indiana University Press,
      2004).
40   See George Berkeley, *An Essay Towards A New Theory of Vision* (1709) (London: Dent,
      1963), 13 and 31–33. At the very beginning of the text, section 2, Berkeley asserts that
      distance, as such, cannot be seen. He develops the argument in subsequent sections and
      concludes this part of his argument in sections 44–46.
41   On this point, see the wonderful account of spatiality in Erwin Strauss, "Forms of
      Spatiality," in *Phenomenological Psychology* (New York: Basic Books, 1966).
42   Merleau-Ponty, "Eye and Mind," 180.
43   I have elaborated this point somewhat in the conclusion to *Topographical Stories: Studies
      in Landscape and Architecture* (Philadelphia: University of Pennsylvania Press, 2004).
44   Three of Strauss's texts are helpful on the spatiality of movement: "Upright Posture,"
      "Man a Questioning Being," and "Awakeness," in *Phenomenological Psychology*.
45   Merleau-Ponty, "Space," 293–94.

CHAPTER 11

The Law of Meander

My aim in this final chapter is to widen the historical framework of the preceding chapters by developing connections between the picturesque tradition and early modern architecture—to show that a number of the spatial structures that characterize modern architecture are outgrowths of pre-twentieth-century history. To demonstrate this I will take up matters of art history, architectural theory, and philosophical anthropology. I have already stated my historical argument, that twentieth-century spatial types such as the free plan, the *Raumplan*, and the open plan developed out of the picturesque tradition. As for matters of theory, I want to show that configurations of this kind emphasized movement through space more than its pictorial aspects. This is not so much a departure from the tradition as it is an elaboration of one of its key aspects. Lastly, I want to argue that the architecture that adopted this manner of design (but not its conventional motifs) enlarged its philosophical anthropology into a set of ideas and symbols that approximate nothing short of a cosmology, one that attempted to overcome the traditional distinction between artifice and nature. Before any of these points can be made, however, I need to set out what I mean by both the picturesque tradition and the spatial structure it developed.

Picturesque space arose in the "informal" garden that emerged in England in the early eighteenth century and then

spread across Europe through the later eighteenth and nineteenth centuries. For the purposes of this study, I will bor-
row John Dixon Hunt's summary of its main characteristics.
Picturesque space offers the experience of a carefully considered
and composed irregularity, featuring the richness and variety of
natural materials arranged in apparent randomness, appealing
to eyes that not only rove across extensive scenery but apprehend its many and varied aspects. These aspects include settings
that appear in a detailed foreground as well as those in a middle
distance of calculated effects and those that lie beyond in the
hazy distance. They appeal all the while to the imagination, often
through exotic buildings, which are designed to be—like their
surrounds—aesthetically and emotionally pleasing, being partly
reminiscent of landscape paintings and engravings.[1] Pictorial
though it often was, the picturesque landscape was also, or just
as often, theatrical, for a principal aesthetic category of gardens
in this tradition was *variety*, which was achieved not through one
prospect but through many—an ensemble, views seen not at
once but one after another in time, like acts or events on stage in
a dramatic performance. Picture making and theater might then
seem to be essentially the same, for both offer their compositions to vision. Yet when one's experience of these compositions
is considered in its temporal dimension, the two are discovered
to be essentially different. Pictorial works offer their contents
all at once, in an instant, notwithstanding the fact that pictorial
understanding takes time. Still, through the duration of viewing,
the pictorial work stays as it is and remains the same when seen
again in the future. Theatrical works, however, unfold in time
in a completely different way. If pictures annul, dramatic works
celebrate time, particularly temporal change, spanning the full
spectrum of human and natural history, from recollection to
anticipation in human experience, and growth and deterioration
in the natural world. Paul Ricoeur has shown in his magnificent

Time and Narrative that story telling and temporal succession necessarily reciprocate one another.[2] No form of experience was more effective in activating garden temporality than movement. Hunt pointed to this in his account of the eye "roving" across extensive scenery, attending to its many and varied aspects, each distinguished from the others by virtue of its specific and identifiable character. Because it will be central to my account of the later architectural interpretation of the picturesque tradition, I would like to offer two additional citations in explanation of movement in the picturesque garden. The sources I cite are from the middle and early period of the garden's development.

In 1764, the poet and amateur gardener William Shenstone made the following recommendation: "[W]hen a building or other object has been once viewed from its proper point, the foot should never travel to it by the same path, which the eye has traveled over before. *Lose the object, and draw nigh, obliquely.*"[3] He attempted to follow this principle in the design and construction of the gardens around his estate called the Leasowes. The "obliquity" of approach recommended by Shenstone was anticipated by Alexander Pope in an earlier statement of principle: "Let not each beauty everywhere be spied, / Where half the skill is decently to hide."[4] Here, delay and roundabout movement are less important than partiality; the garden as a whole is never seen all at once, or all of a piece, for figures that are presently apparent occlude those that are yet to be seen. Pope, like Shenstone, argued for succession. The garden was never more than partially disclosed from a single vantage point; its scenes were to be discovered en route, which is to say, on foot, in the midst of collapsing and expanding distances, noticed through diagonal or oblique views—the kind of optics seventeenth-century set designers had referred to as the *veduta per angolo*. As is well known, spatial structure of this kind was set out along an armature of serpentine paths. All of

William Kent, Chiswick Exedra, Chiswick, c. 1733; Devonshire Collection

the early designers of the picturesque garden were insistent on avoidance of straight lines of movement and on promotion of the meandering route. Two centuries after Pope, Le Corbusier had the same kind of movement in mind when he wrote about "The Law of Meander," to which I will turn at the end of this chapter.

First, though, a little more needs to be said about movement. The passages I have cited from Shenstone and Pope suggest that we analytically separate two sorts of movement, of the eye and of the body—a visual and an ambulatory sort. The latter can be defined most simply as transit from place to place, or change of position, passing from this grove, for example, to that clearing. Obviously, this is not movement *of* but *in* the landscape. On this topic, too, I want to cite Hunt, particularly his differentiation of "kinds of movement": the procession, stroll, or wandering of a perceiving subject.[5] Picturesque gardens were rarely thought of as spaces for processional movement, however; processions happened more frequently in ritualized settings. Further, gardens were only used as sites for wandering when they relaxed their primary order into the uncultivated potentials of the unimproved terrain. If the first kind of movement, procession, has a definite destination and prescribed route, the latter, wandering, has neither. Strolling, by contrast, aims at a destination. Yet it also welcomes unexpected incidents along the way. My proposition is this: just as a strolling sort of movement was central to the picturesque garden, it was key in the development of the new spatiality of early modern architecture.

In 1889, Camillo Sitte, the immensely influential Viennese urban theorist, drew the following comparison between strolling movement in cities and the perception of picturesque spaces: "[A] picturesque effect could be attained by following the natural path of a stroller's feet. Such a graceful curvilinear trajectory is observable in the villages and it is an honor to imitate them."[6] As in picturesque gardens, meandering movement in villages and cities encountered a series of settings, or fragments of them, succeeding one another along an unprescribed passage. Describing movement through medieval towns, Sitte wrote: "[T]he winding character of the ancient streets kept sealing off perspective views in them while offering the eye a new aspect at each succeeding turn. These meanderings, which are wiped out at great expense in our day were not the result of caprice…it was necessary to adapt the layout of the street to its terrain."[7] There are two key points in this passage: one, that winding streets offer successive prospects; and two, that there was a topographical pretext for meandering movement—no matter whether the route was urban or rural. I want to show that that is also the case for modern architecture; the turnings of a modern building's internal routes respond to the characteristics of the surrounding terrain, just as they prompt exploratory movement. I am not the first to draw this comparison between concepts of space in early Viennese urban and architectural theory. Some years ago, George Collins suggested a link between Sitte's concept of *Raumkunst* and Adolf Loos's idea of *Raumplan*.[8] In fact, their shared dependence on the picturesque tradition relates them to one another.

A number of historians have also observed that the concept of the *Raumplan* evident in Loos's houses has as its basis the domestic architecture of England and America in the late nineteenth century.[9] The buildings of Shaw, Webb, Baillie Scott, Voysey, and Lutyens in England and those of Richardson in America exhibited the qualities Loos viewed as representative of the modern way of living. Most important among these qualities were differentiated room levels and heights, open circulation spaces, open stairwells with large landings, fireplaces and bay windows in living spaces, open galleries in halls, terraces, and rooms within the whole ensemble fitted together but not wholly interconnected. The coordination of parts such as these involved the integration and interconnection of interior spaces across all manner of partitions and screens. Presupposed in the design and articulation of these partitions and screens was the subdivision and differentiation of spaces. *Raumplan* spatiality posits both differentiation and integration. What is more, while *Raumplan* configuration depended on the separation and coordination of internal settings, it also assumed their interlocking with the different aspects of the exterior.

As suggested in Chapter 10 and cited on pages 255–58, the most compact definition of the *Raumplan* idea was articulated by Loos himself. While he did not mention the Müller house when explaining this kind of planning, it is clearly an excellent example. The Müller house is situated on a hill overlooking Prague in what was then a suburban village. The principal entry is small, compared to the measure of the expanse of the front facade, and it opens into an equally small-sized entry that leads through a narrow passageway, alongside a vestibule, to a tight semispiral stairway. This sequence is dramatically interrupted at the top of the stairway where the visitor emerges at the side of a vast and beautifully articulated living room. Before this room is entered, looking right, the dining room can be seen at the top of a flight of steps; on the left, another semispiral stairway begins. Straight ahead from the point of arrival on the main level are windows that open onto the rear garden in the foreground and the landscape around Prague in the distance. Thus, from this point, three primary settings are interconnected, albeit through diagonal or oblique views, each setting including more than it actually contains. At the dawn of the picturesque garden tradition, Pope called this "call[ing] in the country."[10] It is also what Frank Lloyd Wright had in mind when he advocated "breaking the box."

As the Müller meander is followed farther, other settings emerge into view. Upon entering the living room, the dining room is visible again through an irregular colonnade or pair of thick piers. Also visible, above and behind the point of entry, is a long internal window. This window joins the living room to a small and intimate sitting space. This space is one part of a very complicated and beautifully interrelated group of settings that lie above the entryway. Joined together there are: the intimate sitting space, a reading space that adjoins a large external window, and the library, which is also attached to a large window. This ensemble can be reached from either the dining room or the living room. Thus it is part of the movement sequence, but at the same time it has autonomy. In fact, other settings in the house are similarly joined to form groups that are only indirectly related to the whole ensemble, but this particular group can be taken as representative.

In the definition of the *Raumplan* alluded to above and cited in Chapter 10, Loos stressed the differentiation of settings according to room level and height. All of the settings I have just named have different ceiling heights. Further, the meander I have followed ascended through at least four levels, although this number could be increased, as some of the landings constitute new levels. Landings such as these seem larger than they are for two reasons: (1) because the stairways of which they form a part are opened onto adjoining settings; and (2) because they are enclosed by screens and partitions that contain built-in furnishings—shelves, seats, and so on. There is no doubt that the metric and shape differentiation of the rooms joined by these stairways and landings is complemented by a refined differentiation of cladding materials, following Loos's principle of making each setting "warm and liveable." Yet just as important as the cladding is the correspondence between these settings and the external or perimeter settings around the house, for the building's surrounds are variously bright and dark, quiet and loud, with near and far prospects that qualify the building's interiors as much as its materials do. As the perimeter varies, so do the size and shape of the internal settings. The large living space is connected to an expansive terrace that overlooks the garden; the tight, intimate spaces for reading and conversation are contained within the enclosure of the side wall; and the entry is positioned on the front facade but drawn in off the main street and reduced in size. The *Raumplan* is a spatial coordination of internal settings with respect to one another and the different aspects of the exterior. Put differently, the interior meander concentrates the variety and richness of the surrounding topography. What Sitte found in the town, Loos arranged inside the house, as if the latter were an image of the former—and the former, of course, understood as a picturesque ensemble.

Let me now move onto my second case and begin by saying that what Camillo Sitte's ideas were to Loos, Hermann Muthesius's were to Mies van der Rohe—that is, a key to the possibility of extending the picturesque tradition (of ordering exterior spaces) into the design of architectural plans and interiors.

In his study of "The Nature of Mies's Space," Barry Bergdoll stressed the importance of the garden, particularly the so-called architectonic garden, in Mies's approach to spatial composition.[11] In explaining the antecedents for this approach, Bergdoll cited both Peter Behrens and Hermann Muthesius on the interconnections between house and garden. Muthesius, for example, spoke of the "continuation of the spaces of the house" into the garden. He wrote that "the same fundamental principles that prevail in the house, the same organic relationship of the individual parts to another, the same unification of the parts into a harmonic whole...must also prevail in the garden."[12] Behrens, for his part, saw the garden as an opportunity for "forming space." Seeing terrain as space allowed the landscape to be assimilated into architecture, for *Raumgestaltung* (giving form to space) "is obviously," Behrens said, "the highest principle of architecture."[13] This assimilation—generally discussed as "continuity"—was, however, only the first step in the development of Miesian space. Bergdoll observed that in his later work, Mies "transposed the dialogue between indoors and outdoors into the architecture itself."[14] This transposition was decisive, for the perceptual possibilities and varied perspectives that are characteristic of his work resulted from just this internalization of the landscape.

My claim, again, is this: Mies's early projects rejected the categorical distinction between the order of the building and the landscape; instead, he allowed the order of the latter to prefigure that of the former. The function of partitions in his plans of the 1920s and 1930s is to orient and lead the strolling kind of movement we have observed in picturesque gardens. Screen walls also open and close the diagonal prospects, such as those Shenstone and Pope recommended. Writing about the garden behind Mies's Riehl House, Bergdoll interpreted its "almost perverse refusal of a direct path from the garden gate to the front door" as "embryonic of a strategy in nearly all Mies's German houses: the visitor is generally obliged to turn several times at right angles before the view is fully unveiled."[15] The strategy of delaying disclosure also explains the transformation of the person into an "ambulant observer." José Quetglas wrote expressively about the lone occupant of Mies's Barcelona Pavilion, whose sole activity was unrequited gazing at theatrical sets of "nothing but space."[16] The opening and closing of views offered to a roving spectator is also what Robin Evans described in his account of Mies's "Paradoxical Symmetries."[17] These essays, together with Bergdoll's arguments about garden spatiality, present Mies as a landscape architect who intended his buildings to offer more terrain than they were really prepared to give. Each view, fragmentary as it was, opened obliquely onto another and then still others. And if the opening was not toward

Mies van der Rohe, Tugendhat House, Brno, 1928–30; interior

a new setting, it was toward a new aspect of a setting that had been seen previously. The sequence is, in principle, without end, the building always exceeding itself. In this, too, it is like the landscape, at least in its visual or optical aspects. Miesian buildings offer a surplus of views, each with its own character, defined largely by aspects of the building itself, together with that part of the ambient landscape it has annexed into its holdings, or allowed to enter into and qualify its several settings.

My third case, Frank Lloyd Wright, presents another example of an early modern architect advocating meandering space in ways that build upon picturesque theory and practice. Intent on preserving the impression of his originality, Wright was never particularly open about his sources. Any attribution of influence in his case will always be suggestive. Still, just a little familiarity with the nineteenth-century landscape tradition in America makes it hard to deny the impact these theories had on Wright. An obvious case in point is Andrew Jackson Downing.

That variety and richness of scenes were characteristic of picturesque landscapes is clear from Downing's definition of the beau ideal in his *Treatise on the Theory and Practice of Landscape Gardening*:

> The *beau ideal* in landscape gardening as a fine art,
> appears to us to be embraced in the creation of scenery
> expressive of a peculiar kind of beauty, as the elegant
> or picturesque, the materials of which are, to a cer-
> tain extent, different from those in wild nature, being
> composed of the flora and arboricultural riches of all
> climates, as far as possible;—uniting in the same scene a
> richness and a variety never to be found in any one por-
> tion of nature.[18]

Obviously, such variety—the riches of all climates compacted into one designed landscape—could not be perceived or experienced all at once, in a single view or at a given moment. Downing, like others before him, imagined and recommended movement through such a landscape. And again, the path of that movement was a meander.

Frank Lloyd Wright's estimation of the importance of the winding path is evident in the fact that he began his *Autobiography* with a short tale about its significance. While it seems clear that the characters of the story—Uncle John and his young nephew—were meant to be understood as ideal types, the young boy can also be seen as Wright himself. The tale begins with a summons from Uncle John:

> "Come now, and I will show you how to go!"...Taking
> the boy by the hand he...started straight across and up
> the sloping fields toward a point upon which he had fixed
> his keen blue eyes. Neither to right nor to left, intent
> upon his goal, straight forward he walked...But soon
> the boy caught the plan of naked weed against the snow,
> sharp shadows laced in blue arabesque...He ran first left,
> to gather beads on stems...then to the right, to gather
> prettier ones...Eager, trembling he ran to and fro...
> his arms growing full of "weeds." [Uncle John's] tracks
> in the snow were [however] straight as any string could
> be straight. The boy came up, arms full, face flushed,
> glowing....The lesson was to come. Back there was the
> long, straight, mindful, heedless line...and there was
> the wavering, searching, heedful line embroidering the
> straight one like some free, engaging vine as it ran back
> and forth across it.[19]

The contrast between topographical types could not be more basic: straight versus wavering. Nor could the modes of perception be more distinct, heedless versus heedful. Nor again, could the kind of movement be more sharply different, processional versus strolling. While Uncle John seems to hold the high moral ground, Wright also recognized the merit of the young nephew's spontaneous conduct, at least the trace of his character in the meandering path. This is implied in his concluding lines: "The boy looked at his treasure and then at Uncle John's pride, comprehending more than Uncle John meant he should. The boy was troubled. Uncle John left out something that made all the difference." If there is any ambiguity about Wright's estimation of the meandering path in this short text, his understanding of its importance is vividly clear in his buildings.

Consider, again, the entry sequence into his Unity Temple. I have already discussed the number of turns and delays involved in the approach. From the street, the building is first seen as a grey cubic mass standing solidly on its corner site. One must follow the sidewalk around one of the sides to the point where the two main volumes (Unity Temple and Unity House) meet. Up a set of stairs and behind a low wall, one finds a bank of doors that lead into the entrance foyer. This foyer is a striking space because of its extremely low ceiling—in fact it is the lowest space in the entire building. The contrast with the expanse outside could not be greater. Although low, the space opens laterally, to the main room in Unity House on one side and a solid wall across the depth of a corridor on the other. The name typically given to this passageway is "cloister," because it allows for a sort of ambulatory movement around the lower level, skirting the main sanctuary. The key moment in this sequence is the indirect connection between the cloister and the sanctuary. Through the opening between the sanctuary floor and the cloister ceiling, one can see from the darkness of the hallway into the warm light of the space above. The main point is the delay, the partial disclosure, or revealing and hiding, in the manner of landscape experience described by Shenstone. Proceeding farther, one must turn and move up the stairs in the back corner

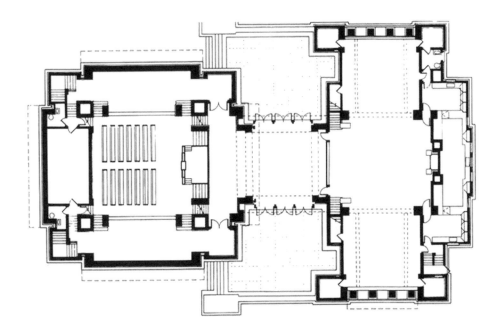

Frank Lloyd Wright, Unity Temple, Oak Park, Illinois, 1906; plan

in order to enter the main space of the sanctuary. Never before had movement into a chapel been structured as such a twisting route through variously qualified settings or scenes. The "flowers" gathered by the young boy climbing the hill are precisely analogous to the gathering of scenes that results from Wright's orchestration of a meandering entry sequence.

The title of my chapter comes from Le Corbusier. It is to him, and his understanding of the law of meander, that I now turn. But as with the other architects I have discussed, here, too, I want to turn briefly to a nineteenth-century theorist whose arguments about picturesque space not only summarized key aspects of the tradition, but also provided a beginning point for architectural developments. The writer I have in mind is Auguste Choisy.

Several historians, Etlin, von Moss, Colquhoun, and Frampton, have pointed to the importance of Choisy's writings for Le Corbusier's ideas about spatial movement. The ideas of Sitte come into this as well, as Allen Brooks in particular has shown.[20] But first Choisy. It is well known that Le Corbusier published plates from Choisy's *Histoire de l'architecture* in *Vers une architecture*. Under an illustration of the Acropolis at Athens, Le Corbusier wrote: "Let's not forget that the ground of the Acropolis is very uneven, with considerable differences of level that were used to create imposing bases for the buildings. The whole thing being out of square makes for vistas that are rich as well as subtle: the asymmetrical masses of the buildings produce an intense rhythm."[21] This observation repeats a principle we have discovered already, that plan and terrain correspond, that the first is not laid onto but built out of the second, despite all of its surface irregularities and asymmetries. Le Corbusier made a related point later in the same chapter in *Vers une architecture*, where the apparent lack of order was explained as a subtle form of balance between near and far geometries. The

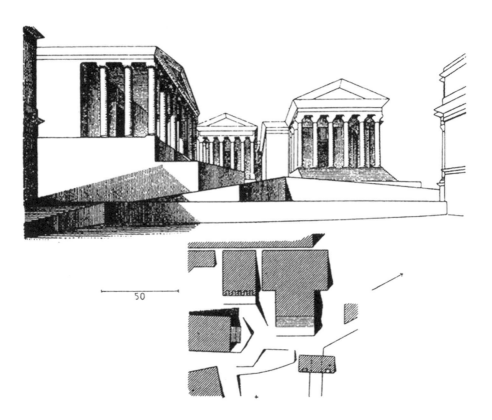

August Choisy, Acropolis, 1899; perspective and plan

Camillo Sitte, Lübeck, 1889

plan's dependence on the surrounds was stated as follows: "[The balance among parts] is determined by the famous landscape which stretches from Piraeus to Mount Pentelicus...the axes [for example] follow the valley."[22] An illustration of the Acropolis taken from Choisy's text appears one more time in Le Corbusier's book, this time illustrating his argument about axes. His first point about axes is that there is not one axis but many. Second, they are perceived in sequence, not all at once. Lastly—and perhaps most importantly—each line of sight hides contents others reveal: "[T]he Acropolis extends its effect right to the horizon. The Propylaea in the other direction, the colossal statue of Athena on the axis, and Pentelicus in the distance. And because they are outside this forceful axis, the Parthenon to right, the Erechtheum to the left, you are able to get a three-quarter view of them, in their full aspects."[23]

All three plates Le Corbusier included are from Choisy's chapter on the picturesque in Greek art. In his account of the function of the Propylaea, Choisy, too, introduced the construction of an oblique or three-quarters view, as if the hilltop ensemble relied on the same optical strategies as landscape gardens: *Lose the object, and draw nigh, obliquely.*

Apart from the geometry of the site, Le Corbusier emphasized the coincidence of the site's near and far horizons, that is, the alignment of the top edge of the hill's stylobates with the shoreline at the foot of the mountains in the distance. Now, going back to Camillo Sitte, Allen Brooks has shown that Le Corbusier also studied Sitte's text very carefully.[24] In fact, early drafts of his first book on city planning amount to little more than commentary on Sitte's arguments. Yet, because the text developed over a number of years, Le Corbusier's appreciation of picturesque planning became somewhat ambiguous or internally conflictual. The difference between his early approval of the meander—rendered as the donkey path—and his later criti-

Le Corbusier, Maison la Roche, Paris, 1923–24; interior

cism can be measured by his recognition of the importance of the automobile. In *Précisions* he wrote:

> Here is a suburban street (a former donkey path) that
> has become very lively with its activities necessary to
> neighborhood life. The automobile has come; numer-
> ous accidents multiply along this old donkey path raised
> to the rank of a national or local highway. It is decided
> to widen and straighten it. Both sides are expropriated.
> Medicine... [but this does not work]. The conclusion is
> simple: in city planning medical solutions are a delusion;
> they resolve nothing, they are very expensive. Surgical
> solution resolve.[25]

Thus, straight streets would be the answer to traffic and congestion problems in the metropolis. This can be seen clearly in Le Corbusier's many urban plans, for Paris of course, but for cities throughout the world as well. Yet, as with Wright, the donkey path was never rejected. It reappeared, for example, as the *promenade architectural*. It also appeared as the pedestrian route through towns. In *The City of Tomorrow*, Le Corbusier recommended straight streets for traffic and meandering lanes for pedestrians: "The curved street has every justification for itself if architectural effect is not aimed at, and if the surrounding countryside, or at least the trees and grass, are picturesque and not overborne by any striking creation of man. Can we impose an architectural character on the winding street? Yes! To sum up the whole matter, the curving street is essentially picturesque."[26]

   That a principle of topographical order could be used to design architectural plans is apparent from Le Corbusier's first use of the term *promenade architectural*. Describing his Maisons La Roche and Jeanneret with this term, he said, first you enter and the spectacle unfolds in succession before your eyes. He then offered a key statement of principle: "[Y]ou follow an itinerary and the perspectives develop with great variety."[27] In this single passage, we have the essential structure of picturesque space: the path, together with its destination, the multiple views succeeding one another, each contributing to the disclosure of unity within topographical variation—concordant discordance. The views Le Corbusier published in his *Oeuvre Complète* catch the principle of obliquity as well, for each is an example of the *veduta per angolo*.

Despite the development of meandering routes in his buildings, Le Corbusier remained ambivalent about the form, as did Wright; he juxtaposed straight and serpentine lines and acknowledged the merits of each. The significant change in Le Corbusier's later period concerns the shift from architectural to cosmological order. He anticipated this enlarged sense of the rambling route in his first account of the law of meander in *The Radiant City*.[28] As with the donkey path, the story in that text begins with an accident: a rock appears in the path of running water. This sets into motion an interplay of consequences, force and counterforce. Instead of flowing normally down to the sea in a straight line, the river is held up in its course by the obstruction in its path. The result is a meander. Given his moral gloss on straight lines—direct means clear, forthright, rational—the meander represents a fall from the grace of the straight line. In the *Poem to the Right Angle*, the same history is offered, but now as an account of world formation:

> ...the spring streams and rivers do the same. From a
> plane one sees them teeming in families on the deltas and
> estuaries of the Indus, the Madgalena or the margins of
> California. Ideas, too, grope their way, tentative search
> in all directions to limit, fix the bounds to left and right.
> They touch one bank and then the other. Settle there?

Run aground! The truth is present only in some spot
where the current always seeks out its bed!...Meander
will live its adventure to its absurd consequence, moreover take its time, millennia if necessary. The inextri-
cable bars the way, the incredible! But life must force
a passage, burst the dam of vicissitude. It cuts through
the meander, pierces the loops, sounding them out just
where licentious passage made them meet. The current
is straight once again...The law of meander is present in
thought and man's enterprise forms renewed examples
there, but the trajectory springs from the mind [and] is
projected by farsighted spirits beyond confusion.[29]

Obviously, architecture, while not an actor on stage in this
drama, is waiting in the wings. The key player is water, sym-
bolized here as the first principle of movement and change, as
it often was in the gardens, where it nourished development
and accelerated deterioration. For Le Corbusier, water is both
precise and amorphous, level on the horizon and straight in its
flow when unobstructed, but willing to take the shape of any
container it enters—formless on its own. The cosmic drama he
describes is most vividly apparent from above. Scenes such as
this first came into his writing after he accustomed himself to
the aerial point of view. From that vantage, the face of the earth
presented the most basic struggles: straight versus curved, light
versus dark, and lawful versus lawless. The law of meander was
so basic that it ruled all manner of terrestrial phenomena: environmental forces, gardens, cities, and buildings. Originating in
natural metamorphosis, the meander was thus taken to be fateful, for the movements of the natural world consign to human
affairs both their orientation and their end.

Endnotes

1   John Dixon Hunt, *The Picturesque Garden in Europe* (London: Thames & Hudson, 2002),
     8–10.
2   Paul Ricoeur, *Time and Narrative*, vol. 2 (Chicago: University of Chicago Press, 1984), esp.
     pt. 3, chap. 4, "The Fictive Experience of Time."
3   William Shenstone, "Unconnected Thoughts on Gardening," in *The Genius of the Place*,
     ed. John Dixon Hunt and Peter Willis (London: Paul Elek, 1975), 291. My italics.
4   Alexander Pope, "Epistle IV. To Richard Boyle, Earl of Burlington," *Moral Essays*, in
     Collected Poems (London: J. M. Dent, 1975), 248.
5   Hunt, "'Lordship of the Feet,' Towards a Poetics of Movement in Gardens," in *Landscape
     Design and the Experience of Motion*, ed. M. Conan (Washington, D. C.: Dumbarton Oaks,
     2003).
6   Camillo Sitte, "City Planning According to Artistic Principles," in *Camillo Sitte: The Birth
     of Modern City Planning*, ed. George Collins and Christiane Craseman Collins (New York:
     Rizzoli, 1986), 249.
7   Ibid., 199.
8   Ibid., 15.
9   See, for example, Dietrich Worbs, "Der Raumplan im Wohnungsbau von Adolf Loos," in his
     Adolf Loos, 1870–1933: Raumplan, Wohnungsbau, (Berlin: Akademie der Künste, 1984).
10   Pope, 248.
11   Barry Bergdoll, "The Nature of Mies's Space," in *Mies in Berlin*, ed. Terence Riley and Barry
     Bergdoll (New York: Harry N. Abrams, 2001), 66–105.
12   Hermann Muthesius, *Das englische Haus: Entwicklung, Bedingungen, Anlage, Aufbau,
     Einrichtung und Innenraum*, vol. 2 (Berlin: E. Wasmuth, 1904–05), 85.
13   Peter Behrens, "Der moderne Garten," *Berliner Tageblatt* 40, no. 291 (10 June 1911): 8.
14   Bergdoll, *Mies in Berlin*, 95.
15   Ibid., 72. See also Caroline Constant, "The Barcelona Pavilion as Landscape Garden:
     Modernity and the Picturesque," *AA Files* 20 (Fall, 1990): 46–54.
16   José Quetglas, "Fear of Glass: The Barcelona Pavilion," in *Architectureproduction*, ed.
     Beatriz Colomina (New York: Princeton Architectural Press, 1988), 122–51.
17   Robin Evans, "Mies van der Rohe's Paradoxical Symmetries," in *Translations from Drawing
     to Building and Other Essays* (Cambridge, Mass.: MIT Press, 1997), 233–77.
18   Andrew Jackson Downing, *Treatise on the Theory and Practice of Landscape Gardening*
     (New York and London: Wiley & Putnam, 1841), 34; cited in Judith Major, *To Live in the
     New World* (Cambridge, Mass.: MIT Press, 1997), 54.
19   Frank Lloyd Wright, "Prelude," *An Autobiography* (New York: Duell, Sloan and Pearce,
     1943), 3–4.
20   H. Allen Brooks, *Le Corbusier's Formative Years* (Chicago: University of Chicago Press,
     1997), 201–08.
21   Le Corbusier-Saugnier, *Vers une architecture* (Paris: Crès, 1923), 32; *Towards a New
     Architecture* (London: Architectural Press, 1927), 43.
22   Le Corbusier, *Vers*, 39; *Towards*, 50.
23   Le Corbusier, *Vers*, 151; *Towards*, 175.
24   Brooks, *Le Corbusier's Formative Years*, 201–08.
25   Le Corbusier, *Précisions* (Cambridge, Mass.: MIT Press, 1991), 172–74; see also Le
     Corbusier, *The City of Tomorrow* (London: Architectural Press, 1929), 280–83.
26   Le Corbusier, *The City of Tomorrow*, 222.

27   *Le Corbusier et Pierre Jeanneret: Oeuvre complète*, vol. 1, 1910–1929, ed. Willy Boesiger
       and Oscar Stonorov (Zürich: Girsberger, 1937), 60; cited in Stanislaus von Moos, "Voyages
       en zigzag," in *Le Corbusier before Le Corbusier*, ed. Stanislaus von Moos and Arthur
       Rüegg (New Haven: Yale University Press, 2002), 41.

28   Le Corbusier, *The Radiant City* (New York: Orion, 1967), 79–80.

29   Le Corbusier, Le Poème de l'angle droit (Paris: Fondation Le Corbusier, 1989), A4.

ACKNOWLEDGMENTS

Colleagues at universities far from my own are to be thanked for invitations to lecture on the topics addressed in this book, topics that have concerned me for several years. Each of the chapters that make up this book developed out of a talk I gave to an audience that welcomed me to their lecture hall, audiences in Europe, Asia, and the Americas. The development of lectures into chapters benefited from the advice and criticism of friends and colleagues closer to home. Colleagues among both groups I would like to acknowledge in particular are: William Braham, Hugh Campbell, Carlos Eduardo Comas, George Dodds, Per Olaf Fjeld, Kenneth Frampton, Edward Ford, Stanislaus Fung, Karsten Harries, Branko Kolarevic, Harry Mallgrave, Ali Malkawi, Philippe Nys, Jo Odgers, Sheila O'Donnell, Andy Payne, Alberto Pérez Gómez, Joseph Rykwert, Adam Sharr, David Summers, Mark Treib, Billie Tsien, John Tuomey, Catherine Veikos, Marion Weiss, Richard Wesley, and Peter Wong.

Current and former students have also helped me think through the questions I have considered in this study, often as a result of discussions of their own work, from which I continue to learn: Michael Asgaard Andersen, Stephen Anderson, Jin Baek, Nathaniel Coleman, Anna Vortmann Hakes, Juan Manuel Heredia, Ross Jenner, Peter Kohane, Gordana Kostich, Anne Lutun, Fernando Moriera, Carlos Naranjo, Rosa Otero, Tonkao Panin, Esra Sahin, and Franca Trubiano.

Finally, I would like to acknowledge the generosity of a number of friends and colleagues who have read parts of this book and given me both suggestions and criticism. I am very grateful to Peter Carl, Richard Francis-Jones, Jamie Horwitz, John Dixon Hunt, Mohsen Mostafavi, Robert Tavernor, Dalibor Vesely, and Enrique Vivoni.

Earlier versions of some of the chapters in this book have appeared in other publications: "Unscripted Performances" in *Performative Architecture*, eds. B. Kolarevic and A. Malkawi (New York: Spon Press, 2005), 5–20; "Materials Matter" in *Structure and Meaning in Human Settlements*, eds. Tony Atkin and Joseph Rykwert (Philadelphia: University of Pennsylvania Museum of Archaeology and Anthropology, 2005), 347–364; "Table Talk" in *Eating Architecture*, eds. Jamie Horwitz and Paulette Singley (Cambridge, Mass.: MIT Press, 2004), 211–228; "Sitting in the City" in *Body and Building*, eds. George Dodds and Robert Tavernor (Cambridge Mass.: MIT Press, 2002), 268–289; "Practically Primitive" in *Primitive: Original matters in architecture*, eds. Jo Odgers, Flora Samuel and Adam Sharr (London: Routledge, 2006), 127–138; and "Landings and Crossings" in *O'Donnell + Tuomey Selected Works* (New York: Princeton Architectural Press, 2007), 176–185.

PHOTOGRAPHY CREDITS

All photographs courtesy of the author unless otherwise noted.

22	AACUPR, University of Puerto Rico
32, bottom left	Fernando Moriera
55, right	Tonkao Panin
56	Anna Vortmann Hakes
59	Carlos Naranjo
77	Carlos Naranjo
79	Carlos Naranjo
109	Margherita Spiluttini
124	Graphische Sammlung Albertina, Vienna
132	Albright Knox Gallery, Buffalo
135, upper	Metropolitan Museum of Art, New York
153	Graphische Sammlung Albertina, Vienna
158	Graphische Sammlung Albertina, Vienna
176	Carlos Naranjo
178	Hagley Museum, Philadelphia
181	Hagley Museum, Philadelphia
184	Hagley Museum, Philadelphia
186	Anna Vortmann Hakes
208	Tonkao Panin
222	O'Donnell + Tuomey
226	O'Donnell + Tuomey
229	O'Donnell + Tuomey
235	British Museum
238	Foundation Le Corbusier
240	O'Donnell + Tuomey
251, lower right	James Hakes
274	Devonshire Collection, Oxfordshire

INDEX